John Timon

Missions in Western New York, and Church History of the Diocese of Buffalo

John Timon

Missions in Western New York, and Church History of the Diocese of Buffalo

ISBN/EAN: 9783743399150

Manufactured in Europe, USA, Canada, Australia, Japa

Cover: Foto ©Lupo / pixelio.de

Manufactured and distributed by brebook publishing software (www.brebook.com)

John Timon

Missions in Western New York, and Church History of the Diocese of Buffalo

IN

Western New York,

AND

CHURCH HISTORY

OF THE

DIOCESE OF BUFFALO,

BY

THE BISHOP OF BUFFALO.

BUFFALO:
CATHOLIC SENTINEL PRINT.

1862.

DEDICATION.

TO THE VENERABLE CLERGY
AND
FAITHFUL LAITY
OF THE DIOCESE OF BUFFALO.

Looking round on a blessed increase of zealous Priests, crowded Churches, and fervent communicants, we, with worshipful thanksgiving to God, affectionate gratitude to our venerable Co-operators the Clergy, and grateful paternal love to the pious Laity—dedicate these hasty memoirs, as a monument of our affection to the worthy Priests, and generous, devoted Catholics of this new Diocese.

Amidst occupations already almost excessive, it seemed wrong to attempt a work like this—when only interrupted moments, snatched from important and necessary duties, could be devoted to examining documents, written at various epochs, during hundreds of years. But the advice of respected friends, and their suggestion that, if not soon began, future steps in this direction might be almost impossible, made us hesitate. Then the desire to aid in preserving interesting details of the Church's first struggles, against error and crime in this region; a wish to invite the attention, of our generous native and adopted citizens, to the heroic virtues, saintly examples, and martyr' sufferings of the holy dead, who once trod the soil, which we now tread; who once labored in the fields of our present labors; who once preached and practiced what we now preach and practice; made hesitation change into firm resolve. Then, far advanced in the midnight vigil; or long before dawn of day, we strove to make a beginning; hoping that our labors might induce others who have time and talent, to follow the glimpses, that may open through these pages, and unfold the shadows which still rest round the dark and stormy past; and even make it bright with evidence that, in America, as in every other land, the truth of God, the promises of God, the power of God, always protected the Church, preserved its light, and matured its fruits of love.

We pause at this first volume. Its last paragraph will tell that we wait, to give ampler testimony, than the modest reserve of God's pious and faithful priests, permitted them to send, of their zealous co-operation in the great work which has been wrought in our midst.

"Being confident of this very thing, that He Who hath begun a good work in you, will perfect it unto the day of Jesus Christ," we pray that God may ever bless those faithful priests, and their generous flocks.

✝ JOHN,
Bp. of Buffalo.

CONTENTS.

CHAPTER I.

Beginning of the Church in America—Vicissitudes—Prosperity and Adversity, in America, as elsewhere—Instructors of another race in America—Ancient Remains—Danes—Irish—Iceland, Christian—Lost to Science by Lutheranism—Greenland converted—America discovered, about the year 1000—Bishop Eric visited it in 1120—Last Mention in 1384.....7

CHAPTER II.

Success of Early Missions—General View—Assertion that Jesuit Missions are always Failures, contradicted—Failure of non-Catholic Missions—Persecution.....19

CHAPTER III.

Earliest Missions—South of the U. S.—Quebec—St. Lawrence—The English destroy it—Rasles.....24

CHAPTER IV.

Indians—Number of Martyred Priests—Indians, hospitable at first—Wronged, before they did wrong—Tribes many and populous in the State of New York—Hudson—Indians kidnapped—Hi-a-wat-ha.....39

CHAPTER V.

Religion, Rites and Ceremonies—Compared with the Ancients and with the Jews.....47

CHAPTER VI.

Catholic Missionaries, Franciscan Fathers—Invite and lodge the first Jesuits—Jesuits among the Hurons—The Franciscan, then the Jesuit approach or reach Niagara River.....60

CHAPTER VII.

Host of Martyrs.....71

(v.)

CHAPTER VIII.

Missions in Western New York—Iroquois—Franciscans instruct them in 1621—Father Joques—Rev. W. J. Kipp—Father Ponset—Torture of Father Le Moyne—Discovers the Salt Springs of Syracuse—Indian Council—Father Chaumont—His Speech—Cayugas—Senecas—Intrigues—Persecution—Adversity..80

CHAPTER IX.

Gospel Fruits—Sanctity of Indians—Catherine Teaghokuita—Miracles...112

CHAPTER X.

Early Indian Missions, in what is now Diocese of Buffalo.......147

CHAPTER XI.

Missions of the Buffalo district continued, in a place of Refuge from Persecution...185

CHAPTER XII.

Missions for our Race—Beginning of Churches—Conflicting vices, but still onward progress.........................207

CHAPTER XIII.

Buffalo, an Episcopal See................................236

Missions in Western New York.

CHAPTER I.

BEGINNINGS OF THE CHURCH IN AMERICA.

In every land, we trace the varying features of God's Church militant; now highly favoured, now chastised, almost crushed; then rising, sometimes rapidly, sometimes slowly, to more than former splendor.

In Africa, what vicissitudes marked the state of the Church; once glorious, then sunk in darkest night; yet now the See of St. Augustine, from which all traces of Christianity seemed effaced, brightens again under Christ's blessed light. England too, twice or thrice had the faith almost to begin, and only lately, after the direst persecution on record, does the English Church again display in triumphs of grace, her undying work of love. Nor were the hours of gloom without blessed fruit. How many generous martyrs did not England and Ireland send to heaven? How many have not Japan and China, (which still daily sends,) sent, in past ages to swell "the glorious choir of martyrs." St. Francis Xavier converted Japan; the same arts which, for commercial purposes, or for domination, were so successfully practiced upon our Indians in this State; brought on, in Japan, a bloody persecution; two millions of martyrs passed heroicly, through dreadful torments, to the Church triumphant. Was this not a gain for earth, as well as for heaven? We even have indications that in the mountains of Japan the ancient faith ever remained: may it not be that now the blood of the martyrs shall soon be the seed of Christians?" For ages the faith has been struggling in China: at times, to men, it seemed extinct: during those ages of struggle, millions of martyrs passed to heaven: yet we are told that there are upwards of 2,000,000 of christians in China: churches, and seminaries, and Sisters of Charity, in every province, penetrating, in their labours of light and love, to the inmost recesses of the country..

It would seem that our America had passed through some of the same phases; had its bright rays of hope; its sad reverses, through the cunning and cruelty of God's enemies; may we not hope for a glorious crop, from the blood of Christian martyrs that once consecrated the soil of America, even here in our State of New York.

In beginning these memoirs that may serve in forming the history of the Church in this diocess; it seemed useful to present an abridgment of historical fragments, on our early history; as curious developements are daily made, through the assidious labours of devoted and learned writers. In the compilation, the sources whence the facts are drawn will often be immediately noticed; more frequently perhaps, the notice, with all due praise, will be given at the end of the work.

Baron HUMBOLDT remarking the evidences, that instructors, of another race, had penetrated into Mexico and South America, suppose that they came from Eastern Asia. Father ANTONIO RUIZ, mentions a miraculous cross, found in that part of Paraguay which is now called "*Holy Cross*," and speaks of a local tradition, pointing to St. Thomas, the Apostle, as the first teacher of the faith, in that Southern part of America. Father DURAN says that in South America, the Indians declare that Saint *Svme*, (which in their language means Thomas,) predicted to their ancestors that priests of the mighty God would, one day, reproduce in their midst, the doctrine which he announced, preach brotherly love, and *teach them to have but one wife.*

In reading what learned men have written, on early American traditions, which gleam, like more than half forgotten truths of Christianity, we almost feel inclined to receive literally the Scripture declaration that on the day of Pentecost, "there were dwelling at Jerusalem Jews, devout men, out of *every nation under heaven*"; that America was represented there, and consequently, to suppose that our country was peopled, not only from the North-east and North-west, but also from the South; and that the West Indian, and other islands, are but the lofty ridges of a connecting land between the old and the new world which sunk to its present state, in some of the mighty convulsions of nature, that occurred at the death of our Lord, and recurred frequently during succeeding centuries.

BANCROFT has a curious passage, relating to the voluntary mortifications and penances of the first discovered Indians: he says: "That man should take up the cross, that sin "should be atoned for, *are ideas that dwell in human "nature;* they are so diffused among the savages that Le "Clercq believed some of the Apostles must have reached the "American continent." His. U. S. 3vol. 291.

DE WITT CLINTON says: "Previous to the occupation of this country by the progenitors of the present race of Indians, it was inhabited by a race of men much more populous, and much further advanced in civilization." Speaking of ancient fortifications he says: "I have seen several of these works. "in the western part of this State. There is a large one in "the town of Onondaga, one in Pompey, and one in Malins; "one in Camillus, eight miles from Auburn; one in Scipio, "six miles, another, one mile, and another, about half a "mile from that village. Between the Seneca and Cayuga "Lakes, there are several;—three within a few miles of each "other. Near the village of Canandaigua there are three. "In a word they are scattered all over that country."

"There is from the Niagara to the Genesee river, upon the mountain Ridge, a line or corden of these ancient fortifications. Upon a slope or offset of the mountain Ridge, three and a half miles from the village of Lewiston, is a marked spot, which the Tuscarora Indians called *Kiennka,* (fort or stronghold,) there is a burial ground, and two eliptic mounds that have a diameter of twenty feet, and an elevation of from four to five. Eight miles east of this, upon one of the most elevated points of the mountain ridge, in the town of Cambria, on the farm owned by John Gould, is an ancient fortification and burial place. . . An area of about six acres of level ground, appears to have been occupied. Nearly in the centre of the area was a depository of the dead. It was a pit, excavated to the depth of four or five feet, filled with human bones, over which were slabs of sand stone. Hundreds of both sexes, and of all ages seem to have been thrown in promiscously. Extreme old age was identified by toothless jaws and the complete absorption of the aveola process; and extreme infancy, by the small skulls and imcomplete ossification. In the position of the skeletons there was none of the signs of ordinary Indian burial. A tree had been cut down, growing directly over the mound, upon its stump could be counted two hundred and thirty concentric circles. Remains of earthernware, pieces of copper, and iron, instruments of rude workmanship, were ploughed up within the area!

" At the head of a deep gorge, a mile west of Lockport, in the early settlement of the country, a circular raised work, or ring fort, could be distinctly traced. Leading from the area, there had been a covered way to a spring of pure cold water, that issues from a fissure of a rock, some fifty, or sixty feet down the declivity."

There is an ancient battle field upon the Buffalo Creek, six miles from Buffalo, near the Mission station. The Senecas have a tradition that here was a last decisive battle between their people and their enemies, the Kah-Kwahs. A mile north of Aurora village in Erie County, there are several small lakes or ponds, around and between which there are knobs or elevations thickly covered with a tall growth of pine; upon them are several mounds, where many human bones have been excavated. Relics around Aurora in Erie county, abound perhaps to a greater extent, than in any other locality in western New York.

An area, from three to four miles in extent, would seem to have been thickly populated. There are in Aurora village and vicinity few gardens and fields where ancient Indian relics are not found at each successive ploughing. Few cellars are excavated without discovering them. In digging a cellar a few years since a skeleton was exhumed, the thigh bones of which, would indicate great height. In digging another cellar, a large number of skeletons or detached bones were thrown out upon the farm of M. B. Crooks, two miles from the village; where a tree had been turned up several hundred pounds of axes were found. The ancient works at Forthill, Le Roy, are especially worthy of observation, they are three miles north of Le Roy. There are undoubted evidences of its having constituted a valuable point of defence to a rude and half civilized people. Such skeletons as have been found, in and about this locality indicate a race of men averaging, *one third larger* than the present race. From the fortification a trench leads to a spring of water. Arrow heads, pipes, beads, gouges, pestles, stone hatchets, have been found upon the ground. The growth of timber would show that these works were over five hundred years old. It even seems possible that other growths may have preceded them!

About one and a half miles west of Shelby centre, Orleans county, is an ancient work—trees of four hundred years' growth stand upon the embankment, and underneath them have been found earthen ware, pieces of plate or dishes, wrought with skill, presenting ornaments in relief of various patterns. Some skeletons, almost entire, have been exhumed; many of giant size—not less than from seven to eight feet in length. The late Hon. S. M. BURROUGH says: "This was doubtless a spot where a great battle had been fought. Were not these people a branch of the Aztecs?"

Upon the middle branch of Buffalo Creek, three and a half miles from the village of Aurora, there are remains of one of the largest class of ancient fortifications. The spot had attractions for successive Indian nations—the Eries, the Neuter Nation, and the Iriquois; for there are evidences of continued occupancy to our own period. When the French Franciscans and the Jesuit Missionaries came to this region, they undoubtedly made it one of their principal stations. In the year 1809, a copper plate was ploughed up, twelve inches broad and sixteen long. It had engraven upon it, in regular lines extending the whole length of the plate, characters that appear to have been some record."—Turner's History of Hol. Pur.

Certain it is that indications, both in the physical and moral order, point to some early but long since forgotten intercourse with the Old World. The learned researches of the Danish antiquaries make it almost certain that our country was discovered long before COLUMBUS.

Baron HENRION, in his "Missions Catholiques," Liv. i., chap. 31, gives in much detail the proofs that the Northmen of Scandinavia discovered Iceland in the ninth century, and that they found on the shores crosses, bells, and sacred vessels of Irish workmanship.

Iceland is about one-fifth larger than Ireland. Its area is estimated at 40,000 square miles. It seems to have been discovered in 861 by Naddor, who called it *Snowland*. Three years after, Garder and Floki visited it, and from the drift ice, along the northern shores, called it "Iceland." In

874, Norwegian nobles who had rebelled, and been defeated in Norway, reached Iceland. Ingolf and Leif conducted them. They finally settled at Reykjawk. Leif, enriched with plunder from Ireland, was killed by some of his captive Irish. The colony was soon augmented by plunder and slaves from abroad. Among their captives were many Christians, monks, priests, and even bishops. The truths of Christianity insinuated themselves, into the hearts of the worshippers of Woden. Frederick, a Saxon bishop, who came, or *was brought there* in 981, seems to have been the apostle of Iceland; we know that Christianity was adopted by the National Assembly in A. D. 1000. In the year 1057, ISLEIF, Bishop of Ikaholt, introduced into Iceland the art of writing and the Latin alphabet, modified according to German forms. As usual, the monks, especially those of the Benedictine Monastery of Thingeyra, were large contributors to Icelandic literature. Nothing can compensate for the national loss sustained by the sack of convents, and the wholesale destruction of valuable manuscripts and relics of antiquity, at the introduction of Lutheranism in 1550.

With the introduction of writing, a great and general educational and literary movement commenced in Iceland; which continued unabated for five centuries. And Iceland became a country which, in point of general education, has hardly, if at all, been equalled. The natural result was a refinement of manners, and an advanced civilization, which seems wonderful in that wild age of lawlessness and violence. The records and memorials of this vanished civilization, and the monuments of this dead literature, still subsist in piles of dusty manuscripts preserved in the Royal Library of Copenhagen, in the British Museum, and elsewhere.

Iceland is about one hundred and eighty miles from Greenland. Grenbiorn, who first discovered Greenland, gave a sad description of its ice-bound shores; a few years later, *Eric* the Red, under more favorable circumstances and a better season, found the same land, was pleased with it, and, from its then verdure, called it Greenland. Notwithstanding awful privations, the colony was established, and began to flourish.

In 999, Leif, son of Eric, was converted to Christianity. All the settlers of Greenland followed his example. A bishoprick was founded at Garde, convents of nuns were established. There were twelve parishes and two houses of religious men in the eastern division, and four parishes in the western. We have an authentic account of a voyage undertaken by some priests of the diocese of Garder, in 1266, in the course of which they penetrated through Lancaster Sound and Barrow's Strait, and examined shores, the re-discovery of which lately has been vaunted as among the most intrepid fruits of modern nautical daring. These priests, fortunately, have given us some astronomical observations, from which it appears that they advanced almost to the seventy-sixth degree of north latitude.

The colonists of Greenland frequently visited the mother countries, Iceland and Norway. There was a continuous intercourse between Greenland and these countries; the inmates of the Greenland monasteries were often sent over to the convents of Iceland and Norway. The Bishops of Garder were Suffragans of the Archbishop of Trondhjem, a city of Norway, on the river "Nid," (whence its ancient name "Nidrosia;") and for their consecration, and for many other reasons, had frequent necessity of going to Europe.

Greenland was the pioneer station, on the road to America. Biorni sailed from Norway to visit Herulf, his father, in Greenland. Driven by storms too far south, he discovered Newfoundland and the mainland of America. Returning northeastwardly with favorable but strong winds, in four days he reached Greenland. Fourteen years after.

Eric Rande bought Biorni's vessel, and with thirty-five companions started to explore this "Newfoundland." They reached Newfoundland, which, from its barren aspect, they called "Helluland," or "The Barren Land." Continuing on west, they reached Nova Scotia; they called it "Markland," or "The Land of Woods." Coasting down, they reached the southern part of Massachusetts; a colony was planted in Vinland, "Land of the Vine," on the continent, opposite to "Martha's Vineyard." The succeeding navigators examined the coast of Long Island, the coasts of Delaware and Maryland, and even farther south. A commerce in furs, etc., began; the intercourse between America, Greenland and northern Europe continued for at least three centuries. The latest mention of it occurs in a document compiled in 1348, where an Icelandic vessel is spoken of as having been to Markland for a cargo of timber, the very commodity, even now, for a vessel in the Canada or Nova Scotia trade.

Some notices in the ancient documents are curious and interesting. One of them speaks of the shipwreck on a part of the American coast called *"Ireland it mikla,"* (Great Ireland,) of Arc Marson, a wealthy Icelandic lord, in 983, during a voyage from Dublin to Reikjavik. The people are represented as white and Christians, speaking a dialect of the Erse. They baptised Arc Marson, and detained him thirty years. Arc Frode, one of the most trustworthy of Icelandic writers, to whom we owe the most detailed account of the settlement of Greenland, and of the American discoveries, was the great grandson of this Arc Marson, who, as well as Arc Frode, believed this American people to be an Irish colony that long before had made their way across the ocean.

Other relations, such as that of Biorni Asbrandson, are equally strange. But they have a counterpart in many

Indian traditions. The southern Indians, before their expulsion from Florida, had a tradition that the Florida, and Carolinas were, ages ago, inhabited by a race of white men, who used iron tools, cultivated the earth, and worshipped the Great Spirit in houses built for that purpose. The Mexicans had similar traditions.

The records of the discovery of America by the Icelanders are too consistent, too truthful to be rejected. The whole Scandinavian people must have conspired to invent a gigantic fiction, were it false, even in one of its leading features; and they must have engaged unborn generations in the conspiracy. Such a fiction, too, must have guessed the configuration of some two or three thousand miles of coast, the distances and bearings of places, hundreds of miles apart, the zoology and botany of countries differing widely in soil, climate, and physical conformation. It was no fiction, surely, when Thornfinn exhibited the ears of maize in the streets of Trondhjem; nor when he sold the slab of bird's-eye maple to the Bishop of Bremen, for a mark of gold. More than eight centuries and a half have rolled away since Leif wintered in Vinland; yet his descriptions are pictures of Newfoundland and the country around Martha's Vineyard, to this hour."—Dublin Review, May, 1861.

Iceland and Greenland, almost from their discovery, had their churches, their convents, their bishops, their colleges, their libraries, their apostolic men, and when the explorers Beorn and Leif and their followers coasted southernly along the Atlantic shore and discovered a great part of the United States, missionaries immediately offered to go and preach the gospel to the savages. In 1120, Bishop ERIC visited in person this country, then called Vinland, or Land of Vines. The colonies of the Northmen on the west coast of Greenland continued to flourish till 1406, when the seventeenth and last Bishop of Garda was sent from Norway; those on the eastern coast subsisted till 1540, when they were destroyed by a physical revolution which accumulated the ice in that zone. Thus a focus of Christianity not only long existed in Greenland, but from it, rays of faith for a time illuminated part of the territory now embraced in the United States.

As to the position of Vinland, there can be little doubt. A careful study of the narratives of the early voyagers, narratives, stamped with the imprint of truth, leaves no doubt that they turned Cape Cod, and entered the water of the Narragansett Bay. To corroborate this, a ruin exists near Newport, evidently of Runic or Scandinavian origin, It was found on the settlement of the country, and is clearly no Indian work; while its resemblance to acknowled Scandinavian works in Greenland and Iceland places the question beyond a doubt.

"The ancient *tholus* in Newport, the erection of which," says the Royal Society of Antiquarians, "appears to be co-eval with the time of Bishop Eric, belonged to a Scandinavian church or monastery, where in alternation with Latin masses, the old Danish tongue was heard seven hundred years ago."

Dr. HOLLAND, in a "Dissertation on the History and Literature of Iceland," remarks that the description given of a great country to the southwest of Greenland, which had *formerly* been visited by Icelanders, proves at least that the discoveries of the Northmen were not entirely unknown in Southern Europe.

ANTONIO ZENO found in Vinland Latin books brought thither by a Bishop of Greenland in the beginning of the twelfth century. Baron HENUION gives a long article on the veneration of the cross by savages along the Saint Lawrence, and on their traditions, which seem to point to a visit from Bishop ERIC about the year 1120. MALTE BRUN thinks that the traditions of the savages on this subject are reasonable, and point to Bishop ERIC, and to deliverance from an epidemic through him. Christianity was forgotten when the missionaries withdrew or were martyred; but the veneration of the cross remained. Father LAFITAU attests, that the veneration of the cross was practiced in America, before the coming of Columbus. "Meurs des Sauvages Americains," vol. i., p. 424. This learned Father makes on this subject the following reflexion: "Although the Evil One might pervert anything, still, can it be thought that he would excite his adorers to venerate the sacred sign by which he was vanquished? Or, may not this be a proof that Christianity had penetrated into America, before the discovery of later days!"

From 1120 up to 1493 we only have vague accounts of Greenland: even these disappear about the time that Columbus discovered America, in which country the light seems to have faded away, amidst the murderous enmities and the dark passions of a savage people, who had perhaps despised and abused their first grace.

"The antiquarian, as he excavates the mounds, and surveys the remains, which are scattered over the Western valleys, meets with relics of a remote antiquity and memorials of a populous race, advanced in civilization, who

 "'Heaped with long toil the earth, while yet the Greek
  Was hewing the Pentelicus to forms
  Of symmetry, and rearing on its rock
  The glittering Parthenon.'

"The various tribes of aboriginal inhabitants which were found in possession of this country at its discovery, exhibited a diversity of institutions, customs, and language, which could only have resulted from a separation at a period far remote in their history." Marshall.

CHAPTER II.

ON THE SUCCESS OF EARLY MISSIONS.

ANCIENT and recent monuments and discoveries, make it then almost certain, that at a very early period Catholic Priests exercised their ministry in this New World. Certain, at least it is, that the first discoverers, and the first settlers were Catholics. Ambition, and the cursed thirst for gold, too much indeed, influenced many, yet, as the most lawless had still faith and conscience, which could restrain unlimited power, they frequently aided the Catholic Priest in his efforts to civilize and save the Indians; hence the Indian race was preserved where Catholics ruled, but exterminated, or nearly exterminated, wherever the Catholic religion was either powerless or persecuted. The results at this day will show how differently the non-Catholics, as a body acted. From the north of Mexico to Cape Horn there yet exists about twenty millions of Indians; they are Christians; their civilization has not reached that of our race; but it may be much less than we imagine, behind that of England or of other countries, 300 years after their conversion. And, though the Christian Indians of the South are far in advance of the Northern tribes, yet are they not now, what they would have been, had not a stronger race, with adverse social and religious ideas, undermined their principles and weakened their morality. Even now, in the far North the Catholic Indians are greatly in advance of the non-Catholic savages. These remarks are not intended as reproach against respected Protestant fellow citizens, who generally condemn, sometimes in stronger terms than we dare use, the wrongs inflicted upon the Aborigines.

But, the Catholic historian is forced, however unwilling,

to make such remarks, in answer to the oft-repeated assertion, of some Protestant writers. The same in substance as the following quotation from Rev. W. I. Kip, M. A.: "Look over the world and read the history of the Jesuit missions. After one or two centuries, they have always come to naught. There is not a recorded instance of their permanency, or of their spreading each generation, wider and deeper, *like our own missions in India*. Thus it has been in China, Japan, South America, and our own land. For centuries the Jesuit foreign missionaries have been like those 'beating the air.' And yet, greater devotion to the cause than theirs, has never been since the Apostle's days. Must there not have been something wrong in the whole system—some grievous error mingled with their teaching, which thus denied them a measure of success, proportioned to their efforts." Kip, Jes. Miss. Pref. It seems a duty respectfully to remove erroneous impressions. Hence we must point out retarding causes, which the Church could not remove. Unless, as in Japan, where about two millions of converts died martyrs; unless, as in the North Eastern States, when the converted tribes were exterminated, the assertion above made is the very reverse of the truth. Jesuits may have been chased away, or murdered like Resles; but other Jesuits, or other Priests took their place; even after a price had been put upon the head of God's minister, as was the case in our own state. Every one knows that the Catholic missions in India are immensely superior, and far more successful than the Protestant missions there, notwithstanding the boast of Mr. Kip. Misrepresentation, craft, and British power, destroyed the Indian missions in this State, but not the entire Indian Christianity of the State, which was transferred to Canada, where very many Catholic descendants of the Christian Indians of New York, still worship with fervor before their

Catholic altars. In many parts of the United States, in Michigan, Kansas, &c., &c., there are many Churches and large congregations of faithful Indians, many of whose fathers had to fly from persecution in this State. Rev. EUGENE VETRANILE, Pastor of Biddeford, says in a letter to the writer of these memoirs: "In the State of "Maine there are two tribes of Indians of the Etchimin, "nation, a division of the great Algonquin family. They "number one thousand, and are all Catholics. There are "no Protestant Indians in the State. These Indians have "a right to send two men to the Legislature of Maine. I "am informed by fishermen, who frequent Labrador, that "they are continually visited by Catholic Esquimeaux In- "dians."

Where are the Protestant Churches, or the Protestant Christian Indians of all the tribes that swarmed in New England and in Eastern New York. The power, the wealth, the religious zeal, of "old" and "New" England were brought to aid the Indian Missions of Rev. JOHN ELIOT and others. Let a Protestant writer tell the result: JOSHUA R. CLARK, A. M., corresponding member of the New York Historical Society, says in "Onondaga," vol. i.: "Two hundred years have not yet rolled around, and a Bible, (the Indian Bible printed through the aid of the British Parliament,) the fruit of many years of diligent labor, translated expressly for a people, whose salvation was the end and aim of the great, the gracious, and the good of that era, lives only as a literary curiosity on the shelves of a very few libraries in Christendom. . . . The race for whose benefit these holy words were arranged, has passed away, and with them their literature, and even their very names." p. 211.

GOV. ANDROS, in his official report in 1678, makes no mention of Catholics, in enumerating the religious denominations in the State; and this, because Catholics, publicly known as such, did not exist in the civilized districts.

Gov. DONGAN, in 1687, in his report to the British Parliament, says, "New York has first a chaplain, belonging to "the Fort, of the Church of England; secondly, a Dutch "Calvinist; thirdly, a French Calvinist; fourthly, a Dutch "Lutheran. Here be not many of the Church of England, "*few Roman Catholics*, abundance 'of Quaker preachers, "men, and women especially, Singing Quakers, Ranting "Quakers, Sabbatharians, Antisabbatharians, some Anabap- "tists, some Independents, some Jews; in short, of all sorts "of opinions there are some, and the most part, of none at "all." Doc. Hist. of N. Y. Vol. I., 116.

Various intolerant laws soon forced most of the *few* in the State to leave it. In 1700, an Act was passed with this preample: "Whereas divers Jesuits, Priests, and Popish "Missionaries have of late come, and for some time have "had their residence in the remote parts of this province," (New York,) It is then enacted that every priest, etc., remaining in or coming into the province after November 1, 1700, "shall be adjudged to suffer perpetual imprisonment." In case of escape and capture, to suffer death! By the same law, harborers of Priests were to pay a fine of two hundred pounds and to stand two days in the pillory. SMITH speaks of this law as "One for hanging any Popish Priest who would come voluntarily into the Province," and he says, "It continues in full force to this day, as it forever ought." A man then did not dare to avow himself a Catholic; it was odious; a chapel then would have been pulled down. It used to be said, "JOHN LEARY goes once a year "to Philadelphia to get absolution." In 1741, JOHN URY was hung in New York ostensibly on account of a pretended participation in a plot, but in reality on account of his being thought to be a Priest, as it seems he was. (This bloody law against Catholics was repealed by special act of the New York State Legislature, in 1784.)

"In the year 1700, the Earl of BELLMONT, Governor of New York, memoralized the Lords of trade and plantations, "to prevent their being practised upon by the French Priests, and Jesuits. (Laws enacted to hang the poor Priests who came into the Province must have appeared quite efficacious.) "The Queen gave directions for the erection of a fort, with a chapel and house for the Clergyman, in the country of the Mohawks. . . . . After about six years of labor, trial, and disappointment, the Reverend W. ANDREWS solicited removal from that Mission, which was done. He gives anything but a favorable report of the success of his labors, saying, "There is no hope of making them better. Heathen they are, and Heathen they still must be."—213. Great efforts were also made among the Onondagas. The result is thus stated by the learned Author: "The general character and condition of the Onondagas, as a body of this day, is not remarkable either for industry, thrift, perseverance, temperance, or any of those higher virtues and graces which tend to exalt and elevate mankind." Clark, Vol. 1. p. 321.

In 1778, in the month of February, a large French ship was taken by the British, near the Chesapeake, and sent for condemnation into New York, at that time still in possession of the English. Amongst her officers was a Priest, of the name of DE LA MOTTE, of the Order of St. Augustin, who was Chaplain of the vessel. Being permitted to go at large in the city, he was solicited by his countrymen, and by those of his own faith, to celebrate Mass. Being advised of the existence of a prohibitory law, he applied to the commanding officer for permission, which was refused: but M. DE LA MOTTE, not knowing the language very well, mistook what was intended for a refusal as a permission, and

B

accordingly celebrated Mass. For this he was arrested, and kept in close confinement until exchanged. This was under Governor Tryon's administration. His. of C. C. in N. Y. p. 29 & 35." That the Catholic Church under such circumstances, could not continue its work of conversion among the Indians, and that the converted Indians would be forced into exile, is evident. That the Protestant religion, under such favorable circumstances, should have *zero* for the result of gigantic efforts and expenditures, can easily be explained, by thinking men.

CHAPTER III.

EARLIEST MISSIONS.

Under God the discovery of America by Columbus, was greatly due to the Franciscan Monk John Perez di Marchena. But for him Columbus could not have sailed from Spain. On the 12th of October, 1492, in the Isle of San Salvador, another Monk, the Reverend Father Solozano, made the hills and forests of the New World witness the solemn rites, and re-echo to the sacred chants of Catholic worship; and, first in the Southern part of America, did that Monk plant the sign of man's salvation, on a soil, the discovery of which saved the life of Columbus. Thence onward, through difficulties, dangers and death, the Catholic missionaries pressed on, in their labors of love, to every part of the New World.

In 1542 The Franciscans Father Padilla and Brother John of the Cross cheerfully died martyrs in the present diocese of Sante Fe. Before the English had formed a single settlement either in Virginia or New England, all the tribes on the Rio Grande were converted and civilized: "The Dominicans, Franciscans and Jesuits labored in Florida. "Villages of converted Indians gathered around the Spanish

"ports. Devotional works were translated and printed in
"the Indian dialect. The 'Doctrina Christiana', of PAREJA,
"is the oldest published work in any Indian dialect of the
"United States. The convent of Saint Helena, in the City
"of St. Augustine, became the centre whence the Franciscans
"spread in every direction. The faith prospered among the
"tribes, and the cross towered in every Indian village, till
"the increasing English colony of Carolina brought war into
"those peaceful regions. In 1703 the valley of the Appa-
"lachicola was ravaged by an armed body of covetous fan-
"atics; the Indian towns were destroyed; the missionaries
"slaughtered, and their neophytes shared their fate, or still
"more unfortunate, were hurried away, and sold as slaves in
"the English West Indies. Fifty years after the whole
"colony of Florida fell into the hands of England, and Cath-
"olicity, under its crushing power, languished or escaped to
"less intolerant rule. The Missions were destroyed, the
"Indians dispersed, and St. Helena, the convent whence
"Christianity had radiated over the Peninsula, became a
"barrack. Driven from their villages, the unhappy Indians
"wandered in the wilderness, and resumed their nomadic
"life, from which Christianity had reclaimed them. Buried
"in the pathless everglades, they took the name of Semi-
"noles, (wanderers,) gradually lost the faith, and became
"the scourge of the whites." Discovery, by Shea.

CARTIER sailed into the Gulf of St. Lawrence on the feast
of St. Lawrence, the 10th of August, 1535. The pious
Frenchmen celebrated the feast of the glorious martyr, and
gave his name to the Gulf and River. The cross was
erected perhaps where Bishop Eric had blessed it three
hundred years before. In 1604, permanent settlements
were begun at Quebec and Port Royal, now Annapolis.
Bancroft says, " In 1608, the Apostolic Benediction of the
" Roman Pontiff was solicited on families which exiled

"themselves to evangelize infidels, and by a compact with De
"Biencourt, the proprietory's son, the Order of the Jesuits
"was enriched by an imposition on the fisheries and on the
"fur trade. The arrival of the Jesuit priests was signalized
"by conversions among the natives. In the following year,
"De Biencourt and Father Biart, explored the coast as far
"as the Kenebeck, and ascended that river. The Canibas,
"Algonquins, of the Abenaki nations, touched by the con-
"fiding humanity of the French, listened reverently to the
"message of Redemption. A French colony within the
"United States followed. Under the auspices of Guerche-
"ville and Mary of Medicis, the rude intrenchments of St.
"Sauveur were raised on the eastern shore of Mount Desert
"Isle. The natives venerated Biart as a messenger from
"heaven; and under the summer sky, round a cross in the
"center of the hamlet, matins [mass, we suppose,] and
"vespers were regularly chanted. France and the Roman
"Religion had appropriated the soil of Maine." Vol. I., p.
27. The English, conducted by Argal, attacked St.
Sauveur; one of the missionaries was mortally wounded,
and his companions were carried off prisoners—the Christian colony was broken up!!

However desirable it is to abridge, yet there is something so touching in the following letter that it would scarcely be right to omit it; particularly as giving the key to the success of the missionaries of God's Church. Let it be read, remembering the axiom, "By one learn what all were."

Letter from Father Sebastien Rasles, Missionary of the Society of Jesus in New France to Monsieur his Nephew:

At Nanrantsouak, this 15th of Oct. 1722.

Monsieur, My Dear Nephew:

The Peace of our Lord be with you.

During the more than thirty years that I have passed in the depth of the forests with the Savages, I have been so occupied in instructing them and training them to Christian virtues, that I have scarcely had time to write many letters, even to those who are most dear to me. I cannot, however, refuse you the little detail of my occupations for which you ask. I owe it, indeed, to the gratitude I feel for the strong interest which your friendship induces you to take in all that concerns me.

I am in a district of that vast extent of country which is between Acadia and New England. Two other Missionaries as well as myself are engaged there among the Abnakis Indians; but we are separated very far from each other. The Abnakis Indians, besides the two villages which they have in the midst of the French Colony, have also three other considerable settlements, on the border of a river. There are three rivers, which empty into the sea to the south of Canada, between New England and Acadia.

The village in which I live is called Nanrantsouak, and is situated on the banks of a river, which empties into the sea at the distance of thirty leagues below. I have erected a church there, which is neat and elegantly ornamented. I have indeed thought it my duty to spare nothing, either in the decoration of the building itself, or in the beauty of those articles, which are used in our holy ceremonies. Vestments, chasubles, copes, and holy vessels, all are highly appropriate, and would be esteemed so even in our churches of Europe. I have also formed a little choir of about forty young Indians, who assist at Divine service in cassocks and surplices. They have each their own appropriate functions, as much to serve in the holy sacrifice of the Mass, as to chant the Divine Offices for the adoration of the Holy Sacrament, and for the processions which are made by great crowds of Indians, who often come from a long distance to engage in these exercises; and you would be edified by the beautiful order they observe and the devotion they show.

They have built two chapels at three hundred paces distance from the village: one, above on the river, dedicated to God under the invocation of the Holy Virgin, and where can be seen her image in relief; the other, under the invocation of the Angel Guardians, is below, on the same river. As they are both on the road which leads, both into the woods and into the fields, the Indians can never pass without offering up their prayers. There is a holy emulation among the females of the village as to who shall most ornament the chapel of which they have care; when the procession is to take place there, all who have any jewelry or pieces of silk or calico, or other things of that kind, employ them to adorn it.

The great blaze of light contributes, not a little, to the beauty of the church and of the chapels, it not being necessary for me to be saving of the wax, for the country itself furnishes it abundantly.

None of my neophytes fail to repair twice in each day to the church, early in the morning to hear Mass, and in the evening to assist at the prayers which I offer up at sunset. As it is necessary to fix the imagination of these Indians, which is too easily distracted, I have composed some appropriate prayers for them to make, to enable them to enter into the spirit of the august sacrifice of our altars. They chant them, or recite them in a loud voice during Mass. Besides the sermons which I deliver before them on Sundays and festival days, I scarcely pass a week-day without making a short exhortation, to inspire them with a horror of those vices, to which they are most addicted, or to strengthen them in the practice of some virtue. After the Mass, I teach catechism to the children and young persons, while a large number of aged people, who are present, assist and answer, with perfect docility, the questions which I put to them. The rest of the morning, even to mid-day, is set apart for seeing those who may wish to speak with me. They come to me in crowds, to make me a participator in their pains and inquietudes, or to communicate to me causes of complaint against their countrymen, or to consult me on their marriages, and other affairs of importance. It is therefore necessary for me to instruct some, to console others, to re-establish peace in families at variance, to calm troubled consciences, to correct others by reprimands mingled with softness and charity; in fine, as far as it is possible, to render them all contented.

After mid-day, I visit the sick and go around among the cabins of those, who require more particular instructions. If they hold a council, which is often the case with those Indians, they depute one of the principal men of the assembly, to ask me to assist in their deliberations; I accordingly repair to the place where their council is held; if I think they are pursuing a wise course, I approve of it; if on the contrary, I have anything to say in opposition to their decision, I declare my sentiments, supporting them with weighty reasons, to which they conform. My advice always fixes their resolutions. They do not even hold their feasts without inviting me. Those who have been asked carry each one a dish, of wood or bark, to the place of entertainment. I give the benediction on the food, and they place, in each dish, the portion which has been prepared. After this distribution has been made, I say grace, and each one retires; for such is the order and usage of their feast.

In the midst of such continued occupations, you cannot imagine with what rapidity the days pass by. There have been seasons, when I scarcely had time to recite my office, or take a little repose during the night; for discretion is not a virtue which particularly belongs to the Indians. But, for some years past, I have made it a rule, not to speak with any person from the prayers in the evening, until the time of it, on the next morning. I have therefore forbidden them to interrupt me during this period, except for some very important reasons, as, for example to assist a person who is dying, or some other affair of the kind which it is impossible to put off. I set apart this time to spend in prayer, or to repose myself from fatigues of the day.

When the Indians repair to the sea shore, where they pass some months in hunting the ducks, bustards, and other birds, which are found there in large numbers, they build on an island a church, which they cover with bark, and near it they erect a little cabin for my residence. I take care to transport a part of our ornaments, and the service is performed with the same decency, and the same crowds of people, as at the village.

You see then, my dear nephew, what are my occupations. For that which relates to me personally, I will say to you that I neither hear, nor see, nor speak to any but Indians. My food is very simple and light. I have never been able to conform my taste to the meat, or smoked fish of the savages, and my nourishment is only composed of corn, which they pound, and of which I make each day a kind of hominy which I boil in water. The only luxury in which I indulge is a little sugar, which I mix with it to correct its insipidity. This is never wanting in the forest. In the spring, the maple trees contain a liquor very similar to that which is found in the sugar-canes of the Southern Islands. The women employ themselves in collecting this in vessels of bark, as it is distilled from the trees. They then boil it, and draw off from it a very good sugar. That which is drawn off first is always the most beautiful.

The whole nation of the Abnakis is Christian, and very zealous to preserve their religion. This attachment to the Catholic faith has induced them, even to this time, to prefer

our alliance to advantages which might be derived from an
alliance with the English, who are their neighbors. These
advantages would be, too, of very great importance to our
Indians. The facility of trading with the English, from
whom they are distant but one of two days' journey, the
ease with which the journey can be made, the admirable
market they would find there for the purchase of the mer-
chandise that suits them—these things certainly hold out
very great inducements. In place of which, in going to
Quebec, it is necessary to take more than a fortnight, to
reach there, they have to furnish themselves with provisions for the journey, they have different rivers to cross,
and frequent portages to make. They are aware of these
inconveniences, and are by no means indifferent to their
interests, but their faith is infinitely more dear to them, and
they believe that if they detach themselves from our alliance,
they will shortly find themselves without a missionary
without sacraments, without a sacrifice, with scarcely any
exercise of their religion, and in manifest danger of being
replunged into their former heathenism. This is the bond
which unites them to the French. Attempts have been
vainly made to break it, sometimes by wiles which were
held out to their simplicity, and sometimes by acts of violence which could not fail to irritate a nation exceedingly
jealous of its rights and liberties. The commencement of
this misunderstanding could not but alarm me, for it made
me fear the dispersion of that little community which Providence had for so many years confided to my care, and for
the sake of which I would willingly sacrifice what remains
to me of life. Let me mention to you, then, some of the
artifices to which the English had recourse to detach them
from our alliance." . . . .

But however striking the instances Father RASLES gives, it

is necessary to refrain. But the poetry of WHITTIER, given by Rev. M. KIP, should not be refused a place here:

> On the brow of a hill, which slopes to meet
> The flowing river, and bathe its feet—
> The bare washed rock, and the drooping grass,
> And the creeping vine as the waters pass—
> A rude and unshapely chapel stands,
> Built up in that wild by unskilled hands;
> Yet the traveler knows a place of prayer
> For the holy sign of the Cross is there;
> And should he chance at that place to be,
> Of a Sabbath morn, or some hallowed day,
> When prayers are made and masses said
> Some for the living, and some for the dead,—
> Well might the traveler start to see
>
> The tall dark forms, that take their way
> From the birch canoe, on the river shore,
> And the forest paths, to that chapel door;
> And marvel to mark the naked knees
> And the dusky foreheads bending these,—
> And stretching his long thin arms over these
> In blessing and in prayer,
> Like a shrouded spectre, pale and tall,
> In his coarse white vesture, Father Balle!"

Omitting the most interesting letters on that mission, space will only suffice to admit the last, which depicts the tragic end:

From Father De La Chasse, Superior General of Missions in New France, to Father —— of the same Society.

AT QUEBEC, 29th of October, 1724.

MY REVEREND FATHER

The Peace of our Lord be with you!

In the deep grief which we feel for the loss of one of our oldest missioners, it is a sweet consolation for us, that he has fallen a victim to his love, and his zeal to preserve the faith, in the heart of his neophytes. You have been already apprized by previous letters of the origin of the war which was kindled up, between the English and the Indians. In the former, the desire to extend their dominions; in the latter, the horror of all subjection and the attachment to their religion, caused at first that misunderstanding, which was at length followed by an open rupture.

Father RASLES, missionary to the Abnakis, had become exceedingly odious to the English. Convinced that his industry in strengthening the Indians in their faith, constituted the greatest obstacle to the design they had formed, of encroaching upon the Indian lands; they set a price upon his head; and, on more than one occasion, endeavored either to capture or destroy him. At last they have effected their object, in satisfying their transport of hate, and freeing themselves from this apostolical man; but at the same time they have procured for him a glorious death, which was always the height of his desires; for we know that, for a long time, he had aspired to the happiness of sacrificing his life for his flock. I will describe to you in a few words, the circumstances of this event.

After frequent hostilities had taken place, on each side, between the two nations, a small force composed of the English and their Indian allies, to the number of about eleven hundred men, came unexpectedly to attack the village of Nanrantsouak. The thick brushwood by which the village is surrounded, aided them in concealing their march, besides not being enclosed by palisades, the Indians taken by surprise, did not perceive the approach of their enemies, until they received a general discharge of musketry, which riddled all the cabins. There were at that time about fifty warriors in the village. At the first noise of the musketry they simultaneously seized their arms, and went forth from their cabins to make head against the enemy. Their design was, not rashly to sustain a contest with so great a number of combatants, but to cover the flight of the women and children, and to give them time to gain the other side of the river, which was not as yet occupied by the English.

Father RASLES, warned by the clamors and the tumult, of the peril which threatened his neophytes, promptly went forth from his house, and, without fear, presented himself before the enemy. His hope was, either to suspend, by his presence, their first efforts, or, at least, to draw on him alone, their attention, and thus, at the expense of his own life, to procure the safety of his flock.

The instant they perceived the missionary, they raised a general shout, followed by a discharge of musket balls, which rained on him. He fell dead at the foot of a large cross, which he had erected in the middle of the village, to mark the public profession they had made to adore, in that place, the crucified God. Seven Indians, who surrounded him, and who exposed their lives to preserve that of their father, were killed at his side.

The death of the shepherd spread consternation through the flock. The Indians took to flight and crossed the river, part by the ford, and part by swimming. They had to endure all the fury of their enemies, even to the moment when they took refuge in the woods on the other side of the river. There they found themselves assembled to the number of about a hundred and fifty. Although more than two thousand musket-shots had been directed against them, they had but about thirty persons killed, including women and children, and fourteen wounded. The English did not attempt to pursue the fugitives, but contented themselves with pillaging and burning the village. The fire which they kindled in the church, was preceded by an unhallowed profanation of the sacred vessels, and of the adorable body of Jesus Christ. The precipitate retreat of the enemy permitted the Nanrantsouakans to return to the village. On the morrow, they visited the ruins of their cabins, while the women, on their part, sought for herbs and plants to dress the wounded. Their first care was to weep over the body of their missionary: they found it pierced with a thousand wounds, his scalp taken off, the skull split by blows of a hatchet, the mouth and eyes filled with mud, the bones of the legs broken, and all the limbs mutilated. They were scarcely able to attribute, except to the Indian allies of the English, such an excess of inhumanity on a body, deprived of feeling and of life.

After these fervent Christians had washed and kissed, many times, the precious remains of their Father, they buried him in the same spot where, the day before, he had celebrated the holy sacrifice of the Mass, that is, on the place where the altar had stood before the burning of the church.

It is by so precious a death that this apostolic man finished, on the 23rd of August of this year, [1724,] a career of thirty seven years passed in the painful toils of this mission. He was in the sixty-seventh year of his age. His fasts and continual fatigues had latterly enfeebled his constitution. During the last nineteen years, he had dragged himself about with difficulty, in consequence of a fall in which he broke his right thigh and his left leg. It happened that the fractured parts having badly united, it became necessary to break the left leg anew. While they were drawing it most violently, he sustained this painful operation with extraordinary firmness and admirable tranquility. Our physician, who was present, appeared so astonished, that he could not forbear saying to him, "Ah, my Father, permit at least some groans to escape you, for you have cause for them."

Father Rasles joined to talents which made him an excellent missionary, those virtues which are necessary for that Evangelical Ministry, to be exercised with effect among our Indians. He enjoyed robust health, and with the exception of the accident I have mentioned, I do not know that he ever had the least indisposition. We were surprised at his industry and readiness in acquiring the different Indian languages. There was not one on this continent of which he had not some knowledge. Besides the Abnakis language, which he spoke for a long time, he knew also the Huron, the Otaonais, and the Illinois. He availed himself of them with great effect in the different missions where they are used. Since his arrival in Canada, he was never seen to act inconsistently with his character; he was always firm and courageous, severe to himself, tender and compassionate in his regard to others.

Three years ago by order of Monsieur, our Governor, I made a journey through Acadia. In conversation with Father Rasles, I represented to him, that in case they declared war against the Indians, he would run the risk of his life; that his village, being but fifteen leagues distant from the English forts, he would find himself exposed to the first irruptions; that his preservation was necessary to his flock, and that he ought to take measures for his own security. "My measures are taken," he answered in a firm tone; "God has committed this flock to my care, and I will share its lot, being too happy, if permitted to sacrifice my life for it." He repeated often the same thing to his neophytes to strengthen their constancy in the faith. "We have had but too good a proof," they themselves have said to me, "that our dear Father spoke to us from the abundance of his heart; we have seen him, with a tranquil and serene air, meet death, and oppose himself alone to the fury of the enemy, to retard their first efforts, for the purpose of giving us time to escape the danger and to preserve our lives."

May it please the Lord that his blood, shed for so just a cause, may enrich these heathen lands so often watered by the blood of the evangelical laborers who have preceded us;

that it may render them fertile in earnest Christians, and that it may animate the zeal of apostolical men to come and reap the abundant harvest which is offered by so many people still shrouded in the shadow of death. Nevertheless, as it appertains only to the Church to declare the names of the saints, I recommend him to your holy sacrifices, and to those of all the Fathers. And I pray you not to forget him who is, with much respect, etc."

We cannot conclude this letter without quoting from Dr. Convers Francis' Life of Rale—to which we have been indebted for many of these notes—a couple of passages describing the present appearance of the spot on which this tragedy of Rasles' death took place: " Whoever has visited the pleasant town of Norridgwock, as it now is, must have heard of Indian Old Point, as the people call the place where Rasles' village stood, and perhaps curiosity may have carried him thither. If so, he has found a lovely sequestered spot in the depths of nature's stillness, on a point around which the waters of the Kennebec, not far from their confluence with those of Sandy River, sweep on their beautiful course, as if to the music of the rapids above—a spot over which the sad memory of the past, without its passions, will throw a charm, and on which he will believe that the ceaseless worship of nature, might blend itself with the aspirations of Christian devotion. He will find, that vestiges of the old settlement are not wanting now; that broken utensils, glass beads, and hatchets have been turned up, by the husbandman's plough, and are preserved by the people of the neighborhood; he will turn away from the place with the feeling, that the hatefulness of the mad spirit of war, is aggravated by such connection with nature's sweet retirements.

With the Rev. W. J. Kip, now Protestant Bishop of California, we close this greatly abridged, yet still most touching narration with another quotation from WHITTIER'S poem of "Mogg Megone," describing RASLES' Indian village after the ruin:

> "No wigwam smoke is curling there;
> The very earth is scorched and bare:
> And they pause and listen to catch a sound
>   Of breathing life, but there comes not one,
> Save the fox's bark and the rabbit's bound;
> And here and there, on the blackened ground,
>   White bones are glistening in the sun.
> And where the house of prayer arose,
> And the holy hymn at daylight's close,
> And the aged priest stood up to bless
> The children of the wilderness,
> There is naught, save ashes sodden and dank,
>   And the birchen boats of the Norridgwock,
>   Tethered to tree, and stump, and rock,
> Rotting along the river bank!"

The spot on which the Norridgwock missionary fell, was marked, some time after his death, by the erection of a cross. This, it is said, in process of time, was cut down by a company of hunters. I believe it was replaced by some rude memorial in stone. But in 1833, a permanent monument was erected in honor of RALE. . . . An acre of land was purchased, including the site of RALE's church and his grave. Over the grave, on the 23d of August, 1833, the anniversary (according to the New Style) of the fight at Norridgwock, and just one hundred and nine years after its occurrence, the foundation was laid and the monument raised with much ceremony, amidst a large concourse of people. Bishop FENWICK, of Boston, directed the ceremonies and delivered an address full of appropriate interest. Delegates from the Penobscot, Passamaquaddy, and Canada Indians were present on the occasion. The monument is about twenty feet high, including an iron cross with which it is surmounted. On the south side of the base, fronting the Kennebec River, is an appropriate and somewhat long Latin inscription." p. 329,

All that is generally read of this interesting mission is contained in the following words of an estimable historian:

"In 1640 the Jesuits were invited, by a deputation from the Abanakis Indians, to resume their missions in Maine. The Jesuit Fathers LA CHASSE, two Fathers BIGOT, LOGARD, and SIRENNE, and AUBRY, preached the gospel so effectually as to convert that powerful tribe. The mission long retained its zeal and fervour. But when Canada was conquered by England, the English from Massachusetts spread fire and death through the villages of the Abanakis; the missionaries were driven away, or slain; the churches destroyed; and the Indians deprived of all the consolations of faith. Yet these poor Indians remained true to their religion. Down to our day, they have resisted the preachers of Protestantism, and the remnants of this tribe, still occupy five villages in Maine and Canada, they are all Catholics, as their forefathers have been for two centuries.

CHAPTER IV.

INDIANS.

IN the preliminary details of this histo.y. t was wished to give an idea of all the early Catholic Missionaries by authentic details of one who, though heroic, was surpassed in austerities and sufferings by many others. O. H. MARSHALL, Esq., passing over the dead and martyred Franciscans, says of the Jesuits: "During this same period, fifty-five of the Order arrived in Canada, of which number sixteen returned. One was frozen, two were drowned, fourteen died, seven suffered martyrdom by the Iroquois, five were otherwise killed, leaving ten remaining in the country in 1657. Thus, in a few years, of fifty-five priests, but twenty-six escaped from violent death or martyrdom. And most of the small remnant soon passed away to eternal rest, on account of fatigues and sufferings for souls redeemed by Christ.

In few but eloquent words, Mr. MARSHALL follows the successors of those martyred missionaries, "as they located at Sault St. Marie and the Fond du Lac of Green Bay, on the picturesque islands of Mackinaw and along the borders of the Illinois and Mississppi rivers. They doubled in their frail canoes, the head lands of Lake Superior, discovered the mines which abound on its shores and founded a mission at its farthest extremity." But it is time to return from heroic personal virtue, to consider those sacred ways of God's Providence by which the light of faith first dawned on Western New-York and on this diocese.

"Savage indeed, in many respects, as the Indians appeared to be," says TURNER, "yet the kindest hospitality, from the purest motives was always readily extended to their foreign guests; and perhaps the golden cord of friendship would forever have remained unbroken, had *the red man* been the first to begin hostilities. "Welcome English;" "welcome English," (The word "English," was too hard for Indian pronunciation, hence, in Indian mouths the welcome was: "welcome Yingees," "welcome Yingees;" hence the name Yankee;) are words intimately associated with early American history. These were the first accents our Pilgrim Fathers heard on the American strand, and ever have the same grateful sounds greeted the ears of the whites, upon their first interview with the rude sons of the forest. Had the disposition of the Aborigines been any other than friendly, the feeble colonies first planted on American soil would have been speedily annihilated." The following is an extract from the first sermon ever preached in New England. It was by one of the Pilgrims. "To us the Indians have been like lambs, so kind, so submissive, and trusty, as a man may truly say, many Christians are not so kind and sincere; when we first came into this country, we were few, and many of us sick, and many died by reason of the cold and wet, it being the depth of winter, and we having no horses or shelter; yet, when there were not six able persons among us, though the Indians came daily to us, by hundreds, with their sachems or kings, and might, in one hour, have made a dispatch of us, yet they never offered us the least injury. The greatest commander cometh often to visit us, often sends us presents, &c."

The Respectable Protestant writer who quotes this sermon, continues thus "And yet aggressions and wrongs commenced on the part of our race, in its earliest intercourse with theirs; were some of his own race, the chronicler of events—commencing with the discovery of Columbus and coming down to our own day of pre-emption bribes, and treaties attained with wrong and outrage—he would gather up a fearful account."—Turner, Hist. of the H. P. 76. "The Pilgrim Fathers" begun the war of oppression "and cruelty; the Indians, savagely retaliated." The last law of the "*Holy Pilgrims*," destroyed the Indian race within their reach. We quote Bancrofts Hist. of U.S. Vol. III. p. 217.

The Indians could not be reduced by the usual method of warfare: hence "a bounty was offered for every *Indian scalp;* to regular forces under pay, the grant was ten pounds; to volunteers, in actual service, twice that sum; but if men would, of themselves, without pay, make up parties and patrol the forests, in search of Indians, as of old the woods were scoured for wild beasts, the chase was invigorated by the promised encouragement of fifty pounds, (two hundred and fifty dollars) for each scalp."

An educated Cayuga chief spoke thus before the New

York Historical Society. "The land of Ya-nun-no, or the "Empire State," as you love to call it, was once traced by our trails, from Albany to Buffalo. Trails that we had trod for centuries—trails worn so deep by the feet of the Iroquois, that they became your road of travel, as your possessions gradually eat into those of my people. Your roads still traverse those same lines of communication, which bound one part of the long house to the other. Have we, the first-holders of this prosperous region, no longer a share in your history? Glad were your fathers to sit down upon the treshold of the Long House. Rich did they hold themselves in getting the mere sweepings from its door. Had our Forefathers spurned you from it, when the French were thundering at the opposite side; to get a passage through; and drive you into the sea; whatever has been the fate of other Indians, we might still have had a nation, and I—I, instead of pleading here for the privelege of lingering within your borders, I—I might have a country." [Turner.]

It is sad, yet often instructive, to take a review of sins long past, and of the retribution in time which follow them. When our forefathers reached this land, the Indians were numerous, confiding and generous. The State of New York, especially, was filled with Indians. In it, and stretching into Ohio, were the Erie or Cat Nation; where Buffalo now stands, and west and east of it, was the Neuter Nation, then, bending eastward, with the course of the waters, were the Senecas, the Cayugas, the Onondagas, the Oneidas, and the Mohawks; on the Susquehana were the Andastas or Canestogues. The Delawares and others dwelt south and west of these tribes.

Thirteen different tribes of Indians, all of whom are now extinct, dwelt on Long Island; many others to the east, amongst which the Massachusetts early attached themselves to the English, their name means "Toward the Big Mountain, Massatzoick.

A writer who supposed Hudson to have been the first to visit our State says: "The first European advent to our State was marked by inflicting on the Indian race a curse, more terrible in its consequences than all else combined. While Hudson's vessel lay in the river, near Albany, great multitudes of savages flocked on board. In order to discover whether "any of the chiefe men of the country, had any treacherie in them," our master and mate took them into the cabin, and gave them so much wine and *aquavitæ*, that they were all merrie. One of them became intoxicated, staggered and fell, at which the natives were astonished." It was "strange to them, for they could not tell how to take it." They all hurried ashore in their canoes. The intoxicated Indian remaining."

In 1609, Hudson entered the Hudson river, he testifies to the friendly disposition of the natives. They soon complained that efforts had beed made on his part to kidnap two Indians. Afterwards some Indians attracted by curiosity, and having, perhaps, imperfect ideas of the rights of property, stole into the cabin window, and pilfered a pillow and some wearing apparel. The Indian was shot at and killed; another Indian was killed in recovering the property. Following after these events, was a concerted attempt on the part of the natives to get possession of the ship. It failed. Nine of the Indians were killed, none of the Europeans. Thus a relation that began in friendship, ended in war. [Turner 83.]

The English " Plymouth Company," in 1613, fitted out two vessels, and placed one of them under the command of Capt. Smith and the other, Capt. Hunt. This expedition explored with care the whole coast from Cape Cod to Penobscot. Captain Hunt, who commanded one of the vessels, instead of returning with Smith, enticed a number of Indians aboard his vessel; and, touching at Malagar, on his homeward voyage, sold them as slaves; thus, upon the threshold of New England civilization, provoking the natives to abandon their pacific policy, and look upon the new comers as enemies. The very next vessel that visited the coast of New England brought news of their vindictive hostility." Turner, 82.

"In the autumn of 1650 and spring of 1651, two frontier villages of the Neutral Nation, one of which was located near what is now Buffalo, were sacked and destroyed by the Senecas. The largest village contained 1,600 men. Those spared from death were taken to Gannogareo, a Seneca village east of the Genesee River, where they were found by Father Fremin, in 1669.

The "relations," which will be here continued, of the mission, will also afford glimpses of the Indian history. When the Indian missions on the American side were crushed, the Indian race rapidly sunk into almost vassalage. The following remarks from a distinguished Protestant writer, may be considered their epitaph:

"It becomes us not to forget those distinguished braves, (the Six Nations,) who so freely shed their blood for their English allies. . . . Had it not been for the long continued friendship of these distinguished people, and the inestimable service rendered by them in the English wars with the French, it is not at all certain that the English would have been successful; and it is possible, if not probable, that the colonies would have been governed by the French." He then tells us that these Indians, in the war of American independence, were on the side of England, "and rendered essential service to the Crown." Page 317. "But, after the war of the Revolution, the English treated their Indian allies with great indifference and neglect." In the treaty there was no stipulation made in behalf of the Indians. By *treaties*, they were gradually deprived of their lands. In 1814, in council at Buffalo, the Oneidas, Onondagas, Cayugas, and Senecas pledged themselves to the American cause, against England. They fought and bled at Chippewa, Lundy's Lane, &c., under the gallant generals, Brown, Scott, Ripley, and Porter. "Their services have never been duly appreciated, and the scanty pittance meted out for their services (he might also say for their land,) is but a common illustration of the gratitude and magnanimity of powerful nations toward the weaker." History of Onondagas, page 346.

Among the old traditions of the Indians, the following speech is stated to have caused the celebrated confederacy of the Indians. The prediction of ruin through division was too well accomplished. God grant that the sad experience of a once powerful race, now fast passing away, may aid in restoring union to our far nobler, our far more prosperous confederacy.

"The council assembled, and all were anxious to hear the words of Hi-a-wat-ha. A breathless silence ensued, and the venerable counselor began:

"Friends and Brothers: You are members of many tribes and nations. You have come here, many of you, a great distance from your homes. We have convened for one common purpose, to promote one common interest, and that is, to provide for our mutual safety, and how it shall be best accomplished. To oppose these hordes of northern foes by tribes, singly and alone, would prove our certain destruction; we can make no progress in that way. We must unite ourselves into one common band of brothers. Our warriors, united, would surely repel these rude invaders, and drive them from our borders. This must be done and we shall be safe.

"You, the Mohawks, sitting under the shadow of the Great Tree, whose roots sink deep into the earth, and whose branches spread over a vast country, shall be the first nation, because you are warlike and mighty.

"And you, Oneidas, a people who recline your bodies against the Everlasting Stone, that can not be moved, shall be the second nation, because you give wise counsel.

"And you, Onondagas, who have your habitation at the Great Mountain, and are overshadowed by its crags, shall be the third nation, because you are greatly gifted in speech, and mighty in war.

"And you, Cayugas, a people whose habitation is the Dark Forest, and whose home is everywhere, shall be the fourth nation, because of your superior cunning in hunting.

"And you, Senecas, a people who live in the Open Country, and possess much wisdom, shall be the fifth nation, because you understand better the art of raising corn and beans, and making cabins.

"You, five great and powerful nations, must unite, and have but one common interest, and no foe shall be able to disturb or subdue you.

"And you, Manhattoes, Nyacks, Montauks, and others, who are as the feeble Bushes; and you, Naragansetts, Mohegans, Wampanoags, and your neighbors, who are a Fishing People, may place yourselves under our protection. Be with us, and we will defend you. You of the South, and you of the West may do the same, and we will protect you. We earnestly desire your alliance and friendship.

"Brothers, if we unite in this bond, the Great Spirit will smile upon us, and we shall be free, prosperous, and happy. But if we remain as we are, we shall be subject to his frown; we shall be enslaved, ruined, perhaps, annihilated forever. We shall perish, and our names be blotted out from among the nations of men. Brothers, these are the words of Hi-a-wat-ha; let them sink deep into your hearts. I have said it."

CHAPTER V.

RELIGION, RITES AND CEREMONIES.

These Indians believe in one Great and Good Spirit, styled in the language of the Onondagas, Ha-wah-ne-u, who is the Creator of the world; the Holder of the Heavens; the Master of Breath; the Maker of men and useful animals. He is the controller of events; He rules the destinies of men; supplies them with the comforts and conveniences of life; makes abundance of game in the hunting grounds, and supplies the streams with fish, and the air with birds. He is believed to be the peculiar Deity of the red man, and they are his peculiar people.

To this Great and Good Being they address their prayers, render thanks for success in hunting, and for victories in war. To him they offer sacrifices and chant their songs of praise. These things they do with a regularity, devotion, and reverence, in the midst of a Christian people, within the influences of the Gospel; and adhere to them with a tenacity that should make their Christian neighbors ashamed.

In each year, they hold five stated festivals, for a general assembling of their clans. Upon these occasions, all join in thanksgiving to the Great and Good Spirit for blessings received from his beneficent hand; the old men converse upon the best means of meriting his favors, and of continuing to merit them in future.

The fifth or last festival, the crowning one of the year, and the one to which most importance is attached, is celebrated late in the month of January, or early in the month of February, according to the phases of the moon. The Indian year is reckoned by moons, and this great national festival is held at the full moon, nearest the first of our month February.

The hunters having all returned from the chase, and having brought in their venison and skins, that have been taken, and a portion of these trophies having been deposited in the council house, two sets of managers are appointed, numbering from ten to twenty young men on a side. These are chosen to superintend all the concerns relative to the grand festival, thanksgiving, and sacrifice, which is immediately to take place.

Arrangements are made at the council house for the reception and accommodation of the whole nation. This being done, the managers are ready to commence their appropriate duties, during the whole of which they act with great formality, order, and decorum.

On the first day, a select number from each party of the managers, some four or five, start from the council house, and run with all possible speed to every cabin in the nation, knocking on the doors and sides of the houses, informing the people that all things are now ready, and that they must immediately repair to the council house, and partake of the festivities of the occasion. The fire is now extinguished in every cabin, the committee enter the dwelling, (the inmates expecting them,) and, with a small wooden shovel, scatter the ashes in every direction. The hearths are made clean; new fire is struck from the flint and rekindled: thus they proceed from house to house till every one is visited and purified. During these proceedings the remaining part of the managers are engaged at the council house in firing guns, hallooing, shouting, &c., to inform the people that the ceremonies have commenced. They meet all those who come to the festival, greet them most cordially, and conduct them into the council house.

This is the course pursued on the first day. The second day, the managers assemble early at the council house, and receive from the master of ceremonies instructions for the day. When ready to depart, several guns are usually fired, accompanied by shouting and hallooing. On this day, the managers are fantastically dressed, and proceed from house to house, with baskets, collecting the gifts of the people with which to grace the festival. These gifts consist of pork, beef, bread, beans, pease, ears of corn, tobacco, savory herbs, small handfuls of straw, nicely bound, and every article is received that is useful for food, for incense, or for sacrifice. Every one is bound to give something, or he is not to be included in the general absolution. Each manager, in his round of alms-gathering, carries a large rattle, made of dried tortoise shell, in which are small stones, pease, or beans. These they rattle violently in the several cabins, earnestly inviting the people to bestow their gifts. These proceedings are continued for several days, according to the time allotted for the continuance of the festival. During all this time, the people who are assembled at the council house, are engaged in leaping, running, dancing, and their native sports.

On the day preceding the last, the managers, having gathered all the sins of the nation to themselves, and made full report of all their proceedings to the person who officiates as high priest, or master of ceremonies, the day is spent in preparation for the great day of sacrifice, which is to take place on the morrow. This day is concluded with demonstrations of joy, festivity and dancing.

The last day, and the one to which most consequence is attached, being the great day of sacrifice, the people assemble at the council house in great numbers. The exercises commence, by building large fires early in the morning, by firing guns, and loud hallooing. The wood for the sacrificial offering is arranged near the council house, by laying near half a cord in alternate layers, crosswise. This is done by a select committee of the managers, who proceed with considerable ceremony.

A house, near the council house, is selected as a place in which to make preparation. To this the managers proceed, and prepare themselves for the occasion. One from each party is selected as a leader. They are dressed in long loose shirts of white; others are appropriately dressed, as managers, &c., according to the duties they are expected to perform. The grand master of ceremonies, or high priest, takes his station at the council house, and to him reports are made of the progress of the proceedings, and he, in turn gives new directions. Messengers are continually passing and re-passing from the council house to the house of preparation. On the occasion, at which notes for this article were taken, the venerable Oh-he-nu presided with great dignity. Having arrived at an early hour, we found this gray-headed chief gravely seated near the center of the council house, discoursing to his people, receiving messages, and giving directions.

About nine o'clock, the managers rushed out of the house of preparation, and two white dogs, fantastically painted with red figures, and adorned with small belts of wampum feathers, and ribbons tied around their necks, legs, and tails, followed them. A long rope, with a single knot in the centre, was instantly passed over the head of one of them, when some eight or ten of the managers seized the rope on either side, commenced pulling lustily, each party occasionally yielding to the other, as if to give greater force to their operations. After a few struggles, the dog was suffocated, and hung up on a ladder, which leaned against the house. The other dog was disposed of in precisely the same manner, and hung beside his fellow. Guns were now fired, and some thirty or forty persons rushed out of the council-house, gave three tremendous yells, and retired. After about half an hour, the dogs were taken down, and carried into the house of preparation. To this house spectators were not admitted, and what particular ceremonies were there performed, we have no means of knowing. These dogs are always white, or as nearly so as they can procure them; spot or blemish renders them unsuitable for sacrifice. A wound producing an effusion of blood would be productive of the same consequences.

By some peculiar manœuvering, the sins of the people, which had become concentrated in the managers, are now transferred to the two individuals, who are clad in the white garments. These, by some peculiar ceremony, again work those sins off, into the dogs. These animals, thus laden with the sins of the nation are raised upon the shoulders of two persons appointed for that purpose, (their legs being tied so as to admit of their being slung, like a pack.) A procession is formed in ranks of double files, preceded by the two men dressed in white, and others of the managers, followed by as many others as may choose to join them. The procession moves slowly and silently, with measured step, around the house of preparation, through the council-house, which has two doors, one opposite the other, and around it. After which they are brought in, and the dogs laid upon a platform, about a foot from the floor. As they enter the council-house for the last time, they break into single file. While these ceremonies were going on at the house of preparation and out of doors, others of importance were observed in the coun -house.

The offerings which h been collected were disposed of upon pins around the counc -room. The master of ceremonies, during the whole progress of proceedings, remained stationary, seated in the centre of the council-room. To him were brought, at different times, at intervals of about two minutes, every article which had been deposited. Every person who brought a piece of pork, a paper of tobacco, a bunch of herbs, or a handfull of straw, stopped about three paces from him, holding it towards him, looking him full in the face with the greatest attention. After he had said a few words, the old chief took it in his hands, over which he uttered a short ejaculatory prayer or thanksgiving, after which a hearty response was made by all present. It was then returned to the place from which it had been taken. Every article of the offerings was presented and returned in like manner. The females present participated in these ceremonies. All the messengers who addressed the chief halted at a respectful distance, and stood a moment in silence before they made their communications. These events all transpired at the council-house before the dogs were brought in. After the dogs were brought in, the procession, in single file, moved three times round the platform, before they were laid down. At each round, the master of ceremonies rose in a sedate and dignified manner, clapped his hands on the shoulders of the bearer of the dog who was foremost in the procession. He stopped in the precise position he was in, when the hand of the chief was laid upon his shoulder, and there remained as motionless as a statue for the space of a minute, during which he was addressed in a whisper by the master of ceremonies. Several other chiefs addressed those who carried the dogs, in the same manner, and again the procession moved on. After this, the dogs were laid upon the platform, and all joined in loud singing and chanting, while the procession continued slowly moving around the dead carcasses of the dogs, with the most devout solemnity.

While these ceremonies were proceeding in the council house, fire had been applied to the altar of wood outside. The pile had become nearly half consumed and yielded great heat; while around it, in a circle, had been drawn a line, within which it was not intended spectators should pass. This, however, availed nothing, for the moment the procession had drawn around the fire, the area was crowded to its utmost capacity.

Under the direction of "Oh-he-nu," the bearers of the dogs again resumed their burdens; a procession was formed in single file, the master of ceremonies taking the lead. Then followed the men in white robes, the persons who carried the dogs, the managers and others promiscuously. As the procession moved along, the principal actors in the scene commenced singing, which continued while the whole marched around the council house to the place of sacrifice. Around the burning pile they moved three separate times, the last of which, the master of ceremonies stopped on the west side, with his face to the east and towards the fire. The remainder of the procession formed around the circle; the persons in white being on the left hand of the high priest, and those bearing the dogs near them.

The leader of the ceremonies offered a short prayer to the Great Spirit; a sacrificial chant was sung; the dogs were laid at the feet of the officiating priest; another prayer was offered; another chant was sung, when one of the dogs was cast into the fire by the high priest. A like ceremony was performed, and the remaining dog was also thrown upon the burning pile, and again followed the chanting. Different individuals now brought forward baskets of herbs, tobacco, and such like, which were at intervals thrown upon the fire, and, with the consuming dogs, produced a variety of scents not easily comprehended. After the dogs were nearly consumed, the procession was again formed and returned to the council house, and the committee were directed to go to the preparation house. The solemnities of this day being concluded, they formally adjourned. The accustomed ceremonies of this interesting season are usually concluded by a war dance and feast on the same day after the sacrifice."

We will fitly close by the following remarks of the same author, Mr. Clark, in his History of the Onondagas, vol. 1, page 70.

"Sacrifices have in all ages and by almost every nation been regarded as necessary to appease divine anger, and to render Deity propitious." Page 70. "The origin of the institution of sacrifices is clearly traceable to Divine authority, and to that pure primeval period when our original ancestor and his sons were yet upon earth." *

Early in the morning, previous to the commencement of the war dance, several large kettles had been placed over the fires, in which were cooking the ingredients, upon which the whole nation were at liberty to feast. The contents were composed of meat, corn, beans, pease, potatoes, turnips, some garden herbs, which served for seasoning, and other things which had been previously gathered in the baskets. After the close of the war dance, and the peace dance; the feast was made ready, by removing the kettles to a convenient distance from the fires.

The mass was frequently stirred till the whole became completely mixed. The contents of the kettles were devoured without regard to politeness or ceremony. Some dipped from the kettles with spoons, others skimmed out the more substantial parts with chips, some were provided with bowls and spoons, while others, as soon as the scalding aliment was sufficiently cooled, thrust in their fingers, and thus

---

*Of course the primeval idea of rewards and punishments beyond the grave, exists among the Indians. But it is strange that an idea common to the Hebrews in their last state before the coming of Christ should also prevail among the Indians. Like those Hebrews, Indians believe that no Indian, who has not quit his national religion will be lost forever. He will, if not good, go to the bad hunting ground, pursue, through briars and thorns, deer so lean that, when taken, they can not be eaten, yet, after expiation, he will be admitted to the good hunting ground. But if he quit his national religion, he is lost for ever.

obtained their share. After a reasonable time, the whole had vanished, and all appeared to be refreshed and satisfied. The pipe of peace was now lighted, and the presiding officer of the past ceremonies drew the first draught, puffed the first whiff, and was very careful that a large quantity of smoke should issue from his mouth at the same time, which he took great pains to make ascend in graceful curls, and watched them with peculiar enjoyment. The pipe was passed from him to the other chiefs present, and from them to the old men, who all partook of it with a commendable relish.

Having concluded the ceremonies of the great festival, and all its requirements being fulfilled, every one feels himself absolved from the sins of the past year, and forms new resolutions for the time to come. Congratulations are exchanged, and new hopes excited; free from iniquity and resolved to follow the path of evil no more; each one repairs to his home, happy in the propitious commencement of a new year, in perfect readiness to embark in all the operations of war, the chase, the council, or the cabin.

During the celebration of these ceremonies, the Indians observe the strictest sobriety and propriety of conduct, and seem pleased with the company of visitors and strangers who are disposed to treat them respectfully.

These dances of the Onondagas, which are similar to those of the other five nations, may, with propriety, be called the descriptive dances. They are intended to exhibit some action, or series of actions, generally relating to war, and the imitation is often so close and so exactly executed, that the most indifferent spectator can follow the intentions of the performers. Dances are rather a business than a pastime. They mingle with all the occupations and enterprizes of life. When war is declared and proclaimed, it is by means of a dance, and the warriors who engage in it, are thereby enlisted. When an alliance is concluded, or peace restored, the event is celebrated by a dance, corresponding to the difference of circumstances. The war dance is the exact image of a campaign.

The Baron Lahontan, speaking of the dances of the American Indians, says: "These dances may be compared to the military dance of Minerva; for these savages observe, whilst dancing, with singular gravity, the harmony of certain songs, which the Greek soldiers of Achilles called Hyporchematiques."

It is not easy to decide whether the savages learned them of the Greeks, or the Greeks of the savages.

Charlevoix, upon the same subject, remarks that the greatest of their feasts, their songs and dances appear to have their origin in religion, and still preserve some traces of it. I have met with some who could not help thinking that our savages were descended from the Jews, and found in everything some affinity between these people and the children of God. Indeed, there are, in some things, a strong resemblance.

The origin of the institution of sacrifice, as before remarked, is clearly traceable to Divine authority. Cain brought of the fruits of the ground an offering; and his brother Abel, of the firstlings of his flock and the fat thereof. From the examples of the early chosen people of God, the Gentile nations received or retained their notions of sacrifice, and on this account, we need not wonder to find so many coincidences in the sacrificial systems of the Jews, and the neighboring nations. All false religions can be considered only as departures from the true. . . . . . .

The principal yearly sacrifice of the Jews, were the Paschal lamb, at the Passover, celebrated at the commencement of the sacred year, the day of Pentecost, or first fruits, lastly, the day of expiation or great day of atonement. Two others were afterwards added. Besides these, were the monthly festivals, and others of less importance; yet they were nevertheless attended with the greatest punctuality, but never more so, than are the five stated festivals of the Six Nations, to this day, at Onondaga. Before the law was given to Moses, burnt offerings served for all purposes of Divine worship, whether they gave thanks for blessings, or deprecated evil, or prayed for good. These sacrifices expiated sins of omission, as well as those of commission. This rite has been transmitted, with more or less of corruption, even to the wilds of America, and continued to the present time, among a people, shut out, we know not how long, from all intercourse with the old world.

The priests office was at first, undoubtedly, exercised by heads of families, and afterwards by heads of clans. And, previous to the consecration of Aaron and his sons to the priesthood, the office of priest and of magistrate were blended in the same person.

Melchisedeck was both a king and priest of Salem and offered sacrifice.

Abraham, who was styled a prince, performed the sacerdotal functions; and Jethro, a prince and priest of Midian, offered burnt sacrifices as a priest, being at the same time a ruler of his people. So the chiefs of the Six Nations, invariably officiate as priests at their festivals or sacrifices.

The place of sacrifice was directed, by the Jewish ceremonial, to be at the door of the tabernacle or place of worship; and, in like manner, is the Indian sacrifice universally made at the door of their council house, their only place of worship.

The Jewish priests, on all sacrificial occasions, were clothed in robes of pure white; and so are those clothed who officiate as priests at the Indian sacrifices.

On sacrificial occasions, the alms and offerings of the Jews were gathered in baskets, brought to the altar, and set before the priest, with the strictest order and propriety. Almost precisely the same practice exists among the Indians, who gather the alms and oblations of the people, and present them to the officiating high priest in a basket.

The Jews offered in sacrifice only oxen, sheep, and goats; other animals, although they might be esteemed good for food, were unsuited for sacrifice. It may be asked, then, why the dog, an animal entirely rejected from the Jewish ceremonial, should be received among the Indians as an animal suitable for sacrifice? Let it be borne in mind that, not many years since, dogs were their only domestic animals; wild animals being nowhere commanded for sacrifice, these were the only ones they could have always at hand. They were forced to adopt them or reject the rite entirely.

By the Jews, in the selection of victims for sacrifice, the utmost care was taken to choose such only as were free from blemish. "Without spot and without blemish," are the terms in frequent use throughout the Jewish ritual. And it was a custom among the nations surrounding Judea, and among the Egyptians, to set a seal upon the victim deemed proper for sacrifice. Among the Indians, a spot, or blemish, or maim, renders the animal as unfit for sacrifice, as did the same faults, among the Jews.

We have endeavored to point out a few of the coincidences which may be supposed to exist between some of the ceremonies of the Jews, and those of the Indians. as practiced at Onondaga. We are satisfied that they prove nothing positively, as to their origin from that peculiar people. If any thing, they may illustrate the common origin of all men, and the high origin of all religious institutions, which at first must have emanated from the same source.

The learned and estimable Protestant author of "Onaudaga," from whom the above is copied, might go further—he might show that nearly the same strange mingling of sublime truth with dangerous or ridiculous error, has been found in every page of human history, whenever men have separated from a teaching Church.

SOPHOCLES, ESCHYLUS, MEANDER assert at times, in sublime language, the unity, eternity and sanctity of God. CLEANTHUS has a hymn or prayer, which was cited by St. PAUL at Athens: "Glorious and immortal King, adored under various names, eternally all-powerful, Author of nature, governing the world by thy laws, I salute thee! Mortals are permitted to invoke thee, *for we are thy offspring!* In the Philosophers and Poets, sometimes most clearly expressed, sometimes mingling with human fancies, we read of the Creation, the Fall, Immortality, and Judgment beyond the grave; the Guardian Angels, the ministering spirits that protect; the evil ones that tempt; the Supreme Mighty God, who directs and modifies their actions. HERODOTUS, who wrote about four hundred and fifty years before Christ, remarks that it was HESIOD and HOMER who first gave a genealogy of the Gods, assigned to each of them a name and form; that before those poets, who, he remarks, lived only four hundred years before him, men adored the Gods who had submitted the universe to order, without giving them any name; for, says he, they never heard their name. Her. c. 2, 6, 52, 53.

EURIPIDES has a strong passage on this subject. He introduces THESEUS reasoning with HERCULES, and alleging the crimes of the Gods in extenuation of those of mortals; HERCULES answers: "I have never believed, nor ever will I believe, that the Gods give themselves up to incestuous love. A God, if he be God indeed, is in need of no one; it is the poets that have invented those miserable fictions."

The learned are now more and more convinced that in Ancient Egypt, philosophy had the same religious foundation as in India—a Supreme and Only God, manifesting his Being under three principal forms or persons, a Creating Word, the Sovereign Intelligence, the Fall of Man, the hope of a Redemption, Divine Incarnations, a Heaven, a Hell, Purgatory, (in most instances, by metempsychosis,) personifications of all that exist, the sun, moon, and stars, the Nile, the winds, the seasons, or rather the Divinity, manifested, reproduced in all these things, in some manner transformed into them; in a word, every truth serving as a base for every error: for no error can be presented unless mixed with some truth. A pure error is an impossibility: as a pure poison is impossible. The most active poison is ever united with water, or with something that is good, without which it could not be exhibited to man.

CHAPTER VI.

CATHOLIC MISSIONARIES.

The eternal Providence of the Saviour God, who died "that he might present to Himself a glorious Church, not having spot or wrinkle," ever watches over it, and, far in advance, directs events to prepare for the sanctification of each member "of his body, which is the Church." Often, as in the Sacred Head, so in the members, this is visibly accomplished by the cross. From Canada began the work of converting the Indians of Western New York: to Canada, when persecution was aided by the penal laws of England, those converted Indians, who did not migrate to heaven, migrated. And there, in their descendants, perhaps more numerous than ever, do they still worship the Son of Mary, in the land whence his blessed light, first shone upon them. It must not, then, seem strange that some space is here devoted, to missions on the Canadian side of the waters, that mark our boundary. A certain knowledge of them is necessary in order to understand our own missions. The rich mine, there glowing in generous, Christian, heroic virtue, may tempt the historian a little farther than is absolutely necessary. Efforts will be made to resist that temptation; and if these efforts be not always successful, the reader will still be edified, and the time lost will be well repaid, by one generous thrill of holy desire, or of generous sympathy.

In 1603, CHAMPLAIN accompanied PONTGRAVE to Canada, and examined carefully the River St. Lawrence. Even then he is supposed to have planned a settlement there. On his second voyage, he reached Quebec in 1608. The place was called by the Indians "Kebbek," which means "a narrow passage." His views were comprehensive, his courage extraordinary, his labors great, his zeal for the missions truly Christian. Of his secular exploits, no judgment can here be pronounced. In 1615, he returned from France with Franciscan Fathers: their steps we will follow, but remark in passing that, in 1633, CHAMPLAIN, worn out by fatigue and preparing for death, established an admirable order among his soldiers. The fort appeared to be a well-regulated Academy. Following the example of CHAMPLAIN, all approached the sacraments; their deportment was edifying. During the repasts, one read: at dinner they read some pious history; at supper, the Lives of the Saints. At night, CHAMPLAIN, like a good father, reunited them in his room, to make the examination of conscience, and recite night prayers. He also established in Canada the custom, so faithfully observed to our day, of ringing the *Angelus Domini* thrice each day. He died on December the 25th, 1635, having received with great piety, the sacraments of the Church. Father LE JEUNE pronounced the funeral discourse. His wife became a nun of the Ursuline Order, lived holily and died in her convent in blessed hopes of eternal life, on the 20th of December, 1654. A splendid monument was erected over his grave, and when the venerable Father CHARLES RAYMBOULD, worn out by apostolic labors, died in 1642, the Government, as a mark of special honor, had the remains of the honored priest, buried alongside of CHAMPLAIN.

The Franciscans who accompanied CHAMPLAIN, on his return to Canada from his visit to France, in 1615, were four in number, and were of the Reform called Recollects. When Father JAMES GARNIER, Provincial of the Recollect Franciscans in Paris, sent a mission to Canada, that Society had already many missions in the New World. In 1621, the Recollects had in Spanish America five hundred convents, distributed in twenty-two provinces. The Papal Brief given to the Franciscan Missionaries for Canada, contains ample powers, and was expedited in 1618. Father DENNIS JAMAY was named first Commissary of the Mission. His companions were Fathers JOHN DOLBEAU, JOSEPH LE CARON, and Brother PACIFIC DU PLESSIS. The missionaries reached Quebec in 1615. The first simple chapel was soon built; the first Mass was celebrated on the 25th of June, 1615. Other chapels were soon built in different places. Since then the "clean oblation" has indeed been perpetual in Canada.

Le Caron soon started westward for the Huron country; through almost incredible fatigues, incessantly working, though half starved, but never complaining, he reached the Huron country, and built the Franciscan chapel and altar, near a Huron village. Great was the humble self-sacrificing zeal of those first missionaries; it is well to publish it, in the following eloquent passage, from the discourse of O. H.

Marshall, Esq. "The glowing narrative of Bancroft has thrown the drapery of romance, over the lifes and labours of the Jesuits, whilst only a bare allusion is made, to the daring intrepidity, and self denying zeal of Le Caron, D'Albion, Du Plessis, and Jamay, the humble Franciscans who with naked feet, and uncovered heads, threaded the forests, and first met the untamed Indian, in his home, on the borders of the northern Lakes."

The labours of these zealous and self-sacrificing missionaries, were repaid by many conversions. Henry de Levi, Duke of Ventadour, in 1623, retired from the Court took holy orders, became a priest, and organized a mission to Canada. Divine Providence thus disposed to meet the wants of the Franciscans; for whilst they were pursuing their labors in the mission, another Franciscan, Father Piat, went to France to obtain the assistance of the Jesuits, who received the invitation with joy, and the following missionaries, (already promised to the noble priest, Henri de Levi,) Father Claude, Sallamant, Father Edmont Massi, and Father John de Broebeuf, were ready to sail early in the year 1625. These first Jesuit missionaries soon arrived in Canada, prepared to announce the gospel to the heathen. Before the Franciscans, none had intercourse with the Aborogines of our land, except either in the character of traders, using every means to overreach, or in the garb of military adventurers. "These sons of the forest, now for the first time saw men entering their villages, whose word breathed peace and love; whose business was only to suffer, and to teach humility; whose sword was the cross, and who preached sobriety, good will, charity, and bright hopes beyond the grave. The privations of the wilderness, and rigors of the climate, were borne with fortitude; native languages were mastered, the dispositions and customs of a strange people were studied, and conformed to; and difficulties sufficient to appal the stoutest heart, were encountered and overcome. These devoted men, and their successors, entered upon their labours, with a zeal that knew no limit; and with a devotedness that shrunk from no trial. They were successful in winning these strange men, to their stranger doctrines and faith. The establishment of missions among the natives naturally led to the exploration of the country. And thus the pioneers of the cross, became the first discoverers and historians of the whole interior of North America. They widely extended geographical knowledge, and did not overlook the importance, of providing the means of education, for the youth of the land. So important have their *Relations* become, that they may well be termed an elaborate history of the country. In proportion to their high value, is, at the same time their scarcity. Clark, History of Onandaga, Vol. 1. p. 128.

BROEBEUF and his associates, under the guidance of the Franciscan priest DALLION, a man no less distinguished for his illustrious birth, than for his piety, and religious zeal; landed in Quebec in 1625, the Jesuits met with a cool reception, on the part of the inhabitants; no one offered to give them a shelter, or to supply them with provisions, and they were on the point of abandoning the enterprise. The Franciscans, after using much persuasion, obtained from the Governor, leave to receive the Jesuits into their establishment. One half of their convent garden, and farm, was generously surrendered to the new comers; and the two societies lived, and labored together, in uninterrupted friendship, and harmony, for two years.

The vows which the Jesuits took, the austerities which they practiced, their rigid discipline and untiring zeal, rendered them peculiarly adapted (says O. H. MARSHALL, Esq.,) to encounter and overcome the obstacles incident to missionary life in the savage wilds of America. There is much in the history of their efforts, which the heralds of a more *spiritual* faith might well admire and emulate." (The learned and estimable writer, would be puzzled to show how, the heralds of any Protestant sect. is, or can be, as spiritual as the heralds of the Roman Catholic Church.) Many of them were of high birth, and entitled to princely fortunes, all of which, with every wordly prospect and advantage, they laid on the altar of their faith, and sacrificed in the course of their missions." In 1624 the Jesuits set out for the Huron country, with DALLION, the Franciscan, over the same painful and toilsome route, which LE CARON had pursued, eleven years before. They had some difficulty in inducing the Hurons to give Father BROEBEUF a seat in one of their canoes, as he was corpulent, and they feared his weight might overset it. They re-established the missions which had been founded by the Franciscans. Father DALLION, of the noble house of the Counts DuLEID, stimulated by the desire of propagating his faith in remote regions, visited the Neuter Nations; he set out the 18th of October, 1626." After a perilous journey, through many villages of the Neuter Nation, he entered the country bordering on the Niagara River, and lying around the western extremity of Lake Ontario. Through many dangers and sufferings, he tried to open a mission among the tribe of Neutrals." They dwelt near and on the Niagara River. He was at first well received, and being adopted by SOUARISSEN, the chief of the whole nation, took up his residence among them. He was, however, soon after robbed and brutally beaten, and returned to the Hurons.

In 1629, the English captured Quebec, and the Catholic missionaries had to return to France.

In 1632, when Canada was restored to France, the Jesuits returned to their missions among the savages. CHAMPLAIN had intended to aid and arm the Hurons. He died.

His successor had not such extensive views. The Hurons were left without aid. But the Jesuits went to their spiritual relief. BROEBEUF, CHAUMONT, and others started for the Huron Mission. BROEBEUF narrates, in simple and touching terms, their great sufferings on the rout. Almost in the last extremity, they reach a Huron Village. BROEBEUF was recognized and most kindly received, a chapel was soon erected, the Mass said, and the Mission dedicated to St. Joseph. Around its altars an extensive mission soon flourished. Before the end of the year 1636, six Jesuit priests were employed in different villages.

BROEBEUF and CHAUMONT resolved to visit the Neuter Nation. The Neuter Nation, which, before the Seneca conquests, occupied both sides of the Niagara River, and claimed the territory west of the Genesee, and west as far as the Eries, were estimated, in 1641, at twelve thousand souls. They were visited by Catholic priests, but no distinct records of their labors have reached us. Their affection or veneration for the dead induced them to treasure up the bones of the departed for ten or twelve years, when, at an appointed time, all repaired, to a fixed spot, a vast grave was made, the bones from every quarter, wrapped in furs, were brought, deposited together with religious rites, and a mound became the memorial. Some of these mounds exist around Buffalo. Many similar tumuli are found, of whose origin the Senecas disclaim all knowledge. They were conquered by the Iroquois, many killed, the rest led into captivity to the Seneca country beyond the Genesee River. Father FREMIN found them there, in 1669, eighteen years after their capture. Many of them had become Catholics.

After leaving Sainte Marie, Broebeuf and Chaumont, pursued a southerly course through the territories of the Hurons, until they reached their last village. Here they procured provisions and a guide for their journey, and pursuing their way, slept, four nights, in the woods, before reaching the territories of the Neutral Nation.

The first village they entered they named "*All Saints*," on their arrival at the residence of the principal chief, whose approval of their mission was necessary, they found him absent on a war expedition. His return was not expected until spring, and they were told by the remaining chiefs, that they must wait that event.

The Jesuits eagerly embraced the opportunity, thus afforded of acquiring a knowledge of the language, character, and genius of the people.

Suspicion was soon excited however, in the minds of the savages, which exposed them to a series of insults and indignities, during their visit. They were accused of witchcraft and of conspiracy with the neighboring Senecas "who "lived," says Broebeuf, "but a days journey from the easter- "most villages of the neutral nation." Their breviaries, inkhorns, and manuscripts, were considered as so many instruments of sorcery, and their prayers as magical incantations. The chiefs withdrew their protection, and there seemed to be no alternative but to retrace their steps. In the course of their travels they visited 18 villages, but they tarried principally in ten, these contained 500 families and 8,000 souls, to whom those Jesuits announced the Gospel.

On the return to Sainte Marie, a deep fall of snow arrested them in a village, beyond which it was impossible to proceed. What they at first considered a calamity, soon proved a providential occurrence. A female of the village received them into her hut, ministered to their wants, and substituted fish and vegetables, for the usual animal diet, during their observance of Lent. She also took great pains to learn them her language, articulating the words, syllable by syllable, as a teacher to a scholar. Notwithstanding the ridicule and jeers, heaped upon her by her own people, she continued these kind offices, until the Jesuits were enabled to construct a dictionary of the language, a work which LALEMANT remarks, would be cheaply purchased, at the cost of many years' residence in the country, inasmuch as the savages are easy of access, to those who speak their language, all others being regarded as strangers.

After undergoing incredible hardships, they safely reached the Huron Mission, where they rejoined their brethren, who had almost despaired of their return. It is not certain how far they penetrated, at this time, towards the River Niagara. It appears from their journal that they acquired, while in this vicinity, an accurate knowledge of the configuration of the lakes which it connects, though no mention is made of the Cataract which constitutes so striking a featuere in its scenery.

In 1623 Father Nicholas Veil, and brother Gabriel Sagard, the first historian of the Huron missions, started for the Huron missions; Sagard in his "Great journey to the Huron country" thus describes the life of the Franciscan Missionaries. "We took our repasts on straw mats, a log of wood served us for a pillow at night, our cloaks, were our blankets, we had no other towel than corn husks, we had a few knives, but they were of little use, we had no bread to cut; and meat was so scarce, that we would pass, from six weeks to two months, without eating a mouthful. Our usual food was *Sagamite*, made with water and corn meal, some pumpkins, or beans were added, and a little parsely, or a kind of spice wood, with wild onions, to give a better taste; our drink was from the stream. If, whilst the sugar maple was running in season, any of our party got sick, we would make an inscission in the tree, which then ozed out its sugary water, and this the sick man would use as a great remedy. Unremittingly the good Franciscans employed every leisure hour, in learning the Huron language, and in composing a Huron dictionary, but during the long nights of winter, they had only the light of the fire, or light from pine, or bark torches, which frequently had to be renewed, and which filled their cabin with smoke. Father Nicholas Viel and a neophyte were cruelly murdered two years after by some brutal savage Hurons, enemies of the faith.

Such, with little variation, amidst great labours, was the life of the missionaries, until in 1634-5, Father Broebeauf returned to the Huron mission. He brought with him from France many articles of great use; but which caused the greatest wonder among the Indians; what most excited their admiration, was a clock. They called it the "Captain of the day." "When it strikes," says BROEBEUF, "they cry out that it speaks; when they come to see us they ask 'How many times has "the Captain of the day" spoken since morning?' They want to know what it *eats*, and what it *says!*" The devotedness, the courage, and the holy perseverance of those missionaries were finally crowned with success; the religion of Christ triumphed. Sixteen years after BROEBEUF's arrival, the Indians were conquered; but whether captives with the Iroquois or safe among the French, they remained faithful. Even those who had not been converted in Huronia, were, for the greater part, converted along the waters of Cayuga and Seneca Lakes.

The "Relations," of 1648 say of the Huron Mission:

"This mission of the Conception is the most fertile of all, both in the number and zeal of the christians; whose faith shows itself with great advantage, and whose sanctity is respected even by Infidels. Three of the principle captains, and some of the men, set an example by the holiness of their lives, which has more effect than our sermons. In a word the Faith of this church emits a fragrance of Christianity all over the country.

The mission of St. Michael, is well founded and is daily increasing, in spite of the opposition of Infidels, who always oppose the commencement of a Church.

The mission of St. Joseph, is still more crowded, but, indeed it is longer founded.

The mission of St. Ignatius, which is later than any of the preceding, has a fervor and innocence which astonishes the Infidels, and which we never expected to see, in so short a time, in the commencement of a church.

The faith has increased far beyond our expectations, in these four missions; so much so, that our chapels are too small for the number of the faithful on festival days, and our missionary is often obliged to say two masses on the Sunday, so that all can assist—still the church is filled, even to the corner of the altars, and numbers of the faithful kneel outside, even during the winter rains or snow!

The mission of Holy Mary, consists of twelve or thirteen villages and has but one Father to attend them, which he does with incessant labor, visiting each at stated times.

We hope to be obliged to form another mission, within eight months, still further from here, among some villages too far for us, and which we shall name, the Mission of St. Mary Magdelane.

We asked permission of the Petun Nation to instruct them, and have sent there two of our Fathers, who have formed missions in two different nations, of which their country is composed; the one is called the Wolf Nation, where we have formed the mission of St. John; the other is called the Stag Nation, among which we have formed the mission of St. Mathias.

There is, without doubt, a great deal to suffer in all these missions, from hunger, as well as from the inclemency of the seasons; from cold and heat; from fatigue in travelling; and from the continual danger of being surrounded by the

Iroquois, taken captive, and made suffer a thousand deaths, before you die *once*.

But after all, all these evils are easier to support, than it is to practice the council of the Apostle, to become "all to all," in order to gain souls to Jesus Christ. Excessive patience is necessary, in order to endure thousands of insults. Invincible courage to overcome everything; a humility, which counts itself to have done nothing, when it has done all; and a longanimity which waits, with patience, the moments of Divine Providence, in fine an entire conformity to His most holy will, that He may one day reward our labors of ten or twenty years. It is on this foundation that we must build these churches, and establish the faith in these countries; this it is what God requires of us.

CHAPTER VII.

HOST OF MARTYRS.

ALMOST incredible, and most affecting, are the simple details of the labors and sufferings of the Franciscan and Jesuit priests. CHAUMONT compiled his Indian Grammar on the frozen earth; BROEBEUF, paralyzed by a fall, with his collar-bone broken, crept on his hands and knees along the frozen ground, and slept unsheltered on the snow! The work of God advanced rapidly, conversions were numerous. In 1644, Fathers BROEBEUF, GARROW, and CHARBONEL became permanent residents at the stations of the Conception, St. Joseph's, and St. Michael's. Through aid given the Iroquois by the Dutch, in supplies of firearms, these pagan savages conquered the Hurons, and made many martyrs. The "Relation," from the writings of eye-witnesses, as translated by O. H. MARSHALL, Esq., is too thrilling, too edifying, not to find place here:

"In this region, which the Jesuits paint as so delightful,

chosen by the Hurons for their homes, and occupied by them for so long a period, that their traditions fixed no era for their arrival, the missionaries were accustomed to assemble thrice in the year, to rehearse their toils and their triumphs, to confess one another, and to devise plans for the more rapid diffusion of the faith they taught. And here, year after year, they continued one uniform round of life, adhering to their simple and austere habits, secluded from the world, and devoted to their missions.

" By night, a bundle of faggots served them for a pillow, and their mantles formed their only covering. Their meals were taken on the ground, while reclining on mats of rushes, or seated on billets of wood. The earth, or their knees, furnished a table, and leaves of Indian corn were their only napkins. Knives they had, but they were useless; for there was no bread to cut, and meat was so rare, that if, by chance, the Indians gave them a portion of their game, it was carefully laid aside and kept for Easter. Their ordinary food consisted of the Indian sagamite, or corn pounded between stones, or in a wooden mortar, and boiled in water. Into this was thrown, to give it relish, some sweet majoram, purslain, or balm, and a kind of wild onion which they found in the woods. Their only drink was water from the brook, or the sap, which they caught from the maple in their trough of bark. Wild grapes, bruised and pressed in a cloth, over a bark vessel, furnished them wine for the mass, or for medicinal purposes.

" While they were thus pursuing their peaceful labors, the Iroquois made an incursion upon one of the villages, comprised within the Huron Mission, and called St. Joseph. Father ANTHONY DANIEL, one of the earliest pioneers to this region, having labored in it fourteen years, had just finished mass, and his neophytes were still engaged in their devotions, when the cry 'To Arms' was heard.

"It was the morning of the fouth of July, 1648. The enemy had approached the village under cover of the night, and thus effected a surprise. The greatest panic and confusion prevailed, and the terror-stricken Hurons flocked around the Father as their protector. He animated them, by his presence, where the danger was most imminent, and encouraged them to defend their village. But it was of no avail. The dreaded name of the Iroquois, was ever sufficient to intimidate a Huron. (The Dutch from New York, as before remarked, had supplied the Iroquois with firearms.) They abandoned all defence and sought for baptism at the hands of the Jesuit, as a preparation for the certain death that awaited them. But the number was too large, and the danger too imminent, to take them singly, and dipping his handkerchief in water, he performed the rite upon the whole crowd by aspersion. In the meantime the enemy took possession of the place, and those who were able to flee, escaped to the neighboring villages. Not so the Father, Forgetful of himself, he eagerly sought out the aged, infirm, and sick, to prepare them for their fate. The whole village was soon in conflagration, and none were spared in the general massacre. DANIEL then repaired to the chapel, which was already crowded with Hurons. Some he baptized, others he confessed and absolved, and upon all he bestowed appropriate words of consolation. 'My brothers,' he exclaimed, 'to-day we shall meet in Paradise.' The enemy soon learned their p'ace of refuge, and sending forth a shrill war-whoop, rushed in a body to the church. The Father, alone and undismayed, advanced to meet them. The savages, astonished at his temerity, and awed by his appearance, recoiled for a moment as he approached. Soon recovering from their surprise, but keeping at a distance, they pierced him with their arrows, and shot him in the heart with an arquebuse; he fell, the first Jesuit martyr of the Huron Mission. His body, stripped and dishonored by his murderers, became a holocaust consumed in the fires of the burning church. A part of the Hurons, who succeeded in escaping found refuge among their brethren, in the neighboring village of Sainte Marie. About seven hundred, consisting principally of women and children, were taken captives by the Iroquois, and carried home to their country, to undergo the torture, or supply the waste of disease and war, by adoption into their tribes. The winter passed away among the Hurons without further disturbance, and the mission continued to flourish until the next year. On the evening of the 16th day of March, 1649, about two thousand Iroquois, well supplied with firearms procured from the Dutch at Albany, arrived at the frontier settlement of the Hurons, and silently surrounded the village called by the French St. Ignace. This place, in additional to the natural strength of its position, was fortified with palisades fifteen or sixteen feet high, and surrounded by a deep ditch. The enemy reconnoitred its situation, and at break of day, while the Hurons were wrapped in profound sleep, effected an entrance, before any resistance could be made. Only ten Iroquois were slain, and all but three of the Hurons, numbering more than four hundred souls, were either immediately massacred, or reserved for the more terrible torture. The three that escaped, nearly naked, made their way over the snow to a neighboring village, to which they carried the alarm.

The Iroquois pursuing their victory, appeared before sunrise in front of the adjacent village of St. Louis, also fortified with palisades. The women and children escaped on hearing the approach of the enemy, leaving about 80 warriors to defend the place. They repulsed with vigour the first and second assault, killing and wounding a large number of the assailants. But they were finally overpowered by numbers.

The Iroquois having cut a passage through the palisades, were enabled to enter, and the fire and smoke from the consuming village, soon revealed to the anxious missionaries at Sainte Marie, about a league distant, that the work of destruction had commenced. The Iroquois raged, like incarnate fiends, among the consuming dwellings. The old men and children, the sick, the infirm, and the wounded, were alike thrown into the devouring flames, as useless incumbrances upon their captors. Two Hurons escaped to Sainte Marie and told the sad particulars. At the time of the attack, the Jesuits Brœbeuf and Lalemand, were residing in the village. They had charge of the five contigous settlements, which were all comprised under the name of St. Ignace, and formed one of the eleven Huron missions, then carried on by the Jesuits. The Huron neophites besought the Fathers to flee, and it would be easy for them to have done so, but they considered the few moments of that terrible conflict, as the most precious of their existence, and laboured incessantly during the heat of the combat, for what they deemed the welfare of their chosen flock. One stationed himself at the point, where the enemy had made a break in the palisades, baptizing the converts, and giving absolution to the neophites. Both encouraged the Christian Hurons to suffer death, under the influence of those sentiments with which their teachings had inspired them.

The Iroquois captured and secured the two Fathers, with many Huron prisoners, and returned to St. Ignace. In the evening their scouts reconnoitred Sainte Marie for the purpose of an attack next morning. The Hurons in the latter village, remained all night under arms, in momentary expectation of an assault, but it passed away in profound silence. On the 19th, a sudden panic seized the enemy, and disregarding the remonstrances of their chiefs, they commenced a rapid and disorderly retreat.

Loading their captives like beasts of burden, they compelled them to carry the spoils which they secured. Those not needed for the purpose were put to death, with excruciating torture. Some were bound to stakes driven within the consuming dwellings, and the captors regaled their ears with the cries, uttered by their dying victims. Parents and children were tortured side by side, a spectacle at which it would seem that even cruelty itself, would have revolted. When it was ascertained that the Iroquois had retreated, a detachment of seven hundred Hurons were sent in pursuit, but the scarcity of provisions, and their fear of the fire arms of the enemy, induced them soon to abandon the chase. They found on their way, many of the captives, who, not being strong enough to keep pace with the Iroquois, had been knocked on the head, or half burned at the stake. When the Jesuit RAGUENEAU and his companions at Sainte Marie, had full assurance of the departure of the enemy, they searched for the remains of BROEBEUF and LALEMAND, of whose death they had been informed. Their eyes rested on a spectacle of horror, and they heard a tale of cruelty, of which history scarcely affords a parallel.

As soon as the Jesuits had been captured, they were stripped, their nails were torn out, and on entering the village of St. Ignace, they were compelled to run the gauntlet. Their bodies were covered with bruises, inflicted by the clubs of their captors.

BROEBUEF sunk under the weight of their blows, but his spirit was unsubdued. The savages now resorted to every species of cruelty to torture their victims. They cut off the hands of one of the Fathers, and pierced those of the others with sharp awls and pointed irons. They applied to their arm-pits and loins, red hot hatchets, with which they also formed necklaces, to hang around them in such a manner, that every movement of their bodies would cause excruciating pain. Whether they leaned backwards of forwards, the red hot iron would enter the flesh. They bound bark girdles around their persons, filled with pitch, which, being set on fire, roasted the whole surface of their bodies. In the height of these agonies, Father LALEMAND, of gentler mould than his companion, his strength scarcely equal to his will, joining his hands from time to time, supplicated heaven for aid.

Father BROEBEUF endured like a rock. Insensible to torture, without a groan, he maintained unbroken silence for a long time, to the great astonishment of his tormentors. At length he began to speak, and to preach to the Iroquois and to his companions in misery. Indignant at his zeal, the captors mutilated his mouth, and cut off his nose, but he continued, as far as he was able, to encourage those around him. In derision of the baptism, which the priests had administered so freely, in the hottest of the conflict, these fiends in human guise, poured boiling water over their naked persons. "We baptize you," said they, "that you may be happy in heaven, for no one can be saved unless baptized;" others said, "What we thus do, is in friendship, since we will be the cause of your highest happiness in Heaven. Thank us for our kindness, for the more you suffer, the more your God will recompense you."

They tore out the eyes of LALEMAND and placed burning coals in their sockets. Both did not suffer at the same time. BROEBEUF was undergoing the severest of his torments for nearly three hours, of the same day he was captured and expired about four o'clock in the afternoon. LALEMAND suffered, from six in the evening until nine the next morning.

While they were yet alive, pieces of flesh were cut from their bodies, broiled on coals, and devoured in their presence. Into the wounds thus made, red hot axes were repeatedly thrust. To complete the tragedy, their hearts were torn out, and the inhuman barbarians drank their blood gushing warm from its source.

It appeared from the examination of their remains, that BROEBEUF had been scalped, that his feet were cut off, and his jaw split open, with an axe.

LALEMAND had a gash over his left ear, which had laid bare his brain. There was no part of his body which had not been burnt, while he was yet living. Their tongues had been destroyed by thrusting into their mouths at various times firebrands and bark torches. Thus perished these devoted Jesuits. LALEMAND, at the age of 39, having labored six months, among the Hurons; and BROEBEUF at the age of 56, after a residence of eighteen years in the same mission.

"But let us leave these objects of horror, and these monsters of cruelty, since, in one day, all their victims were robed in the glory of immortality; since, also, the greater their torments, the richer their crown, and since they now live in the repose of the saints, which they will enjoy for eternity.

"On Sunday, the 21st of March, we buried these precious relics, with so much consolation from the tender sentiments of those who assisted at the ceremony, I think that not one present did not desire death; not one who feared the thought of it, and who would not have believed himself happy to be at once in a place where God would give him the grace to sacrifice his blood and life in a similar manner. Not one of us can make up our minds to pray for them, as though they needed our prayer; but our minds rise continually to heaven, where we believe their souls are. I pray God that it is so, and that he will accomplish his holy will in us, even unto death, as he has done with them." "Relations, 1649," p. 15.

The Huron country was now desolated. The Nation despaired of recovering from the disastrous effects of these warlike incursions, and in less than eight days, accompanied by the remaining Jesuits, they abandoned their homes, and bid farewell forever, to their ancient domains. The Lake, which bears their name, still washes the shores they so long inhabited, an abiding memorial of the race; but, scattered by the exterminating hand of the Iroquois, they from thenceforth ceased to exist as a nation, (Not far from their old grounds, through Upper Canada, and Michigan, many villages of faithful christian Hurons still exist,) and wandered in fugitive bands, seeking shelter in remote Islands and secluded and inaccessible retreats. A few, under the auspices of Father RAGNENEAU, settled in the Island of Orleans near Quebec, and even there deemed themselves scarcely safe under French protection. Others escaped to the Islands of Lake Huron, from whence they subsequently joined their brethern near Quebec. Some went South of Lake Erie and buried themselves in the forests of Pennsylvania and we find them at a later day in the vicinity of Sandusky under the name of Wyandots.

The greater part however found the death from which they fled, and more perished by famine and disease, than by the hand of the enemy.

The prisoners were, for the most part, adopted by the Iroquois, and, subsequent to that period, settlements were found among the latter, composed almost entirely of Huron captives, and which will be more fully noticed, when treating of the Jesuit missions among that people. The Iroquois engaged in this foray, were principally Senecas. Father LEMOYNE in his mission to that tribe five years afterwards found the testament of BROEBEUF in their possession, which he preserved as a precious relic of the martyr.' O. H. MARSHALL.

CHAPTER VIII.
MISSIONS IN WESTERN NEW YORK.

The holy Providence of God displayed itself, in a wonderful manner, by making the cruelty of the Iroquois against the Hurons, a source of many noble virtues, producing rich crops of generous martyrs for heaven; whilst it also sent the captive Hurons to be the nucleus of Christianity, among their conquerors. The five nations, among whom the Jesuits labored, on the south side of Lake Ontario and Erie, have long had the nick-name of Iroquois, from the word "Hiro," I have said it, (dixi) with which they end every discourse, and the exclamation, "Koue," denoting joy or sadness, according to the manner in which it is pronounced. Charlevois, says that their right name is "Agonnonsionnis," (Makers of Cabins.) Nor was Huron more than the nick-name for that people. When the French saw them, with their cropped, and bristling hair, they cried out in French, "Quelles Hures," (what wild boar heads,) hence Huron.

The Iroquois Confederation was, by them, compared to a Long House, the eastern door of which opened on the Hudson, guarded by the Mohawks, the western on Lake Erie guarded by the Senecas. The council fires of the Senecas burned, for a long time, within what is now the limits of Buffalo city.

The Recollect Franciscan, Father William Poulain, was a prisoner in the hands of the Indians, in 1621, and, in his suffering, consoled himself, by instructing in the faith some of the Iroquois prisoners. When the Jesuits came to the aid of the Franciscans, it was resolved, that some priests from the Huron missions should cross the river, and found a mission among the Senecas. Various causes retarded the mission. Father JOQUES, and other missionaries, who had just planted the Cross in Michigan, set out for Quebec, they were captured by the Iroquois. JOQUES might have fled, but "could a minister of Christ abandon the wounded and the dying?" JOQUES, after stopping to baptise a catechumen in his canoe, surrendered himself up, and joined the captives. The savages rejoiced at taking so important a prisoner. They led their captives towards the valley of the Mohawk. The wearied prisoners had, several times, to run the gauntlet; most painful were the wounds and bruises they received. Torture soon began. The brave Frenchman COUTURE had slain a chief, in the struggle at the capture; he was stripped, beaten, and mangled: and Father JOQUES, who consoled and strengthened in faith, the mangled victim, was himself violently attacked, and beaten until he fell senseless; they rushed on him like wolves, and not content with blows, tore out his nails, and gnawed his fingers to the very bone. Terrible were the tortures which JOQUES and RENE endured on their route to the River Mohawk. "God alone," writes JOQUES, "for whose love and glory it is sweet and glorious to suffer, can tell what cruelties they then perpetrated on me." O. H. MARSHALL, Esq., in his lecture to the New York Historical Society, says: "In 1642, Father JOQUES, and RENE GOUPIL were tortured by the Iroquois, at different points along the Mohawk River: one of the village scenes of torture, was at Fort Plain; another at East Canada Creek. At length, RENE was killed, and thus the soil of New York drank the blood of the <u>first martyr</u> who sacrificed his life in the New World, in the cause of the Jesuit Missions." Who will give us, in popular form, and in full detail, the touching incidents of the devoted zeal, the patient, meek, heroic sufferings of these and other early martyr priests and Christians, on the virgin soil of America? It would prove that truth is stranger than fiction. No romance could create the thrilling interest which true, sublime, heroic virtue, in scenes like these, would excite. Another WISEMAN might here, in true history, write, with all the charms of FABIOLA, historic truth, "in thoughts that breathe, and words that burn." It seems that but one has attempted this labor of love, and he was a Protestant minister, the Rev. W. I. KIPP, M. A.. now Protestant Bishop of California, in his "Early Jesuit Missions," which are simply a translation of a few of the most interesting letters of the early Jesuit missionaries.

Though abridging so closely, as to lose some of the charm and unction of the narratives, it may appear that these hurried details, have allured this history from the main object, by flowers of sweetest fragrance, blooming with unearthly charms, amidst thorns of direst suffering. Yet even this wandering will lead back, whilst affording some bright vistas into the past, present and future of the region to be explored. Suffice it *here* to say, that the devotedness of these Apostles of a new world, so well rivalled the devoted heroism of the first Apostles, that the Protestant minister above alluded to, speaks of them in these words:

"There is no page of our country's history, more touching and romantic than that, which records the labors, and sufferings, of the Jesuit Missionaries. In these western wilds they were the earliest pioneers of civilization and faith. The wild hunter or the adventurous traveller, who, penetrating the forests, came to new and strange tribes, often found that years before, the disciples of Loyola had preceded him in that wilderness. Traditions of the "Black robes" still lingered among the Indians. On some moss-grown tree, they pointed out the traces of their work, and in wonder deciphered, carved, side by side on its trunk, the emblem of our salvation, and the lilies of the Bourbons. Amid the snows, of Hudson's Bay—among the woody islands, and beautiful inlets of the St. Lawrence, by the council fires of the Hurons, and the Algonquines; at the sources of the Mississippi, where, first of the white men, their eyes looked upon the Falls of St. Anthony, and then traced down, the course of the bounding river, as it rushed onward to earn its title of "Father of Waters"—on the vast prairies of Illinios, and Missouri;—among the blue hills, which hem in the salubrious dwellings of the Cherokees, and in the thick canebrakes of Louisiana—everywhere, were found the members of the "Society of Jesus." MARQUETTE, JOLIET, BROEBEUF, JOQUES, LALEMAND, RASLES, MARSST, are the names which the West should ever hold in remembrance.

"But it was only by suffering and trial, that these early laborers won their triumphs. Many of them too were men who had stood high in camps and courts, and could contrast their desolate state, in the solitary wigwam, with the refinement and affluence, which had waited on their early years. But now all these were gone. Home—the love of kindred—the golden ties of relationship—all were to be forgotten, by these stern and high-wrought men, and they were often to go forth into the wilderness, without an adviser on their way, save their God.

Through long and sorrowful years they were obliged to "Sow in tears" before they could "reap in joy." Every self-denial gathered around them, which could wear upon the spirit, and cause the heart to fail; Mighty forests were to be threaded on foot, and the great lakes of the West, passed in the feeble bark canoe. Hunger and cold, and disease, were to be encountered, until nothing but the burning zeal within, could keep alive the wasted and sinking frame. But worse than all were those spiritual evils, which forced them to weep and pray in darkness. They had to endure contradiction from those they came to save, who often, after listening for months with apparent interest, so that the Jesuit began to hope they would soon be numbered with their converts, suddenly quitted him, with cold and derisive words, and turned again to the superstitions of their tribe.

Most of them, too, were martyrs to their faith. It will be noticed in reading this volume, how few of their number "died the common death of all men," or slept at last in the grounds which their Church had consecrated. Some, like JOQUES, and DU POISSON and SOUEL; sunk beneath the blows of the infuriated savages, and their bodies were thrown out, to feed the vulture, whose shriek, as he flapped his wings above them, had been their only requiem. Others like BROED UF and LALEMAND and SMMT, died at the stake, and their ashes "flew, no marble tells us whither," while the dusky sons of the forest stood around, and mingled their wild yells of triumph, with the martyrs' dying prayers. Others again, like the aged MARQUETTE sinking beneath years of toil, fell asleep in the wilderness, and their sorrowing companions, dug their graves in the green turf where, for many years, the rude forest ranger stopped to invoke their names, and bow in prayer before the cross which marked the spot.

But did these sufferings stop the progress of the Jesuits? The sons of LOYOLA never retreated. The mission they founded in a tribe, ended only with the extinction of the tribe itself. Their lives were made up of fearless devotedness and heroic self sacrifice. Others, whilst sorrowing for the dead, pressed forward at once to occupy their places, and if needs be, share their fate. "Nothing"—wrote Father le PETIT after describing the martyrdom of two of his brethren—"nothing has happened to these two excellent missionaries, for which they were not prepared, when they devoted themselves to the Indian missions." If the flesh trembled, the spirit seemed never to falter. Each one indeed felt that he was "baptized for the dead," and that his own blood, poured out in the mighty forests of the West, would bring down perhaps greater blessings, on those for whom he died, than he could win for them by the labors of a life. He realized that he was "appointed unto death." "Ibo et non redibo," "I will go, but will not come back" were the prophetic words of Father Jogues, when, after previous most horrible torture, he for the last time, departed to the Mohawks. When Lalemand was bound to the stake, and for seventeen hours his excruciating agonies were prolonged, his words of encouragement to his companions were, "Brothers! we are made a spectacle unto the world, and to angels, and to men.' When Marquette was setting out, for the sources of the Mississippi, and the friendly Indians who had known him, wished to turn him from his purpose by declaring "Those distant nations never spare the strangers," the calm reply of the missionary was, "I shall gladly lay down my life for the salvation of souls." And then, the red sons of the wilderness bowed with him in prayer, and before the simple cross of cedar, and among the stately groves of elm, and maple which line the St. Lawrence, there rose that old chant, which the aged man had been accustomed to hear, in the distant Cathedrals of his own land—

"Vexilla Regis prodeunt;
Fulget Crucis mysterium."

"But how little is known of all these men! The history of their bravery and sufferings, touching as it is, has been comparatively neglected." Rev. W. I. Kipp, Early Jesuit Missions.

In March, 1649, the Iroquois, chiefly Senecas and Onondagas, destroyed the Huron Missions, and brought many Huron captives back with them. Five years after, the Jesuit, LeMoyne, found the martyred Broebeuf's New

Testament and the prayer-book of GARNIER in the hands of those captive Hurons.

"On the 20th August, 1653, a party of Mohawks, lying in ambush near Quebec, captured the Jesuit, Father JOSEPH PONCET, and another Frenchman, and hurried them away to the Mohawk country, to a place at or near the more recent site of Fort Hunter. They were compelled to sing for the amusement of their captors. Father PONCET chanted the Litanies of the Holy Virgin, the Veni Creator, and other hymns of the Church.

"Whilst we were crossing the river of the Dutch," says he, "I confessed my companion, who wished to prepare for death, as we had perceived forty or fifty Iroquois, waiting for us on the other side, with clubs in their hands. They stripped us nearly naked, and compelled us to pass through two rows of the savages, (to run the gauntlet.) They struck me several blows with their sticks upon the back; and, as I increased my pace, one of them seized me by the arm, which he extended, in order to strike me a blow with a short heavy club, which he held in his hand. I surrendered my arm, thinking he was about to break, and beat to pieces, the bone between the elbow and wrist. But the blow fell upon the joint, and I escaped with a bruise which disappeared in time.

"As soon as I reached the village, they compelled me to ascend a scaffold, elevated about five feet, in the middle of the public place. My companion soon after arrived, bearing the marks of the blows he had received. I saw, among other wounds, a cruel and painful cut across his breast."

The details of the torture that was inflicted upon Father PONCET and his companion must be passed over. It continued for several days, when the latter was condemned to the stake and burnt. PONCET was spared by adoption, and, soon after, succeeded in inducing his new relatives, to carry him to the Dutch settlement at Fort Orange, (Albany.)

In 1654, an embassy of fifty Onondagas appeared before Quebec. They, impelled by some unseen power, demanded peace, asked for missionaries, and invited them to visit their cantons, and establish their missions within their borders. The opportunity was eagerly embraced, and on the 2d day of July, 1654, Father Simon LeMoyne departed from Quebec for the country of the Onondagas, by a route which the fear of the Iroquois, had hitherto prevented the French from pursuing. He ascended the St. Lawrence into Lake Ontario, coasted along its southern shore, and landed at a convenient point, from whence he went overland to the principal village of the Onondagas. They received him with marked attention, and permitted him to commence his ministerial labors.

The readers of this history will surely prefer the very words of the holy missionary, written about two hundred and eight years ago, and translated from the missionary letters:

"On the second day of the month of July, 1654, the festival of the Visitation of the Most Holy Virgin, always friendly to our undertakings, Father LeMoyne departed from Quebec on a voyage to the Iroquois and Onondagas. He passed Three Rivers, and from thence by Montreal, where a young man of good courage, and an old inhabitant, joined him, with much piety.

"On the first day of the month of August, some Iroquois fishermen having perceived us from a distance, got together to receive us. One of them runs towards us, advancing a half a league to communicate the earliest news, and the state of the country. It is a Huron prisoner, and a good Christian, whom I formerly instructed during a winter that I passed among the savages. This poor lad could not believe that it was I, whom he never hoped to see again. We disembarked at a little village of Fishermen. They crowd to see who might carry our baggage. They are apparently Huron squaws, and for the most part Christian women, formerly rich and at their ease, whom captivity has reduced to servitude. They requested me to pray to God, and I had the consolation to hear their confessions, and that of HOSTAGEHTAK, our ancient host of the Petun Nation. His sentiments and devotion drew tears from my eyes. He is the fruit of the labors of Father CHARLES GARNIER, that holy missionary, whose death has been so precious before God. The second day of August, we walked from twelve to fifteen leagues through the woods. We camp wherever the day-close finds us.

"The 3d.—At noon we were on the bank of a river, one hundred or one hundred and twenty paces wide, beyond which there was a hamlet of fishermen. An Iroquois whom I, at one time, had treated kindly at Montreal, put me across in his canoe, and through respect, carried me on his shoulders, being unwilling to suffer me to wet my feet. Every one received me with joy, and these poor people enriched me from their poverty. I was conducted to another village, a league distant, where there was a young man of consideration, who made a feast for me, because I bore his father's name, ONDESSONK. The chiefs came to harrangue us, one after the other. I baptized little skeletons, (sick children,) who awaited perhaps only this drop of the precious blood of Jesus Christ.

"The 4th.—They ask me why we are dressed in black, and I take occasion to speak to them of our mysteries. They listened with great attention. They bring me a little moribund whom I call Dominick. The time is passed when they used to hide the little innocents from us. They took me for a great Medicine-man, though I had no other remedy for the sick but a pinch of sugar. We pursued our route, in the middle of which we found our dinner waiting for us. The nephew of the first chief of the country, who is to lodge me in his cabin, is deputed by his uncle to escort us, bringing us every delicacy that the season could afford, especially new corn bread, and ears, (of corn,) which we had roasted at the fire. We slept again that night by the beautiful light of the stars.

The 6th. I was called to divers quarters to administer my medicine, to weakly and hectic little things. I baptised some of them. I confessed some of our old Huron Christians, and found God everywhere, and that He is pleased to work in hearts where faith reigns. He builds himself a temple there, where He is adored in spirit and in truth. Be He blessed for ever!

At night our host draws me aside, and tells me, very affectionately, that he always loved us, that finally his heart was satisfied, seeing all the tribes of his nation demanded nothing but peace; that the Senecas had recently come to exhort them, to manage this matter well for peace, and that in this view, he had made splendid presents; that the Cayuga had brought three belts, for that purpose; and that the Oneidas were glad to get rid of such bad affairs, through his means; and that he desired nothing but peace; that the Mohawk would, no doubt, follow the others, and thus, I might take courage, since I bore with me the happiness of the whole land.

7th. A good Christian named TERESE, a Huron captive, wishing to pour out her soul to me, away from noise and tumult, invited me to visit her in a field cabin where she lived. My God! What sweet consolation to witness so much faith, in savage hearts, in captivity, and without other assistance than that of heaven. God raises up Apostles everywhere. This good Christian woman had with her, a young captive of the Neutral Nation, whom she loved as her own daughter. She had so well instructed her, in the mysteries of the faith,

and in sentiments of piety, in the prayers they make in
this holy solitude, that I was much surprised. "Eh! sister,'
I asked, "why did you not baptize her, since she has the
faith, like you; and she is Christian in her morals, and she
wishes to die a Christian?" "Alas, brother," this happy
captive replied, "I did not think it was allowed me to baptise, except in danger of death. Baptise her now yourself,
since you consider her worthy, and give her my name."
This was the first adult baptism at Onondaga; we are indebted for it to the piety of a Huron captive.

* * * * * * * *

On the 10th day of August, the deputies of the three
neighboring nations having arrived, after the usual summons
of the chiefs, that all should assemble in ONDESSONK's cabin;
I opened the proceedings by public prayer, which I said on
my knees, and in a loud voice, all in the Huron tongue, I
invoked the great master of heaven and earth to inspire us
with what should be for *His* glory, and *our* good. I cursed
all the demons of Hell, who are spirits of division; I prayed
the Guardian Angels of the whole country, to touch the
hearts of those who heard me, when my words should strike
their ear.

I greatly astonished them, when they heard me naming
all by nations, by tribes, by families, and each particular
individual of any note; and all by aid of my manuscript,
which was a matter as wonderful, as it was new to them.
At each present they heaved a powerful ejaculation from
the bottom of the chest, in testimony of their joy. I was
full two hours making my whole speech, talking like a chief,
and walking about like an actor over a stage, as is their
custom.

After that they grouped together apart in nations and
tribes, calling to them a Mohawk, who by good luck, was
there. They consulted together for the space of two hours

longer. Finally they called me among them, and seated me in an honorable place.

The Chief, who is the tongue of the country, repeated faithfully, as orator, the substance of all my words. Then all set to singing in token of their gratification; I was told to pray God on my side, which I did very willingly. After these songs he spoke to me in the name of his nation. 1. He thanked ONNONTIO for his good disposition towards them; he brought forward, for this purpose, two large belts of Wampum. 2. He thanked us, in the name of the Mohawk Iroquois, for having given their lives to five of their allies of the Mohegan nation. Two other belts for that. 3. He thanked us, in the name of the Seneca Iroquois, for having drawn five of their tribe, out of the fire, two more belts; ejaculations, from the whole assembly, follow each present.

In concluding these remarks, the Onondaga Chief took up the word. Listen, ONDESSONK, said he to me; five entire nations speak to thee through my mouth; my breast contains the sentiments of the Iroquois Nations; and my tongue, responds faithfully to my breast. Thou wilt tell ONNONTIO, the Governor of Canada, four things, the sum of all our councils.

1. We are willing to acknowledge Him of whom thou hast spoken, who is the Master of our lives, who is as yet unknown to us.

2. Our council tree is this day planted at Onondaga, (meaning that there would be, henceforth, the place of their meetings, and of their negotiations for peace.)

3. We conjure you to select, on the banks of our great lake, an advantageous site, for a French settlement. Fix yourself in the heart of the country, since you ought to possess our hearts. There we shall go for instruction, and from that point you will be able to spread yourself abroad

in every direction. Be unto us careful as Fathers, and we shall be unto you, submissive as children.

4. We are now engaged in new wars; ONNONTIO encourages us; we shall entertain no other thought towards him, than those of peace.

They reserved their richest presents for these last four words; but I can assure you that their countenances told more than their tongues, and expressed such joy, mingled with gladness, that my heart was full. What appeared to me most endearing in all this, was that our Huron christians and the captive women lighted this fire, which melts the hearts of the Iroquois. These poor captives had told them much good of us, and spoke so often of the great value of the Faith, that they prize it, without being acquainted with it; and they love us, in the hope that we shall be for them what we have been for the Huron Indians.

The 12th of August. Our Christian captives, wishing to confess before my departure gave me employment, or rather the repose which I wished for, I baptised a little girl of four years who was dying. I recovered from the hands of these barbarians, the New Testament of the late Father JEAN DE BROEBEUF, whom they put to a cruel death five years ago, and a small book of devotion, which was used by the late Father CHARLES GARNIER, whom they also killed four years ago.

The 13th. Came the leave taking. Observing the custom of friends on similar occasions, having convoked the council, I made them two presents to console them. And with this view, I first planted in the name of ACHIENDASSE; (which is the general appellation of the General Superior of all our Society's missions in this country,) the first post of which to begin a cabin. This is like laying in France, the first or corner stone of a house, one intends to build. My second present was to place the first strip of bark to cover the cabin. This evidence of affection satisfied them, and three or four of their chiefs thanked me publicly in speeches which, one could not be persuaded, issued from the lips of men called savages.

We arrive at the entrance of a small lake, in a large half dried basin; we take the water of a spring that they durst not drink, saying that there is a demon in it, which renders it fœted, having tasted it I found it was a fountain of salt water; and, in fact, we made salt from it, as natural as that from the sea; of which we carried a sample to Quebec." (When the report reached New York, then New Amsterdam, that LE MOYNE had made the discovery of salt water at Onondaga, the Dutch pronounced it, "a Jesuit lie!"

The 17th. We enter their river, and at a quarter of a league meet on the left the Seneca river, which increases this; it leads they say to Cayuga (Ouion) and to the Senecas in two sunsets. At three leagues of a fine road from there, we have the river Oneida, (Oneiout) which appears to us very deep. Finally a good league lower down we meet a rapid which gives the name to a village of fishermen. I found there some of our Christians and some Huron Christian women whom I have not yet seen.

Before the return of LE MOYNE an embassy of Onondagas arrived at Quebec, soliciting the Jesuits to establish a permanent residence among them.

This request was immediately granted and Father CHAUMONOT, a veteran Missionary in New France, and CLAUDE DABLON, who had recently arrived in the country, were assigned to the duty.

They left Quebec on the 19th of September 1655, and proceeding by the way of St. Lawrence and Lake Ontario, arrived on the 5th of October within a quarter of a league of the Onondaga village. Here they were met by a deputation of chiefs, who received them with speeches and welcomed them to their country. As they passed to the Council House, the roof of the wig-wams were crowded with persons, anxious to obtain a sight of the pale faces.

The Jesuits immediately assembled the scattered members of the church which had formerly existed in the Huron country, now captive among the Onondagas, but which might serve as a nucleus for their future operations.

They visited the salt springs, which they describe as near the Onondaga lakes, and as flowing through a beautiful meadow, surrounded by trees of lofty height. Near by the Springs, and within one hundred paces, they found fresh water issuing from the same hill.

On the 12th of November, they witnessed the torture of a young Erie, nine or ten years old, who was burnt alive before a slow fire, and expired in two hours, without uttering a groan or complaint.

On the 17th they finished their chapel, which they named the church of St. Peter and Paul, it being the first house dedicated to Christian worship in the Northern or Western part of our State. D'Ablion remained with the Onondagas until the following Spring, when, leaving Chaumont in the Mission, he returned to Montreal.

In September 1655, three distinguished Seneca Chiefs arrived at Quebec from the Genesee country; called Sonontonan, for the purpose of forming a friendly alliance with the Algonquins, French and remnants of the Hurons. They were followed by a larger delegation in January 1656, consisting of ten Chiefs, the principal one of whom is described as wise and skillful in managing the affairs of the nation, and possessed of rare and persuasive eloquence. They desired the Jesuits to visit their country, and teach them those truths, of which their Huron captives had informed them.

The cantons of the Five Nations being now apparently

thrown open to the operations of the Jesuits, preparations were made to occupy the field in full force.

There was still great distrust of the sincerity of the Iroquois, for their former perfidy and cruelty and the tragedies they enacted in the Huron country, were still fresh in the memory of the French.

A captive Huron, who had escaped from Onondaga, told them the design was, to induce as many French as possible, to trust themselves in the country, and then to put them all to death.

"But it was no part of the Jesuit creed to shrink from danger. 'The blood of martyrs is the seed of Christians,' was his axiom; and the blood shed by the Iroquois cried not for vengeance, but for pardon and mercy. The Mission must go on, and Fathers MESNARD, D'ABLON, FRENIEU, BROAR and BOURSIER, under the guidance of their spiritual head, FRANÇOIS LE MERCIER, left for the Central Iroquois tribe on the 17th May, 1656." (O. H. MARSHALL.) They suffered much in their journey. Not far from the present village of Liverpool, on the northern shore of the Lake, they fixed their habitation. The "Te Deum" was sung; a firm treaty of peace was ratified, and the Onondagas and Senecas were adopted as brothers; the Oneidas and Cayugas as children of the great ONNONTIO, Governor of New France.

On their arrival, they met twenty Christian Huron captives, who showed their unbounded joy at seeing Father CHAUMONT, whom they had known in the Huron country. Some threw themselves on his neck; some invited him to a feast; others gave him presents. Prayers were said in the open air, a cabin being too small to contain them. The Father heard their confessions, and instructed these poor souls who had heard nothing of God since their captivity. He also says: "The Hurons of the upper country, who had never been instructed, on account of their aversion to the faith, have also begun to yield; so true it is, that affliction gives a right understanding. We have baptised in different times, in sundry places, more than four hundred and fifty savages, of all ages, notwithstanding the obstacles of the wars in which they are engaged. If we can sustain preachers of the Gospel in these countries, which I call the country of martyrs, many more will be baptised." Truly they might expect success for these missionaries, since all could truly utter the words of Father CHAUMONT, who spoke the Indian language fluently, and who, in his address to the assembled Council of savages, said: "Not for traffic, do we appear in your country; our aim is much higher. Keep your beaver, if you like, for the Dutch. What comes to *our* hand shall be employed for *your* service. We seek not perishable things. For the faith alone, have we left our land; for the faith, have we traversed the ocean; for the faith, have we left the great ships of the French, to enter your tiny canoes; for the faith, I hold in my hand this present, and open my lips to summon you to keep your word, given at Quebec. There you solemnly promised to hearken to the words of the Great God: they are in my mouth; hear them!" Then running over the principal doctrines of Christianity, he called upon them to say whether they were not just, and summoned them by their hope of bliss, or fear of chastisement, to embrace the faith. His discourse produced a profound sensation: they built the Church of St. Mary, the Christian captives hastened to receive the sacraments, many were baptised. "From that time the missionaries performed all their duties with the same freedom as if they were in the midst of a colony of French, and the missionaries well knew, in their hearts, those of whom the Holy Spirit had taken possession." The next year, it became necessary to enlarge the chapel, which

could not contain all those who wished to be instructed."—
CLARK.

In the year 1657, the harvest appearing plentiful in all the villages of the upper Iroquois, (Cayugas and Senecas,) the common people listening to the words of the Gospel with simplicity, and the chiefs with a well-disguised dissimulation—Father PAUL RAGUENEAU, Father FRANÇOIS DU PERON, some Frenchmen and several Hurons, departed from Montreal, the 26th July, to aid their brethren and compatriots.

On the third day of the month of August, of the same year, 1657, the perfidy of the Iroquois chiefs, urged on by emissaries from New York, began to develop itself, by the massacre of the poor Hurons who had been brought into the country, after thousands of protestations of kindness, and thousands of oaths, in Indian style, that they should treat them as brothers. Had not a number of Iroquois remained among the French, near Quebec, to endeavor to bring with them the rest of the Hurons, who, distrusting these traitors, would not embark with the others, the Fathers and the Frenchmen who ascended with them, would have then been destroyed; and all those who remained on the banks of Lake Ganatoa, near to Onnontaque, would, shortly after, have shared the same fate. But the fear that the French would wreak vengeance on their countrymen retarded their design, of which our Fathers had had secret intelligence, immediately on their arrival in the country. Even a captain, who was acquainted with the secret of the chiefs, having taken some liking to the preachings of the Gospel, and finding himself very sick, demanded baptism; having received it with sufficient instruction, he revealed the evil designs of his countrymen to those who attended him, and went a short time afterwards to Heaven.

The diplomacy of the Dutch, who from New Amsterdam,

now New York, sought to detach the Indians from the French; and the jealousies of trade, caused the Indian mind to be poisoned by hundreds of slanders, vain fancies, and suspicions; to this a missionary adds, at the disastrious time just mentioned, the following:

"I believe rather that the Onnontaque Iroquois, demanded some Frenchmen in sincerity, but with views very different. The chiefs, finding themselves engaged in heavy wars, against a number of nations whom they had provoked, asked for Hurons as reinforcements to their warriors; they wished for the French to obtain firearms for them, and to repair those which might be broken. Further, as the Mohawks treated them very ill, when passing through their villages to trade with the Dutch, they were anxious to rise out of this dependence, by opening a trade with the French. This is not all, the fate of arms being fickle, they demanded, that our Frenchmen should erect a vast fort in their country, to serve as a retreat for them, or at least for their wives and children, in case their enemies pressed too close on them. Here are the views of the Iroquois politicians. The common people did not penetrate so far ahead; curiosity to see strangers, come from such a distance and the hope of deriving some little profit, created a desire to see them; but the Christian Hurons and captives among the people, and those who approved their lives and conversations, which they sometimes held regarding our belief, desired nothing in the world so much, as the coming of preachers of the Gospel, who had brought these Hurons to the faith of Jesus Christ. But, as soon as the Cheif saw the dreaded Cat, or Erie nation, subjugated by, their arms, their policy changed."

The political and commercial intrigues of the day, entraped the Indians to a course which has been their ruin, and which leaves their sad remnant still pagan. They were taught to suspect the missionaries, whose death was planned. But almost by miracle, the missionaries and their companions, all escaped on the 20th March 1658. Thus ended for a time, after a brief existence, the mission of St. Marys of Ganentau, in the Onondagas country, with its dependant missions among the Oneidas, Cayuga, Senecas, it was now crushed; but its effect was not lost, many had been brought to the faith, and more were convinced of the truth and beauty of Christianity but for motives of policy, they still hung back. A powerful Indian, Garacontie, though up to their departure, no sign had betrayed his favorable opinion of Christianity, now became openly the protector of the Chritians. Garacontie, by presents and arguments rescued as many Christians as he could, in all the cantons. At Onondaga, morning and night, by a bell, he called twenty four of those rescued Christians to prayer. On Sundays he gave feasts, now in one cabin, now another, to enable the Chiristians to spend the day in prayer. It is to be hoped that the Cayuga chief Saonchiogua, the warm friend of Garacontie, did the same for Cayuga; and others, for the Senecas.

This friend of Garacontie, in July 1660 presented himself with a flag of truce, before the walls of Montreal, and demanded, "That the holy women, (nuns) may come to see us, both those who take care of the sick, and those who instruct the young. We will build them fine cabins, and the fairest mats in the country are destined for them. Let them not fear the currents, or rapids,—*we have removed them all, and rendered the river so smooth, that they could themselves, without pain or fear, ply the light paddle.* A black-gown must come with me, otherwise no peace; and, on his coming depends the lives of twenty Frenchmen at Onondaga." The returned captives declared that the Indian women were unanimously for Christianity, &c. The intrepid missionary LE MOYNE, then nearly sixty years of age, joyfully prepared for a mission which seemed to promise martyrdom. On the 12th August, 1660, Father LE MOYNE was solemnly received at the Mission-house, by the sachems of Onondaga, Cayuga and Seneca. In his poor chapel, French, Huron and Iroquois assembled around the same altar, each chaunting in his own tongue the words of truth and life. Ever on the march, village after village, received his missionary visits, and everywhere his presence was gladly welcomed. But he passed through many dangers. An enraged savage once burst into his chapel, to destroy the crucifix: Father LE MOYNE sprang between the altar and the savage, and bared his own head for the blow; but the murderer's hand was caught by sachems, who were present, as the tomahawk glistened in the air."

The simple words of the Jesuit missionary will here not be out of place; in 1668, the missionary writes:

"I am going to finish this letter by the baptism of a captive brought from the Andastoques. He was about fifty years of age, and he appeared to have been of considerable note among his own nation. They held him for some days in the uncertainty of death, during which time, he thought far more of making his escape, than of securing the salvation of his soul. At length, being assured by Father GARNIER that there was no chance of their allowing him to be delivered for any presents, he thanked the Father with as much affection as if he had given him assurance of life: and he commenced with a good will to repeat the instructions which they had taught him in the chapel.

Father MILLET after having duly prepared, baptized him. The captive was immediately afterwards carried back to the same cabin, where he was kept, the rest of the day, for the amusement of those who came to see him, and who made him sing according to their custom. Fortunately for him the

Father met him on the way, when they were carrying him to another cabin to burn him. "I approached him" said the Father in one of his letters "and after having consoled him, and encouraged him to suffer with constancy, doubted whether I should go further; but a savage, having told me to go boldly with him, to instruct him, I determined to go, and arrived at the cabin as soon as the captive, and sat down by him.

They were already preparing the fires and irons, with which he was to suffer, on seeing this sad preparation, he turned towards me, and asked if he would go to heaven; this question moved me, and I told him he *would* go to heaven, that he should take courage, that he would only suffer for a short time, and that he would then be eternally happy. He then repeated with me, over and over again: Lord have mercy upon me, until they told me the time for instruction was up, and that I should retire. I left him with regret resolved to return the next day. True enough, I returned the next morning at break of day; I approached the captive, and told him I was sorry to see him in such a state. He assured me that I gave him great pleasure by speaking so: and when an Iroquois was ready to place a red hot iron upon his foot, I saw him rise it up himself, and keep it thus raised up against the red hot iron, until it had lost the greatest part of its heat.

They had not as yet burnt him any higher than his knees; but scarcely had the sun rose, when they uttered the cry through the village, for every one to assemble; they then conducted him towards the gate, where they had built two fires, and had driven a stake with which to fasten his hands and feet. When this miserable captive saw himself, thus fastened between two fires, he commenced trembling all over his body, and I never saw anything that reminded me more of our Lord, at the pillar, and the fear which caused his bloody sweat in the garden of Olives. The more I saw him afflicted, the more I endeavored to console and comfort him. During the time of his sufferings, I kept close to him, sometimes throwing myself on my knees, and praying for the salvation of his soul, sometimes saying some good word to him, when they gave him some relaxation; and encouraging him to turn his eyes to heaven, and to pray for his eternal salvation. He suffered with so much constancy, that he was admired by every one; all believed, that the rain, which fell for some days afterwards, was caused by his death.

The savages were edified by the manner in which I assistted him in his sufferings, and they asked so many questions as to give me the opportunity of instructing them upon our mysteries.

This work of assisting captives, when they are burned alive, and when they are eaten, in the presence of the missionary, requires a great deal of courage, and for one who has a natural horror of seeing men burnt and eaten, as is the case with a new missionary, there is great need of being well fortified with grace. Besides this captive, there were thirty others baptized this year, in the mission of the Onontagues, the most of them are dead and in heaven, praying to God for the salvation of their brethren."

Dutch traders soon flooded the canton with intoxicating liquors; hence Father LE MOYNE disgusted, gladly accepted an invitation to visit Cayuga, then ravaged by an epedemick. He ministered to the sick, and saved many. A month was too short for him to confess the Christians, baptise their children, and instruct them all. He then returned to Ouondaga. GARACONTIC had, during his absence, baffled the war party who had plotted the death of LE MOYNE. The fervent missionary returned. He had preached to captive Indians of ten different tribes, baptised two hundred infants, and won several adults to the faith. During his stay at

Onondaga, Christian Indians, especially women, came frequently from other cantons, under various pretexts, to profit by his sacred ministry. Some of them, by their piety and virtue, won their mistresses to the faith, and brought them to receive instruction from him. After the departure of Le Moyne the war broke out anew; the Mohawks and Oneidas were defeated by the Chippewas. Near Conestogues, (called by the Hurons, Andastes, Andastogues, and Gandastagues,) pressed hard on the Western Cantons. The scattered Algonquins resumed courage, and cut off Iroquois parties, but being now Christians, they did not perpetrate on their prisoners, the fiendish cruelties usual with them before their conversion. Giving the prisoners a missionary, and time for instruction, they led them out and shot them. The pagan Indians, seeing this exclaimed: "Good, good! when we will become Christians, we shall do so too." In the spring of 1664, the Indians, especially the Senecas, asked for missionaries. Le Moyne offered to go, but the French, so often deceived, refused. A Cayuga chief headed a delegation of his tribe, but he also failed. LeMoyne died November 24, 1665. His death was mourned as a public loss by the French. The Iroquois sent presents to wipe away the tears for his death. His place was soon filled by Fathers JAMES FREMIN and PETER RAFFAIX.

We cannot follow the zealous missionaries in their devoted labors on the Mohawk River. Many are the traits of truly apostolic zeal shown by these missionaries—many the instances of saintly virtue in their neophytes. At Canawago. Montgomery county, the child, CATHERINE TEAGHOKUITA, already began to develop the high sanctity which has made her name famous. "Fervor pervaded all, and converts were made who never swerved from the faith. The Catholic Indians of the Mohawk were now known and ridiculed by the people of Albany, who had never made an attempt to introduce Christianity there. The burghers of Albany and New York even threatened the squaws for displaying their 'beads and popish trumpery' in their villages; but, far from concealing these marks of their faith, the noble Mohawk women were ready to die for it."

Onondaga, the central mission, was now established on a firm basis; the Offices of the Church were celebrated, the sacraments administered, and Christian virtues practiced as regularly and carefully as in the most Catholic parts of Europe. In a short time, two hundred were baptised— among them, five chieftains, pillars of the Church; one of whom, in a public assembly, advocated the faith as the only hope of saving their country, by restoring morality, and, above all, fidelity in marriage, and in their relations with each other, the want of which had been more destructive than armies.

The women, especially listened to the words of truth and the 'Relations' of the missionaries dwell with interest on the noble death of MAGDALEN TIOTONHARASON, who had gone to Quebec to learn the *prayer*, (Christianity,) and who remained steadfast to her last sigh, amid the seductions and persuasions of her unbelieving relatives. The bold stand of the missionaries against polygamy, had won to their cause all the women, who felt indeed the crimes, to which their actual state often gave rise.

The Church was composed of three nations—Onondagas, Hurons and Neutrals—all bound together by the common tie of faith, which made master and slave kneel down side by side. Obstacles were no longer raised by the medicine-men, no sachem opposed the missionaries, and all gloried in the name of Christian.

The reader will understand better the cause, not of the failure of the mission, but of its being chased off by men, and transferred by God to another region—by reading the following letters: one, from a New York Governor, who professed to be a Catholic, but who placed his politics high above his religion, who promised the Indians "English Black-Gowns," (they got Protestant ministers, who would not stay with them;) and one from a Jesuit priest—both copied from "Documents Relating to the Colonial History of New York," Vol III., pages 438, etc.:

"Propositions to the Five Nations westward, viz.: to the cheife Sachems and Captains of the Senekes, Cajouges, Onondages, Onneydes and Maquasse by the Govr in the Citty Hall of Albany, the fifth day of August, 1687, in the third year of his Maj^{ties} Reigne:

"BRETHREN:—

"I am verry gladd to see you all here in this house and am heartely gladd that you have sustained no greater losse by the French, tho' I beleive there intention was to destroy you all, if they could have surprised you in your castles; and as soon as I heard of there designe to warr with you, I gave you notice of itt, and came up here myselfe that I might bee ready to give you all the assistance and advice, that soe short a time would allow me. . . . . . My advice is, further, to you, that Messengers goe in the behalfe of all the Five Nations to the Christian Ind^{ns} att Cannada, to persuade them to come home to their native Country, and to promisse them all protection, which will be another great means to weaken your Enemies, and if they will not be advised, then you know what to doe with them. I think itt verry necessary for the Brethren's security and assistance, and to the endamaging the French, to build a Fort upon the Lake, where I may keepe stores and provisions in case of necessity, and therefore I would have the Brethren let me know what place will be most convenient for itt. . . . There is no advice or proposition that I made to the Brethren, all the while that the Priest lived att Onondaga, butt hee writt itt to Cannada, as I have found by one of his letters that hee had given to an Indyan to carry to Cannada, and was brought here; therefore I desire the Brethren not to receive him or any French Priests any more, having sent for English Priests, whom you can be supplyed with, all to content."

REV. DEAN DE LAMBERVILLE TO GOV. DONGAN.

ONONTAQUE 10th Sept. 1685.

MY LORD

"I had the honor not long since to write to you; it was last month. Since the dispatch of my last letter, the Senecas who were desirous to make trouble and to persuade the Mohawks and other villages to unite with them against Mons. DE LA BARRE, have changed their minds; since they were assured that the peace concluded last year, as you desired, would not be broken by M. DE LA BARRE, as they were maliciously told, and as a hundred false reports which are never ceased being related would persuade them. * * * Since peace, through your care, will apparently last, we shall continue to carry the Christian faith, through this country, and to solicit the Indians, whom your honor with your friendship, to embrace it as you yourself embrace it, for this is the sole object that has caused us to come here, that the blood of Jesus Christ shed for all men may be useful to them, and that His glory may be great throughout the earth.

If you will please to honor me with a line from your hand you can have your letter given to one named GARAKONTIE who is deputed from the Onnontagues to repair to the Diet which you have convoked at Albany. Do him the charity to exhort him to be a good Christian, as he was whose name he bears, and who was his brother. Recommend him I beseech you not to get drunk any more, as he promised when he was baptized, and to perform the duties of a Christian. One word from you will have a wonderful effect on his mind, and he will publish throughout that it is not true that the English forbid them to be Christians since you who command them will have exhorted him to persevere therein."

The border war ended with the peace of Ryswick, in 1697, and the French then hoped as much as the English dreaded, to see the restoration of the Jesuits' missions. The seed of opposition sown by DONGAN had now grown to ripeness, and a new Governor, an Irish peer, of deep-rooted fanaticism, ruled the destines of New York.

One of his first acts was to warn the Indians against the French priests. Mindful of DONGAN's promise of English Black-gowns, the deputies asked BELLAMONT to fulfill it. Accordingly, DELLIUS, the Dutch pastor at Albany, was appointed missionary to the Mohawks, although he never took up his residence among them, and limited his ministry to occasional visits, when he preached by an interpreter, and to the administration of baptism, to such children as were brought to him in Albany. Such a man hardly seemed to the Indians a successor of zealous Catholic priests whose cabins had so long been seen in their villages. Disappointed in their application to New York, they naturally turned to Canada for religious teachers. BELLAMONT was provoked, and resolved to exclude the Jesuits, unblushingly declaring, "that the Five Nations had earnestly implored him to drive out the Jesuits who oppressed them," although he knew that since 1685 there had been no missionary in the cantons, except Father MILET, and he not an oppressor, but oppressed, a prisoner and a slave.

To carry out his plan, he sent to the Assembly the draft of a bill against Jesuits and priests. It was not relished: several of the missionaries had, at various times, visited the colonies; they were known and esteemed by the leading men, who had thus been enabled to see Catholicity in its workings, which the infatuated Governor had not. The Council negatived the bill: BELLAMONT, voting as a member, made a tie, and then voting again as Governor, carried his point, and made it the law of the land. Assuming the Iroquois to be subjects of the English monarch, and with still greater disregard of truth, averring that "Jesuit priests and popish missionaries, had *lately* come into, and for some time had their residence in remote parts of the province, to excite hostility against the English government," the bill enacts that every priest in the colony, "after the 1st of November, be deemed an incendiary, a disturber of the public peace, and an enemy of the Christian religion;" and condemned him to perpetual imprisonment, and, in case of escape, to death, if retaken.

The generous burghers, and their clergy, who had so often showed hospitality to the French missionaries, were, by the same act, threatened with a heavy fine, and with the pillory, should they ever again harbor a priest under their roofs.

BELLAMONT had sought to prevent the Iroquois from making any separate peace with the French; but on FRONTENAC's death, the cantons sent deputies to the St. Lawrence to condole with the colony. This was not, however, their only care; they asked that Father BRUYAS should be sent among them, and the elder DE LAMBERVILLE, be recalled from France to resume his old mission. The answer was deferred, but on the coming of a second embassy, Father BRUYAS, with JONCAIRE and MARICOURT, adopted Iroquois, set out for Onondaga. Here they were received by TEGAMISSORAN with much solemnity, and all terms having been arranged, peace was signed at Montreal, on the 8th of September, 1700, by deputies of all the nations.

To carry out its provisions, BRUYAS visited Onondaga

again in 1701, and having brought back the French prisoners, there, a new treaty was signed at Montreal by the French, Iroquois, Abnakis, Hurons, Ottawas, Illinois, and Algonquins.

No mention was made of the missions in this document; but a deputation sent, at the request of TEGAMMISSORAN, in 1702, invited the return of the missionaries to their former posts. "Fathers were accordingly sent everywhere," says CHARLEVOIX, "and a cotemporary list numbers as Iroquois missionaries Father JAMES DE LAMBERVILLE, JULIAN GARNIER and LE VAILLANT, who renewed their labors among the Onondagas and Senecas." These missions the cantons bound themselves to maintain; and though a new war between England and France soon broke out, the missionaries won the cantons to neutrality; so that New York and Canada, then escaped all the horrors of Indian war.

The missions accordingly continued, but we have no tidings of them. Father JAMES D'HEU, and Father PETER DE MARENIL joined the rest, and they labored on till 1708, when the English finally induced all but the Senecas to take up arms.

By the extract of a letter from M. DE VAUDRENIL to M. DE PONTCHAATRAIN, dated Quebec, 14th November 1709, it will be seen that anti-Catholic diplomacy outwitted the Jesuits; proving what Our Lord said: "the children of this world are wiser in their generations, than the children of light."

"ABRAHAM SCHUYLER having had a long conversation with the Reverend Father DE LAMBERVILLE, and having likewise expressed to him his regret at being obliged to present the hatchet to the Indians, managed so well that he persuaded this good Father to come himself to Montreal to give me an account of what was passing; and, as he desired nothing better than to send off Father DE LAMBERville, of whose influence over the Onontagues he was aware, he took advantage of his absence, as soon as he saw him depart, and told the *Reverend Father De Marinel, who had remained, that his life was not safe, insinuated to him that the only means of extricating himself from certain danger, to which he was exposed was to accompany them to Orange, which this good father complied with, as appears by a copy of a letter, which he himself addressed to Father D'Heu, Missionary at Seneca, and which I annex hereunto. In order to engage the Onontagues the more to declare war against us, Abraham Schuyler immediately made some drunken Indians set fire to the Father's chapel and house, which he first caused to be pillaged."—Documents, etc., Col. Hist. of N. Y., Vol. IX. p. 829.

In 1700 Earl Belmont writes his instructions to Romer, about locating a fort at Onondaga; he concludes thus: "You will do well to assure them, (the Indians,) of my kindness, provided they continue faithful to the king, and keep no correspondence with the French in Canada, *nor receive any of the priests and Jesuits among them.* All which instructions you are carefully to observe and perform for His Majesty.

3d September, 1700. Signed Belmont."

A fitting close, showing why New York Indians did not become Christians, will be found in the following dispatch. In the official letter of Secretary Wraxall to Sir William Johnson, of January, 1756, we read: "The French debauched many of our five nations to their religion and interests, actually drew several off to go and live in Canada, and laid the foundation of that formidable and fatal seduction, which now forms the Cagnawaga nation.

"Still profiting by our supineness, and presuming on the weakness of our Indian management, the French push a point not less insolent than alarming, with the consent of some Onondaga Indians whom they had debauched to their interests. They built a fort, and were building a chapel at the Onondaga castle. Our Albany commissioners awoke; Coll Schuyler went up there with a party of men, destroyed both the fort and chapel, drove the French away, and strengthened our Indian interest. However we relapsed into our former indolence, and the French, though not so boldly, yet steadily pursued their measures."

An unaccountable thirst for large tracts of land, without the design of cultivation, hath prevailed over the inhabitants of this and the neighboring provinces, with a singular rage. Patents have been lavishly granted, (to give it no worse term,) upon the pretence of fair Indian purchases, some of which the Indians have alleged were never made, but forged. Others bought of Indians who were no proprietors; some by making two or three Indians drunk, and giving them a trivial consideration. They say also, the surveyors have frequently run patents vastly beyond even the pretended conditions or limits of sale.

But at the same time it appeared, Firstly, That the confederate nations, at their meeting with Coll Johnson, did with great reluctance take up the hatchet against the French and their Indians.

Secondly, That they declined sending any of their people to join General Braddock.

Thirdly, That they were not inclined to join General Shirley. He then advises that

"The soldiers to be encouraged by some gratuities and advantages to marry such Indian women as will embrace Protestant Christianity."—Documents relating to Colonial History, Vol. VII, p. 16, etc.

Who can tell what would have been the happy lot of the Indians, and that, still more glorious than at present, of our noble state, had not politics, and cupidity, and frantic hatred of the Catholic religion wrested from the New York Indians all means of becoming Catholic Christians; other than that they never will be. In time, through great efforts and sacrifices, some may be made tolerably decent gentiles; Christians, *never*, but through the full form our Lord established.

It would scarcely be just to pass onward, without giving some correct notion of the sanctity to which poor New York Indians had reached, long before their Christianity was placed *under penal law*.

CHAPTER IX.

GOSPEL FRUITS—SANCTITY AMONG THE INDIANS.

A distinguished feature of the Catholic Church is, that the "good oder of Christ, will ever be found" wherever exterior or interior secular power, does not impede the sacred movements of the Christian Priesthood; fetter the divine Hierarchy of the Church of the Living God, "which is the body of Christ, and the fulness of Him;" or impede the due action of the Visible Head, on the living but scattered numbers. Then, always and everywhere, will be found many who can, in some just and true degree, say with St. Paul: "I live; now not I, but Christ Jesus lives in me."

How wonderful a change did not the Jesuits effect in Paraguay! An infidel combination chased away the Pastors; "and the sheep of the flock were dispersed!" Most touching are the early annals of Mexican Christianity. The innocence and piety of the devoted early Mexican Christian Indians; still linger, with holy freshness, round many secluded spots, to which liberal, (illiberal, *almost infidel*) Christians had no access. Our General PIKE, (who during the war of 1812, died heroically, the Patriot's death at Fort Erie, opposite Buffalo,) having, before the Mexican revolution, strayed, with a small band of soldiers, into the Mexican territory, was made prisoner, and led to the City of Mexico. Treated with the greatest kindness, led through almost the whole country, abiding long enough to become intimately acquainted with it, he wrote a work on Mexico, in which he praised the general innocence and piety of the people, the estimable character of the priesthood, and its beneficent action on the Indians.

In 1810 the revolution began. More than twelve years of civil war, injured the vineyard of the Lord. But when the *so called Liberals*, adopted a form of Government for which, neither the traditions, nor the habits of the people were prepared, the Bishops and Spanish Priests, that is nearly all the well instructed clergy of the country were banished. The poor Indians were left with a handful of Priests, each often forced to say six or eight masses, every Sunday, in different and distant churches. Instruction, the frequentation of the Sacraments, &c., became for many, an impossibility. Add to this, that most of the Indian Christians, after having been *legally* robbed of their lands, by *liberal* speculators, were driven up the mountains, towards the region of eternal snow, whither the few, over worked missionaries, could not follow them; strange then would it be, if many were not now sadly different from what they were when General PIKE uttered his words of high commendation. It has been seen already, and will be seen yet more clearly, that here, also hostile opposition struggled, from the beginning, against "*the grain of mustard seed.*" Still, almost from the beginning, the fruits of sanctity, gave evidence to the work of God. And that, too, in the very way which Scripture notes, as distinguishing God's work, from the work of the Father of lies.

If the Redeemer was to be " Emmanuel," "*God with*

us," he was also to be "The Son of David," "*The man of sorrows.*" He sought not to please himself; he watched; he fasted; he suffered. David, who had seen the Lord, in distant blessed vision, caught his spirit, and says of himself: " I covered my soul in fasting; and it was made a reproach to me. And I made hair cloth my garment. I have labored in my groanings; every night I will wash my bed; I will water my couch with my tears. I have watched, and become as a sparrow, all alone on the house top. For I did eat ashes like bread, and mingled my drink with weeping!" The holy youth Daniel tells us almost the same. St. Paul is eloquent, when he often alludes to how severely "he chastised the flesh, and brought it into subjection. In labor and painfulness, in watchings often, in hunger and thirst, in fastings often, in cold and nakedness." Must not a Christian admire, and adore in his work, the Saviour God, who is "the same yesterday, to-day and forever:" when he sees the poor Indian, unknown to the Priest, and with an exaggerated zeal, which the Pastor checks as soon as known, practice the penances to which the spirit of God impelled his saints in every age. But it is time to begin the life of one, who, we will find, had many imitators.

Letter from Father Cholonec, Missionary of the Society of Jesus to Father Augustine Le Banc, Procurator of Missions in Canada:

At Sault de St. Louis, 27th Aug. 1715.

My Reverend Father:

The peace of our Lord be with you:

The marvels which God is working every day through the intercession of a young Iroquois female who has lived and died among us in the order of sanctity, have induced me, to inform you of the particulars of her life. You have yourself been a witness of these wonders, when you discharged here, with so much zeal, the duties of a missionary, and you know that the exalted Prelate who governs this Church, touched by the prodigies, with which God has deigned to honor the memory of this holy maiden; has, with reason, called her "the Genevieve of New France." All the French who are in the colonies, as well as the Indians, hold her in singular veneration. They come from a great distance to pray at her tomb, and many, by her intercession, have been immediately cured of their maladies, and have received from Heaven other extraordinary favors. I will write you nothing, my Reverend Father, which I have not myself seen, during the time she was under my care, or which I have not learned of the missionary, who conferred on her the rite of holy baptism.

TEAGHOKUITA, (which is the name of this holy woman, about whom I am going to inform you,) was born in the year 1656, at Gandaugue, one of the settlements of the lower Iroquois, who are called Agnez, (Mohawks.) Her father was an Iroquois and a heathen; her mother, who was a Christian, was an Algonquin; taken prisoner by the Iroquois, she remained a captive in their country. We have since learned that, in the midst of heathens, she preserved her faith, even to her death. By her marriage she had two children, one son and one daughter—the latter of whom is the subject of this narrative—but the poor mother died, without having been able to procure for them, the grace of baptism. The small pox which ravaged the Iroquois country, in a few days removed her husband, her son, and herself,. TEAGHOKUITA was also attacked like the others, but she did not sink, as they did, under the violence of the disease. Thus, at the age of four years, she found herself an orphan, under the care of her aunts; and in the power of an uncle, who was the leading man in the settlement.

When a little older, she occupied herself in rendering to

her aunt, all those services of which she was capable. She ground the corn; brought water and wood; for such, among these Indians, are the ordinary employments of females. Any spare time, she spent, in the manufacture of little articles, in which she displayed extraordinary skill.

By this means she avoided two rocks which might have been fatal to her innocence—idleness, which is the source of many vices; and the extreme passion which Indians have for gossipping visits, and for showing themselves in public places, where they can display their finery. The young TEAGHOKUITA had naturally a distaste for all vain display, but she could not oppose the persons who stood to her in the place of father and mother, and to please them, she had sometimes recourse to ornaments. But after she became a Christian, she looked back upon this as a sin, and expiated her compliance by severe penance, and almost continual tears.

M. DE TRACY, having been sent by the government to chastise the Iroquois, who had laid waste our colonies; carried the war into their country, and burned three villages of the Mohawks. This expedition spread terror among the Indians, and they acceded to the terms of peace which were offered them. Their deputies were well received by the French, and a peace concluded to the advantage of both nations.

We availed ourself of this occasion, which seemed a favorable one, to send missionaries to the Iroquois. They had already some smattering of the Gospel which had been preached to them by Father JOQUES, and particularly those of the Onontagues, among whom this Father had fixed his residence. It is well known that this missionary received there that recompense of martyrdom which well befitted his zeal. The labors of his two companions were crowned with the same holy death of martyrdom, and it is without doubt, to the blood of these first Apostles of the Iroquois nation, that we must ascribe the blessings, which God poured out on the zeal of those, who succeeded them.

Father FREMIN, Father BRUGAS, and Father PIERRON, who knew the language of the country, were chosen to accompany the Iroquois deputies. The missionaries happened to arrive, at a time when these people are accustomed to plunge into all kinds of debauchery; hence they found no one in a fit state to receive them. This, however, procured for the young TEAGHOKUITA the advantage of early knowing those, whom God sent to instruct her in the way of perfection. She was charged with the task of lodging the missionaries, and attending to their wants. The modesty and sweetness with which she acquitted herself of this duty, touched her new guests; while she, on her part, was struck with their affable manners, their regularity in prayer, and their daily pious exercises. God even then, disposed her to the grace of Baptism, which she would have requested, if the missionaries had remained longer in her village.

The third day after their arrival they were sent for to Tionnontoquen, where their reception was to take place; it was very pompous.

TEAGHOKUITA being now marriageable, her relatives were anxious to find a husband for her; because, according to the custom of the country, the game which the husband kills in the chase, is appropriated to the benefit of his wife, and the other members of his family. But the young Iroquois had inclinations, very much opposed to the designs of her relations. She had a great love for purity, even before she knew the excellence of this virtue, and anything which could in the least soil it, impressed her with horror. When, therefore, they proposed to establish her in life, she excused herself, under different pretexts; alleging, above all, her extreme youth, and the little inclination she had for marriage.

The relations seemed to approve of these reasons; but a little while after they resolved to betroth her, when she least expected it; and, without even allowing her a choice in the person to whom she was to be united. They, therefore, cast their eyes upon a young man, whose alliance appeared desirable, and made the proposition both to him and to the members of his family. The matter being settled on both sides, the young man, in the evening, entered the wigwam, which was destined for him, and seated himself near her. It is thus that marriages are made among the Indians; and, although these heathens extend their licentiousness to the greatest excess, yet is there no nation which in public, guards so scrupulously that outward decorum, which is the attendant of perfect modesty. A young man would be forever dishonored, if he should stop to converse publicly with a young woman. Whenever marriage is in question, the business is to be settled by the parents, and the parties most interested, are not even permitted to meet. It is sufficient that they are talking of the marriage of a young Indian with a young woman, to force them to shun seeing each other. When the parents on both sides have agreed, the young man comes by night to the wigwam of his future spouse, and seats himself near her; which is the same as declaring, that he takes her for his wife, and she takes him for her husband. TEGAHKOUITA appeared utterly disconcerted, when she saw the young man seated by her side. She at first blushed, and then rising abruptly, went forth, indignantly, from the wigwam, nor would she return until the young man left it. This firmness rendered her relatives outrageous. They considered it an insult to them, and resolved not to be disappointed. They, therefore, attempted other stratagems;

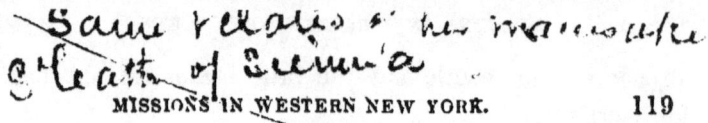

which served only to show, more clearly, the firmness of their neice.

Artifice not having proved successful, they had recourse to violence. They now treated her as a slave, obliging her to do everything painful and repulsive, and malignantly interpreting all her actions, even when most innocent. They reproached her, without ceasing, for want of attachment to her relations, and for stupidity. They attributed it to a secret hatred of the Iroquois nation, because she was herself of the Algonquin race. In short, they omitted no means of shaking her constancy.

The young girl suffered all this ill-treatment with unwearied patience; and, without ever losing her equanimity of mind, or her natural sweetness, she rendered them all the service they required, with an attention and docility, beyond her years and strength. By degrees her relatives were softened, restored to her their kind feelings, and did not further molest her.

At this very time, Father JACQUES DE LAMBERVILLE, was conducted by Providence, to the village of our young Iroquois, and received orders from his superiors to remain there, although it seemed most natural that he should go on to join his brother, who had charge of the mission to the Iroquois of Onnontague. TEAGHKOUITA did not fail to be present at the instructions, and prayers, which took place every day in the chapel, but she did not dare to disclose the design, which she had for a long time formed, of becoming a Christian.

But at length, the occasion of declaring her desire presented itself, when she least expected it. A wound which she had received in the foot, detained her in the village, whilst the greater part of the women were in the field, gathering the harvest of Indian corn. The missionary had selected this time to go his rounds, and instruct at his leisure, those who were remaining in the wigwams. He entered that of Teaghokuita. This good girl, on seeing him, was not able to restrain her joy. She at once opened her heart to him, even in the presence of her companions; declaring the earnest desire she had to be admitted into the Christian fold. She disclosed, also, the obstacles on the part of her family; and in this first conversation, showed great courage. The goodness of her temper, the vivacity of her spirit, her simplicity and candor, caused the missionary to believe, that one day she would make great progress in virtue. He therefore, applied himself particularly to instruct her in the truths of Christianity; but he did not judge it proper to yield to her entreaties, for the grace of Baptism should not be accorded to adults, particularly in this country, but with great care, and after long probation. All the winter, therefore, was employed in her instruction, and in a rigid investigation of her conduct.

It is surprising, that, notwithstanding the propensity these Indians have for slander, the missionary found none, that did not give high encomiums to the young catechumen. Even those who had persecuted her most severely, were not backward in giving their testimony to her virtue. The Priest, therefore, no longer hesitated to administer to her holy Baptism, which she craved so earnestly. She received it on Easter Day, in the year 1676, and was named Catherine, and it is thus that I shall call her, in the rest of this letter. The only care of the young neophyte, was now to fulfil the engagements she had contracted. She did not wish to restrict herself to usual observances; for she felt that she was called to a more perfect life. Besides the public instructions, at which she was present punctually, she requested particular directions for the regulation of her private and hidden life. Her prayers, her devotions, and her penances, were arranged with the utmost exact—

ness, and she was so docile in herself, conforming to the plan of perfection, which had been marked out for her that, in a little time, she became a model of virtue.

In this manner several months passed away very peaceably. Even her relations did not seem to disapprove of the new course of life, which she was leading. But the Holy Spirit has warned us, that the faithful soul, which begins to unite itself to God, must prepare for temptation: this was verified in the case of CATHERINE. Her extraordinary virtue drew upon her the persecutions, even of those who admired her. They looked upon a life so pure, as a tacit reproach to their own irregularities and with the design of discrediting it, they had recourse to divers artifices. But the confidence which the neophyte had in God, the distrust she felt of herself, her constancy in prayer, and that delicacy of conscience, which made her dread even the shadow of sin, gave her a perfect victory over the enemies of her innocence.

The exactness with which CATHERINE observed the festival days in the chapel was the cause of another storm. The chaplet recited by two choirs, is an exercise of holy days: this kind of psalmody awakens the attention of the neophytes and animates their devotion. They execute the hymns and sacred canticles, which our Indians chant, with much exactness and harmony; for they have a fine ear, a good voice, and a rare taste for music. She never omitted this exercise. But her relations took it ill, that on these days, she abstained from going to work, with the others, in the field. At length, they came to bitter words, cast upon her the reproach, that Christianity had made her effeminate, and accustomed her to an indolent life. They did not even allow her anything to eat, to oblige her by means of famine, to follow her relations and to aid in their labor. The neophyte bore, with constancy, their reproach and contempt;

and preferred on those holy days, to do without nourishment, rather than violate the law, which required the observance of festivals, or to omit the ordinary practices of piety.

This firmness, which nothing could shake, irritated more and more her heathen relatives. Whenever she went to the chapel, they caused her to be followed by drunken people, or those who feigned drunkenness; so that, to avoid their insults, she was often obliged to take the most circuitous paths. Even the children pointed their fingers at her, and in derision called her "The Christian." One day, when she had retired to her wigwam, a young man entered abruptly, his eyes sparkling with rage, and a hatchet in his hand, which he raised as if to strike her. Perhaps he had no other design than to frighten her. But whatever might have been his intentions, CATHERINE contented herself with modestly bowing her head, without showing the least emotion. This intrepidity, so little expected, astonished him to such a degree, that he immediately took to flight, as if terrified by some invisible power.

It was in such trials of her patience and piety, that CATHERINE spent the summer and autumn which followed her baptism. The winter brought her a little more tranquillity. Still she had to suffer from one of her aunts. This woman, who was deceitful and dangerous, could not endure the regular life of her niece, and therefore constantly condemned even her most innocent actions and words. It is a custom among these Indians, that uncles give the name of daughters to their nieces, and nieces reciprocally call their uncles by the name of father. It happened, however, once or twice, that CATHERINE called the husband of her aunt by his proper name, and not by that of father; but it was entirely owing to mistake or want of thought. Yet the evil-minded aunt pretended to believe that this expression, which seemed too familiar, was an evidence of criminal intimacy, and immediately went to seek the missionary to decry CATHERINE to him.

"Well!" she said, "so CATHERINE, whom you esteem virtuous, is, notwithstanding, a hypocrite who deceives you. Even in my presence, she solicited my husband to sin!"

The missionary, who understood the ill-will of this woman, wished to know on what she founded an accusation of this kind, and having learned what had given occasion to this odious suspicion, he administered to her a severe reprimand, and sent her away utterly confounded. When he afterwards mentioned it to the neophyte, she answered him with a candor and confidence, which showed the absence of all falsehood. It was on this occasion, that she declared—what perhaps we should not have known, if she had not been placed on this trial—that, by the kindness of the Lord, she could not remember that she had ever sinned against purity, and that she did not fear any reproach on this point, at the Day of Judgment.

It was sad for CATHERINE, to have to sustain so many conflicts, and to see her innocence incessantly exposed to the outrages and railleries of her countrywomen. She had also everything to fear in a country, where so few of the people, had imbibed a taste for the maxims of the Gospel. She, therefore, earnestly desired to be transplanted to some other mission, where she might serve God in peace and liberty. This was the subject of her most fervent prayers, and it was also the advice of the missionary; but it was not easy to bring it about. She was entirely in the power of an uncle, watchful of all her actions, and, through the aversion which he had for Christians, incapable of appreciating her resolution. But God, who listens favorably even to the simple desires of those who place their trust in Him, disposed all things for the repose and consolation of the neophyte.

A colony of Iroquois, had lately been formed among the French; the peace which existed between the two nations, gave these Indians an opportunity of coming to hunt on our lands. Many of them stopped near the prairie of the Madeleine, where the missionaries of our Society conversed with them, on the necessity of salvation. These Indians were converted, renounced their country, and settled among us. They received baptism, after the usual instructions and probation.

The example and devotion of these new converts, drew to them many of their countrymen, and in a few years the Mission of *St. Francis Xavier du Sault*, (thus it was named,) became celebrated for the great number of its neophites, and their extraordinary fervor. If an Iroquois made even a short visit to that mission, he seemed to lose all desire of returning to his own country. The charity of these neophites, led them even to divide, with the new comers, the fields which, with much labor, they had cleared. Their Christian feeling appeared to the greatest advantage, in their eagerness to instruct pagans in the truths of our faith. To this work they devoted entire days and even a portion of the night. Their conversations, full of unction and piety, made the most lively impression, on the hearts of their guests, and transformed them, so to speak, into different beings. He, who a little while before, thought but of blood and war, became mild, humble, teachable, and obedient to the most difficult maxims of religion.

This zeal extended, not only to those who came to visit them, but also urged them to make excursions into other settlements, and they always returned accompanied by large numbers of their countrymen. On the very day that CATHERINE had received baptism, one of the most powerful of the Agniez, returned to the mission, in company with thirty of the Iroquois of that tribe, whom he had gained to Jesus Christ.

It was not until the following year, that CATHERINE obtained the facilities she wished, for the execution of her design. Her adopted sister, had retired with her husband, to the Mission, Du Sault. The zeal of the recent converts, to draw their relatives and friends to the new colony, inspired her with the same thoughts, in regard to CATHERINE, and disclosing her designs to her husband, he gave his consent. He joined himself therefore to an Indian of Loretto, and some other neophytes, who travelled to the villages of the Iroquois, with the intention of engaging their acquaintances to follow them, and to share in the blessings of their conversion.

With difficulty he reached the village in which CATHERINE lived, and informed her secretly of the object of his journey, and of his wife's desire, that she should be with her, at the Mission Du Sault. The neophite appeared transported with joy at this disclosure; he then warned her to hold herself in readiness, immediately on his return from his journey to the English. The uncle was then absent, without having any suspicion of his niece's design. CATHERINE went immediately to take leave of the missionary, and to ask his recommendation to the Fathers, who directed the Mission Du Sault. The missionary could not withhold his approval of her resolution, and exhorted her to place her trust in God, giving her good counsels.

As the journey of her brother-in-law was only a pretext, the better to conceal his design, he almost immediately returned to the village; and, the day after his arrival, departed with CATHERINE, and the Indian of Loretto, who kept him company. It was soon discovered in the village, that the neophite had disappeared, and they had no doubt, but that she had followed the two Indians. They immediately, therefore, dispatched a runner to her uncle, to give him the news. The old chief foamed with rage at the intelligence,

and immediately loading his gun with three balls, set out
in pursuit of those, who had accompanied his niece. He
made such haste, that in a very short time he came up with
them. The two Indians, who well knew that he would not
fail to pursue them, had concealed the neophite in a thick
wood, and had stopped, as if to take a little repose. The
old man was very much astonished, at not finding his niece
with them, and after a moments conversation, coming to
the conclusion that he had credited, too easily, the first
rumor which had been spread, retraced his footsteps to the
village. CATHERINE regarded this sudden retreat of her
uncle, as one effect of the protection of God which she enjoyed; and, continuing the route, arrived at the mission Du
Sault, in the end of Autumn of the year 1677.

She took up her abode with the family of her brother-
in-law. The cabin belonged to one of the most fervent
Christians in the place, named ANASTASIA, whose care it
was to instruct such of her own sex as aspired to the grace
of Baptism. The zeal with which she discharged her duty,
in this employment, her conversation, and her example
charmed CATHERINE. But what edified her exceedingly,
was the piety of all the converts, composing this numerous
mission. Above all, she was struck at seeing men become
so different from what they were, when they lived in their
own country. She compared their exemplary life, with the
licentious course they had been accustomed to lead, and recognized the hand of God in so extraordinary a change;
and thanked Him for having conducted her into this land
of blessings.

To make a suitable return for such favors, she felt that
she ought to give herself up to God, without reserve, or
thought of self. The chapel became, thenceforth, all her
delight. She repaired thither at four o'clock in the morning, attended the mass at dawn of day, and afterwards

assisted at that of the Indians, which was said at sunrise. During the course of the day she, from time to time, broke off from her works, to go and hold communion with Jesus Christ, at the foot of the altar. In the evening she again returned to the Church, and did not leave it until the night was far advanced. When engaged in her prayers, she seemed entirely unconscious, of what was passing without, and, in a short time, the Holy Spirit raised her to so sublime a devotion, that she often spent many hours in intimate communion with God.

To this inclination for prayer, she joined an almost unceasing application to labor. She sustained herself, in her toils, by pious conversations, which she held with ANASTASIA that fervent Christian of whom I have already spoken, and with whom she had formed a most intimate friendship. The topics, on which they most generally talked, were, the delight received in the service of God; the means of pleasing Him, and advancing in virtue; the horror we should have for sin; and the care with which we should expiate it, by penitence. She always ended the week, by an exact investigation of her faults and imperfections, that she might efface them by the Sacrament of penance, which she approached every Saturday evening. For this, she prepared herself by different mortifications, with which she afflicted her body, and when she accused herself of even the lightest faults, it was with such vivid feelings of compunction, that she shed tears, and her words were choked with sobs and sighs. The lofty idea she had of the majesty of God, made her regard the least offence with horror.

Virtues so marked, did not permit me long, to refuse her the permission which she so earnestly desired, that on the approaching festival of Christmas, she might receive her first communion. This is a privilege, which is not granted to those, who come to reside among the Iroquois, until after some years of probation, and many trials: but the piety of CATHERINE, placed her beyond the ordinary rules. She participated, for the first time in her life, in the holy Eucharist, with a degree of fervor, proportioned to the reverence she had for this Sacrament, and the earnestness with which she had desired to receive it. And subsequently whenever she approached the holy Sacrament, it was always with the same disposition. Then her deportment alone, inspired the most lukewarm with devotion, and, when a general communion was about to take place, the most virtuous neophytes strive, with emulation, to be near her, because, said they "the sight alone of CATHERINE serves as an excellent preparation for communicating worthily."

After the festival of Christmas, it being the proper season for the chase, she was not able to excuse herself from following her sister and brother-in-law into the forests. She, however, showed that one can serve God, in any place to which His providence calls. She did not omit any of her ordinary pious exercises, while her fervor even suggested to her holy practices, in place of those which were incompatible with a residence in the forests. There was a time set apart for everything. In the morning, she applied herself to her prayers, and concluded with those which the Indians make in common, according to their custom; and in the evening she repeated them again, continuing in prayer until the night was far advanced. While the Indians were taking their repast, to prepare themselves for the day's chase, she retired to offer up her devotions. A little before the time when, at the mission, all were accustomed to hear mass, she fixed a cross on the trunk of a tree, at the side of a stream, and made this solitary spot her Oratory. There, she placed herself, in spirit at the foot of the altar, united in spirit with the adorers before the altar; she prayed her

Guardian Angel to be present for her, at that holy sacrifice, and to apply to her its benefits. The rest of the day she spent in laboring; but to banish all frivolous discourse, and preserve her union with God, she always introduced some religious conversation, or perhaps invited them to sing hymns or anthems, in praise of their Lord. Her repasts were very simple, and often she did not eat till night. At other times, she secretly mixed ashes with the food provided for her, to deprive it of everything which might afford pleasure to the taste. This is a mortification, which she always practiced when she could do so without being seen.

The sojourn in the forests was not agreable to Catherine, although generally pleasant to the Indian women, because, freed from domestic cares, they pass their time in amusements and feasting. She longed without ceasing to return to the village. The church, the presence of Jesus Christ in the august sacrifice of the mass, the frequent exhortations, and the other exercises of the mission, of which she was deprived while engaged in the chase—these were for her the only objects of interest. She therefore formed the determination that, if she lived to return once more to the mission, she would never leave it. She arrived there about Passion Week, and for the first time assisted at the ceremonies of those holy days.

I shall not stop, my Rev. Father, to describe to you here, how deeply she was affected by a spectacle, so touching, as that of the sorrows and death of a God-man, for our salvation. She shed tears almost continually, and formed a resolution to bear, for the rest of her days, in her own body, the cross of Jesus Christ. From that time she sought all occasions of mortification—perhaps to expatiate those slight faults, which she regarded as outrages against the Divine Majesty; perhaps to trace in herself the image of a God crucified for love of us. The conversations of Anastasia, who often talked with her of the pains of hell, and of the severity which the saints exercised upon themselves, strengthened the desire she had for austerities. She found herself also animated to this course, by an accident which placed her in great danger of losing her life. She was cutting a tree in the woods, which fell sooner than she expected; she had sufficient time, by drawing back, to shun the body of the tree, which would have crushed her by its fall; but she was not able to escape from one of the branches, which struck her violently on the head, and threw her senseless to the ground. She recovered from her swoon, and those around heard her softly ejaculating, "I thank thee, O good Jesus, for having succored me in this danger." She thought that God had preserved her, to give her time to expiate her sins by repentance. This she declared to a companion, who felt herself, like CATHERINE, called to a life of austerity, and with whom so close was the intimacy, that each communicated to the other the most secret movements of their innermost souls. This new association had indeed so much influence on the life of CATHERINE, that I cannot refrain from speaking of it.

THERESE, this pious Indian, had been baptised by Father BRUYAS, in the Iroquois country; but the licentiousness which prevailed among her people, and the evil example she always had before her eyes, caused her shortly to forget the vows of her baptism. Even a subsequent sojourn at the Mission, only produced a partial change in her life. A most strange adventure, however, caused, at last, her conversion.

She had gone with her husband and a young nephew to the chase, near the river of the Outattuacks. Some other Indians joined them, forming a company of eleven persons, four men, and four women, with three children. THERESE was the only Christian. The snow, which, this year, was very late, prevented them from having any success in hunting; they soon consumed their provisions, and they were reduced to eat skins which they had brought with them to make moccasins; they even eat the moccasins; and finally, pressed by hunger, they sustained life by herbs, and the bark of trees. In the mean time, the husband of THERESE fell dangerously ill, and the hunters were obliged to halt. Two among them, an Agniez and a Tsonnontouan, asked leave of the party to make an excursion to some distance in search of game, promising to return, at the farthest, in ten days. The Agniez, indeed, returned at the time appointed; but he came alone, and reported that the Tsonnontouan had perished by famine and misery. They suspected him of having murdered his companion, and then fed upon his flesh; for, although he declared that he had not found any game, he was nevertheless in full strength and health. A few days afterwards, the husband of THERESE died, expressing, in his last moments, deep regret that he had not received baptism. The rest of the company then resumed their attempt to reach the banks of the river, and gain the French settlements. After two or three days' march, they became so enfeebled by want of nourishment, that they were not able to advance farther. Desperation then inspired them with a strange resolution, which was to put some of their number to death, that the lives of the rest might be preserved.

They therefore selected the wife of the Tsonnontouan and her two children, who were thus in succession devoured. This spectacle terrified THERESE, for she had good reason to fear the same treatment. Then she reflected on the deplorable state of her conscience; she repented bitterly that she had entered the forest, without having first purified herself by a full confession; she asked pardon of God for the disorders of her life, and promised to confess as soon as possible and do penance. Her prayer was heard, and after incredible fatigues she reached the village with four others, who alone remained of the eleven. She fulfilled one part of her promise—she confessed soon after her return—but she was backward in reforming her life, and in doing penance.

One day, while she was looking at the new Church then building at the Sault, (after they had removed the Mission thither which before had been at the prairie of the Madeleine) she met with CATHERINE, who was also inspecting it. They saluted each other for the first time, and entering into conversation, CATHERINE asked her which portion of the Church was to be set apart for the females. THERESE pointed out the place which she thought would be appropriated to them. "Alas?" answered CATHERINE, with a sigh, "it is not in this material temple that God most loves to dwell. It is within ourselves that He wishes to take up His abode. Our hearts are the Temple which is most agreeable to Him. But, miserable being that I am, how many times have I forced Him to abandon this heart in which He should reign alone! And do I not deserve that, to punish me for my ingratitude, they should forever exclude me from this temple, which they are raising to His glory?"

The humility of these sentiments deeply touched the heart of THERESE. At the same time, she felt herself pressed by remorse, to fulfil what she had promised to the Lord; she thought that God hath directed to her this holy woman to support her, by counsel and example, in the new kind of life she wished to embrace. THERESE therefore opened her heart to CATHERINE, on the holy desires with which God had inspired her; and, insensibly, the conversation led them to disclose to each other their most secret thoughts. To converse with greater freedom, they sat down at the foot of a cross erected on the banks of the River St. Lawrence. This first interview, which revealed the uniformity of their sentiments and inclinations, began to strengthen the bonds of a holy friendship, which lasted even to the death of CATHERINE. From this time they were inseparable. They went together to the church, to the forest, and to their daily labor. They animated each other to the service of God by their religious conversations—they mutually communicated their pains—they disclosed their faults; they encouraged each other to the practice of austere virtues.

It was thus that God prepared CATHERINE for a new contest, which her love of celibacy obliged her to undergo. Interested views inspired her sister, with the design of getting her married, she supposed that there was not a young man, then in the Mission du Sault, who would not wish to marry so virtious a woman, and that thus, having the whole village from which to make her choice, she would be able to select for her brother-in-law, some able hunter, who would bring abundance to the cabin. She expected indeed to meet with difficulties on the part of CATHERINE; for she was not ignorant of the persecutions, this generous girl had already suffered, and the constancy with which she had sustained them; but she persuaded herself that reason would finally vanquish opposition. She selected therefore her time, and, after having shown CATHERINE even more than usual affection she addressed her with that eloquence which is natural to these Indians, when they are engaged in anything that concerns their interest.

"I must confess, my dear sister, said she, that we are under great obligations to the Lord for having brought you, as well as ourselves, from our unhappy country, and for having brought you to the Mission du Sault; where every thing is favorable to your piety. If you are rejoiced to be here, I have no less satisfaction at having you with me. You every day indeed increase our pleasure, by the wisdom of your conduct, which draws upon your general esteem approbation. There only remains one thing for you to do, to complete our happiness; which is, to think seriously of establishing yourself by a good and judicious marriage. All the young girls among us take this course; you are of an age to act as they do, and you are bound to do so, even more particularly than others, either to shun the occassions of sin, or to supply the necessities of life. It is true that it is a source of great pleasure to us, both to your brother-in-law, and myself, to furnish you, your wants; but you know that he is in the decline of life, and that we have the care of a large family. If you were to be deprived of us; to whom could you have recourse? Think of these things CATHERINE; provide for yourself a refuge from the evils which accompany poverty."

There was nothing which CATHERINE less expected than a proposition of this kind; but the kindness and respect which she felt for her sister, induced her to conceal her pain; and she contented herself with merely answering, that she thanked her for this advice, but the step was of great consequence, and she would think of it seriously. It was thus that she warded off the first attack. She immediately came to seek me, to complain of these importunate solicitations of her sister. As I did not appear to accede entirely to her reasoning, and, for the purpose of proving her, dwelt on those considerations which ought to incline her to marriage, "Ah, my father," said she, "I am not any longer my own. I have given myself entirely to Jesus Christ, and it is not possible for me to change masters. The poverty with which I am threatened gives me no uneasiness. So little is requisite to supply the necessities of this wretched life, that my labor can furnish this, and I can always find some miserable rags to cover me." I sent her away, saying that she should think well on the subject, for it was one which merited the most serious attention.

Scarcely had she returned to the cabin, when her sister, impatient to bring her over to her views, pressed her anew to end her wavering by forming an advantageous settlement. But finding from the reply of Catherine that it was useless to attempt to change her mind, she determined to enlist Anastasia in her interests; since they both regarded her as their mother. In this she was successful. Anastasia was readily induced to believe that Catherine had, too hastily, formed her resolution, and therefore employed all that influence, which age and virtue gave her over the mind of the young girl, to persuade her that marriage was the step she ought to take.

This effort, however, had no greater success than the other; and Anastasia, who had always until that time found so much docility in Catherine, was extremely surprised at the little deference paid to her counsels. She even bitterly reproached her, and threatened to bring her complaints to me. Catherine anticipated her in this, and after having related how they made her suffer, to induce her to enter the state of marriage, she prayed me to aid her in consummating the sacrifice which she wished to make of herself to Jesus Christ; and to provide her a refuge from the opposition she had to undergo. I praised her design, but at the same time advised her to take yet three days, to deliberate on an affair of such importance, and, during that time, to offer up extraordinary prayers, that she might know the will of God; after which, if she still persisted in her resolution, I promised her to put an end to the importunities of her relatives. She at first acquiesced in what I proposed, but in less than a quarter of an hour came back to seek me. "It is settled," said she, as she came near me, "it is not a question for deliberation; my part has long since been taken. No, my Father, I can have no other spouse but Jesus Christ." I thought that it would be wrong for me any longer to oppose a resolution which seemed to me inspired by the Holy Spirit, and therefore I exhorted her to perseverance, assuring her that I would undertake her defence against those who might thenceforth disturb her on that subject. This answer restored her former tranquility of mind, and re-established in her soul that inward peace, which she preserved even to the end of life.

Scarcely had she left me, when Anastasia came to complain, in her turn, that Catherine would not listen to any advice, but followed only her own whims. She was running on in this strain, when I said that I was acquainted with the cause of her dissatisfaction, and was astonished that a Christian, as old as she was, could disapprove of an action which merited the highest praise; and that if she had faith, she ought to know the value of a state so sublime as that of celibacy, which rendered feeble men like to the angels themselves. At these words, Anastasia seemed to be in a perfect dream; and as she possessed true devotion, she almost immediately began to turn the blame upon herself. She admired the courage of this virtuous girl, and, at length, became the first to fortify her in the holy resolution she had taken. Thus God turned these different contradictions into good for his servant. And it also furnished Catherine with a new motive to serve God with greater fervor. She therefore added new practices to her ordinary exercises of piety. Feeble as she was, she redoubled her diligence in labor, her watchings, fastings, and other austerities.

It was then the end of autumn, when the Indians are accustomed to form their parties, to hunt during the winter. The sojourn, which Catherine had already made in the forest, and the pain she had suffered at being deprived of religious privileges, made her form the resolution that she would never more return to it. I thought, however, that the change of air and the diet, which is much better in the forest, would restore her to health. It was for this reason that I advised her, to follow the family and others, who went to the hunting grounds. She answered me, in that deeply devotional manner which was so natural to her: "It is true, my Father, that my body is served, most luxuriously, in the forest; but the soul languishes there, and is not able to satisfy its hunger. On the contrary, in the village the body suffers; I am contented that it should be so, but the soul finds its delight in being near to Christ. Well, then, I will willingly abandon this miserable body to hunger and suffering, provided that my soul may have its sweet nourishment."

She remained, therefore, during the winter in the village, where she lived only on Indian corn, and was subjected indeed to much suffering. But, not content with allowing her body only this insipid food, which could scarcely sustain it, she subjected it also to austerities and excessive penances, without taking counsel of any one, persuading herself that while the object was mortification, she was right in giving herself up to anything, that could increase her fervor. She was incited to this by the noble examples of mortification, which she always had before her eyes. The spirit of penance reigned among the Christians at the Sault. Fastings, discipline, etc., were their most common austerities. And some of them, by these voluntary macerations, prepared themselves, when the time came, to suffer the most fearful torments for their religion.

The war was once more rekindled between the French and the Iroquois; and the latter invited their countrymen who were at the Mission du Sault, to return to their own country, where they promised them entire liberty, in the exercise of their religion. The refusal with which these offers were met, rendered them furious; and the Christian Indians who remained at the Sault, were immediately declared enemies of their nation. A party of Iroquois surprised some of them, while hunting, and carried them away to their country, where they were burned at a slow fire. But these noble and faithful men, even in the midst of the most excruciating torments, preached JESUS CHRIST to those who were torturing them so cruelly, and conjured them, as soon as possible, to embrace Christianity, to deliver themselves from eternal fire. One, in particular, among them, named ETIENNE, signalized his constancy and faith. When environed by the burning flames, he did not cease to encourage his wife, who was suffering the same torture, to invoke with him the holy name of JESUS. Being on the point of expiring, he rallied all his strength, and in imitation of his Master, prayed the Lord with a loud voice, for the conversion of those, who had treated him with such inhumanity. Many of the savages, touched by a spectacle so new to them, abandoned their country, and came to the Mission du Sault, to ask for baptism, and live there, in accordance with the laws of the Gospel.

The women were not behind their husbands, in the ardor they showed for a life of penance. They even went to such extremes, that, when it came to our knowledge, we were obliged to moderate their zeal. Besides the ordinary instruments of mortification, which they employed, they had a thousand new invenions to inflict suffering upon themselves.

Although those, who inflicted these mortifications on themselves, were careful to conceal them from the knowledge of the public; yet CATHERINE, who had a mind quick and penetrating, did not fail, from various appearances, to conjecture that, which they held so secret, and as she studied every means to testify, more and more, her love to Christ, she applied herself to examine everything that was done, pleasing to the Lord, that she might herself immediately put it in practice. It was for this reason that while passing some days at Montreal, where, for the first time she saw the nuns, she was so charmed with their modesty and devotion, that she informed herself, most thoroughly, with regard to the manner in which these holy sisters lived, and the virtues which they practiced. Having learned that they were Christian virgins, who were consecrated to God, by a vow of perpetual continence, she gave me no peace until I had granted her permission, to make the same sacrifice of herself, not by a simple resolution to guard her virginity, such as she had already made, but by an irrevocable engagement, which obliged her to belong to God, without any recall. I would not, however, give my consent to this step until I had well proved her, and been anew convinced that it was the Spirit of God, acting in this excellent girl, which had thus inspired her with a design, of which there had never been an example, among the Indians.

For this great event she chose the day, on which we celebrate the Festival, of the Annunciation of the most holy Virgin, for whom she had a most tender devotion; praying her to present to her son the oblation of herself, which she had just made; after which she passed some hours, at the foot of the altar, in holy meditation and in perfect union with God.

From that time CATHERINE seemed to be entirely divorced from the world. Her aspirations were continually for heaven, where she had fixed all her desires. She seemed even to taste, in anticipation, the sweetness of the heavenly state; but her body was not sufficiently strong to sustain the weight of her austerities, and the constant effort of her spirit, to maintain itself in the presence of God. She was at length siezed with a violent illness from which she never entirely recovered. There always remained an affection of the stomach, accompanied by frequent vomiting and a slow fever, which undermined her constitution by degrees, and threw her into a weakness, which insensibly wasted her away. It was, however, evident that her soul acquired new strength, in proportion as her body decayed. The nearer she approached the termination of her career, the more did she shine forth in all virtues. But I need not stop here to particularize them to you, except to mention a few of those, which made the most impression, and were the source and spring of all the others.

She had a most tender love for God. Her only pleasure seemed to be to keep herself in contemplation of his majesty and mercy; to sing His praises, and continually to seek new ways of pleasing Him. It was principally to prevent distraction, that she so often withdrew into solitude. Anastasia and Therese were the only two Christians with whom she wished much to associate; because they talked most of God, and their conversations breathed nothing but love.

From thence arose the peculiar devotion, she had for the Holy Eucharist, and the passion of our Saviour. These two mysteries of the love of the same God, concealed under the veil of the Eucharist, or dying on the cross, ceaselessly occupied her spirit, and kindled in her heart the purest flames of love. Everyday she was seen to pass whole hours at the foot of the altar, immovable as if transported beyond herself. Her eyes often explained the sentiments of her breast by the abundance of tears she shed; and in these tears she found so great a delight, that she was, as it were, insensible to the most severe cold of winter. Often seeing her benumbed with cold, I have sent her to the cabin to warm herself; she obeyed immediately, but, the moment after, returned to the Church, and continued there in long communion with Jesus Christ.

To keep alive her devotion for the mystery of our Saviour's Passion, and to have it always present to her mind, she carried on her breast a little crucifix. She often kissed it, with feelings of the most tender compassion, for the suffering Jesus, and with the most vivid remembrance of the benefits of our redemption. One day, wishing particularly to honor Jesus Christ, in this double mystery of love, after having received the Holy Communion, she made a perpetual oblation of her soul to Jesus in the Eucharist, and of her body to Jesus attached to the Cross; and thenceforth she was ingenious to imagine every day, new ways of afflicting and crucifying her flesh.

During the winter, while she was in the forest with her companions, she would follow them at a distance, taking off her shoes, and walking with her naked feet over the ice and snow. Having heard Anastasia say, that of all torments, that of fire was the most frightful, and that the constancy of the martyrs, who had suffered this torture, would be a great merit before the Lord; the following night she burned her feet and limbs with a hot brand, very much in the same way, that the Indians mark their slaves; persuading herself that, by this action, she had declared herself the slave of her Saviour. At another time she strewed the mat on which she slept, with large thorns, the points of which were very sharp, and after the example of the holy and thrice happy Saint Louis de Gonzague, she rolled herself for three nights in succession on these thorns, which caused her the most intense pain. In consequence her countenance was wasted and pale, which those around her attributed to her illness. But Therese, the companion whom she had taken so much into her confidence, having discovered the reason of this extraordinary paleness, aroused her scruples, by declaring that she might offend God, if she inflicted such austerities on herself without the permission of her confessor. CATHERINE, who trembled at the very appearance of sin, came immediately to find me, to confess her fault and demand pardon of God. I blamed her indiscretion, and directed her to throw the thorns into the fire. She did so immediately, for she had an implicit submission to the judgment of those, who directed her conscience, and, enlightened as she was by that illumination, with which God favored her, she never manifested the least attachment to her own will.

Her patience was the proof of her virtues. In the midst of her continual infirmities, she always preserved a peace and serenity of spirit, which charmed us. She never forgot herself, either by uttering a complaint, or giving the slightest sign of impatience. During the last two months of her life her sufferings were extraordinary. She was obliged to remain, night and day, in the same position, and the least movement caused intense pain. But when these pains were felt with the greatest severity, then she seemed most content, esteeming herself happy, as she herself said, to live and to die on the Cross, uniting her sufferings, to those of her Saviour.

As she was full of faith, she had a high idea of everything relating to religion, and this inspired her with a particular respect, for those whom God called to the holy ministry. Her hope was firm, her love disinterested; serving God for His own sake, and influenced only by the desire to please Him. Her devotion was tender, even to tears; her communion with God intimate and uninterrupted, never losing sight of him in all Her actions; this it was that raised her in so short a time, to so sublime a state of piety.

There was nothing more remarkable in CATHERINE, than evangelical purity, of which she was so jealous, and which she preserved even to her latest breath. It was indeed a miracle of grace, that a young Iroquois should have had so strong an attachment to a virtue, so little known in her own country, and that she should have lived, in such innocence of life, during twenty years, that she remained in the very midst of licentiousness. It was this love of purity which produced in her heart so tender an affection for the Queen of Virgins. Catherine could never speak of Our Lady but with transport. She had learned by heart her Litanies, and recited them all, particularly in evening, after the common prayers of the cabin. She always carried with her a rosary, which she recited many times in the course of the day. The Saturdays, and other days which are particularly consecrated to honor Mary, she devoted to extraordinary austerities, and devoted herself to the practical imitation of some of her virtues. She redoubled her fervor when they celebrated one of these Festivals, and she selected such holy days, to offer to God some new sacrifice, or to renew those which she had already made.

It was to be expected, that so holy a life, would be followed by a most happy death. And so, it was in the last moments of her life, that she edified us most, by the practice of her virtues and above all by her patience and union with God. She found herself very ill about the time when the men are accustomed to go out to the hunting grounds in the forest, and when the women are occupied, from morning until evening, in the fields. Those who are ill, are therefore obliged to remain alone, through the whole day, in their cabins, a plate of Indian corn, and a little water having, in the morning, been placed near their mat. It was in this abandonment, that Catherine passed all the time of her last illness. But what would have overwhelmed another person with sadness, contributed rather to increase her joy, by furnishing her with something to increase her merit.

Accustomed to commune alone with God, she turned this solitude to her profit, and made it serve to attach her more to her Creator, by her prayers and fervent meditations.

Nevertheless, the time of her last struggle approached, and her strength, each day, diminished. She failed considerably, during the Tuesday of Holy Week, and I therefore thought it well to administer to her the Holy Communion, which she received with her usual feelings of devotion. I wished, also, at the same time, to give her Extreme Unction, but she told me, that there was, as yet no pressing necessity; and, from what she said, I thought I would defer it till the next morning. The rest of that day, and the following night, she passed in fervent communion with our Lord. On Wednesday morning, she received Extreme Unction, with the same feelings of devotion; and at three hours after mid-day, having pronounced the holy names of Jesus and Mary, a slight spasm came on, when she entirely lost the power of speech. As she preserved a perfect consciousness even to her last breath, I perceived that she was striving to perform inwardly all the acts which I suggested to her. After a short half-hour of agony, she peaceably expired, as if she was only falling into a sweet sleep.

Thus died CATHERINE TEAGHOKUITA, in the twenty-fourth year of her age, having filled the mission with the odor of of her sanctity. Her countenance, which had been extremely attenuated, by sickness and constant austerities, appeared so changed, and beautiful, some moments after her death, that the Indians who were present, were not able to restrain the expression of their astonishment, and declared, that a beam of that glory she had gone to possess, even then was reflected back on her body. Two Frenchmen, who had come from the prairie of the Madeleine, to assist in the services of Thursday morning, seeing her extended on her mat with her countenance so fresh and sweet, said, one to the other, "See how peaceably that young female sleeps." But they were very much surprised when they heard a moment after, that it was the body of CATHERINE who had just expired. They immediately retraced their steps, and, casting themselves on their knees, at her feet, recommended themselves to her prayers. They even wished to give a public evidence, of the veneration they had for the deceased, by assisting to make the coffin, which was to enclose these holy relics.

I make use of this expression, my Reverend Father, with the greater confidence, because God did not delay to honor the memory of this virtuous girl, by a great number of miraculous cures, which took place after her death, and which still continue to take place daily through her intercession. This is a fact well known, not only to the Indians, but also to the French at Quebec and Montreal, who often make pilgrimages to her tomb, to fulfill their vows, or to return thanks for favors, which she has obtained for them. I could here relate to you, a great number of these miraculous cures, which have been attested by individuals the most enlightened, and whose probity is above suspicion; but I will content myself with making you acquainted with the testimony of two persons, remarkable for virtue and merit, who having themselves proved the power of this sainted woman before God, felt they were bound to leave a public monument for posterity, to satisfy at the same time their piety and their gratitude.

The first testimonial is that of M. DE LA COLOMBIERE, Canon of the Cathedral of Quebec, Grand Vicar of the Diocese. He expresses himself in these terms: "Having been ill at Quebec, during the past year, from the month of January, even to the month of June, of a slow fever, against which all remedies had been tried in vain, and of a diarrhœa, which medicine could not cure, it was thought well that I should make a vow, in case it would please God to relieve me from these two maladies, to make a pilgrimage to the Mission of St. Francis Xavier, to pray at the tomb of CATHERINE TEAGHOKUITA. On the very same day the fever ceased, and the Diarrhœa having become better, I embarked some days afterwards to fulfill my vow. Scarcely had I accomplished one-third of my journey when I found myself entirely cured. As my health is something so very useless, that I should not have dared to ask for it, if I had not felt myself obliged to do so, by deference for the servants of the Lord, it is impossible reasonably to withhold the belief that God, in granting me this grace, had no other view than to make known the credit, which this excellent maiden had with Him. For myself, I would fear that I was unjustly withholding the truth, and refusing to the Missions of Canada the glory which is due to them, if I did not testify, as I have done, that I am a debtor, for my cure, to this Iroquis virgin. It is for this reason that I have given the present attestation, with every sentiment of gratitude of which I am capable, to increase, as far as is within my power, the confidence which is felt in my benefactress, but still more to excite holy desires by imitating her virtues."

"Given at Villmarie, the 14th Sept. 1696.

J. DE LA COLOMBIERE, P. J.

Canon of the Cathedral of Quebec."

The second testimonial is from M. DU LUTH, Captain in the Marine Corps, and Commander of Fort Frontenac. It is thus he speaks: "I, the subscriber, certify to all whom it may concern, that having been tormented by the gout, for the space of twenty-three years, and with such severe pains that it gave me no rest for the space of three months at a time, I addressed myself to CATHERINE TEAGHOKUITA, an Iroquois virgin, deceased at the Sault St.

Louis, in the reputation of sanctity; and I promised her to visit her tomb, if God should give me health through her intercession. I have been so perfectly cured at the end of one novena, which I made in her honor, that, after five months, I have not perceived the slightest touch of my gout. Given at Fort Frontenac, this 15th day August, 1696.

"J. Du Luth,
"Capt. of the Marine Corps, and Com. Fort Frontenac."

I have thought that a narrative of the virtues of this holy female, born thus in the midst of heathenism and among savages, would serve to edify those, who, having been born in the bosom of Christianity, have also every possible aid for raising themselves to the height of holiness.

I have the honor to be, etc.

CHAPTER X.

EARLY INDIAN MISSIONS IN THE NOW DIOCESE OF BUFFALO.

Though several books of the "Relations" are probably lost, though to others little access can be had; yet, from many statements and frequent allusions, it would seem, that the first Franciscan missionaries among the Hurons had, almost from the beginning, sown "the grain of mustard seed," among the nations dwelling in the western part of the now diocese of Buffalo. Of the Neutral Nation, many of whom dwelt on the Buffalo side of Niagara River, the old "Relations" say:

"The first village of the Neutral Nation which we reached, in going from the Hurons, is about four days' journey, in a southerly or south-easterly direction from where the celebrated river of that nation empties into Lake Ontario. On the west, and not on the east side of that river, are *most* of the villages of the Neutral Nation. But there are three or four on the *east* side, extending from east to west, towards the Erie or Cat Nation. This river is that, by which the great Lake of the Hurons, or fresh sea, empties first into Lake Erie, and from thence enters the territories of the Neutral Nation, and takes the name of Niagara, ('Onquiaahra,') until it discharges into Lake Ontario. It again issues from the latter Lake, and passing before Quebec it is called the St. Lawrence."

The Franciscan Father DALLION, set out from the Huron Missions on the 18th day of October, 1626, and, after passing five nights in the woods, arrived in the first village of the Neutral Nation. He was well received, and, continuing his course southwardly, passed through fifteen villages. In the sixteenth village the chiefs assembled; DALLION requested permission to remain in their country, and teach them the knowledge of the true God. His desire was granted, and ratified with presents.

He was afterwards adopted by the nation, and placed under the protection of the principal chief. He found the number of villages and cantons to be twenty-four. The country, he describes, as exceedingly beautiful; the climate fine compared to that of Quebec; the country fertile, and abounding in deer, elk, beaver, etc.

After remaining in the country three months, explaining the sacred mysteries of faith to the savages, about the middle of January, 1627, he was forced to return to the Huron Missions.

Ten years afterwards; the Jesuit Fathers BROEBEUF and CHAUMONT again visited the Neuter Nation; a short detail of their sufferings and generous exertions among this people has already been given. In eighteen villages of the Neuter Nation lived about three thousand souls, to whom they preached the gospel. Their Breviaries, ink-horns and manuscripts, after some time, excited suspicions. The Fathers had to return. After undergoing incredible hardships, they safely reached the Huron Mission, where they rejoined their brethren, who had almost despaired of their return.

About 1642, Father Jogues, the heroic martyr missionary, made the first opening for the gospel, in the eastern part of western New York. About the same time, as we learn from the following letter, in the Relations of 1644, blessed fruits of the former missions began to appear in the neighborhood of Buffalo.

The "Relations" of the year 1644 give the following, as Chapter VI.

"OF THE MISSION OF ANGELS AMONGST THE ATIOUENDAROUK, OR NEUTER NATION.

"The fewness of our numbers renders it difficult for us to attend the nearer settlements, and we were obliged to discontinue the mission to the Neuter Nation, where, two years ago, we cast the first rays of the Gospel. Some Huron Christians have been there, in our stead, performing the duty of apostles, and, perhaps, up to this time, with as much success as if we had been there ourselves.

"Stephen Totiri, from the mission of St. Joseph, having set out with a lay brother, for the frontier settlements, found the Indians well disposed, and so anxious to hear the truths of faith, that, with difficulty, could they find three or four hours of the night for sleep. They wore their beads around their necks, which caused much curiosity among these barbarians, who immediately asked them to explain the reason of this wearing the beads. 'It is,' said they, 'a mark that we recognize for our master, Him who made heaven and earth. He is invisible to us, although he fills the whole world with his presence; he sustains all things, in the same manner that our souls sustain and invigorate the body; nevertheless he appears not to our eyes.' They then went on explaining the principal mysteries of faith. But that which had the most effect upon this people, was the fear of hell-fire, which the missionaries told them was inevitable, if they did not adore this Great Master of nature. ' Why, then,' replied they, ' did your missionaries not continue to instruct us? Why tell us the evils which await us, if you do not, at the same time, aid us to escape from them?'

"Barnabe Otsinnonanuhont, an excellent Christian, from the mission of St. Michael, having penetrated far into the country, made a longer sojourn; and as he is a man of great authority amongst this people, his zeal did much to establish the faith, while his example did even more than his words. They sometimes, however, quarrelled with him, on account of his refusing to take part in their immorality. And when they represented to him that the yoke of faith was insupportable, obliging them to break off all indecent marks of friendship, and depriving them of the greatest pleasures of life, ' Well!' said he, 'if I knew a road leading to Paradise, even if it were filled with precipices, I would go headlong, and would consider myself too happy to die on that road. A happy eternity is cheap at any price.'

"At length, when about to return, he was called to baptise his little girl. ' Remember, my child,' said he, ' that you preserve most preciously the grace which you will receive by baptism. When the devil, or the voice of the wicked, tempt you to do wrong, think that God sees you, and if this is not sufficient to strengthen you, think that the greatest grief that you could inflict on me, your father, is to commit a sin which would cause you to be separated for ever from me.'

" Towards the end of the winter, a band of about one

hundred of the Neuter Nation, came to visit us in this country. They had seen the church of the Hurons, they were informed of the articles of our faith, from our Christians, and they left, regretting that they could not remain in such company. They even promised that distance should not hinder them from embracing the faith; they also said that we, having made sufficient impression upon the Hurons, should try to give the same chance to them. God willed that this seed should bear fruit, in its time.

"Some Hurons, worthy of credit, who traffic year after year with the Algonquin nations, tell us that they have found Christians there, who kneel down like us, join their hands and look towards heaven, pray to God, night and morning, and also before and after meals; and that the best mark of their Faith is, that they are no longer dishonest or wicked, as they once were. They call them Ondontaonaherounon. These are people about a hundred leagues below Saguene towards the North, who having received instruction, the one from Tadosusac, the other, at the Three Rivers, where they came like birds of passage; carry thence to their woods, their lakes, and their solitary mountains, the faith and fear of God, which finds a sojourn everywhere."

It would be impossible to say how extensive this early Christian movement was, or how it influenced the vague, almost Christian ideas that often mingle with wild Indian traditions. The Quapeaux, very lately located below Little Rock, in Arkansas, have many striking remembrances of this kind; and it seems, that they were remnants of the Neutre or Cat Nation, that fled south from the victorious Iroquois.

BROEBEUF and CHAUMONT tell us, that in the very early time of the visit, to the Eighteen villages of the Neutral Nation: "The Senecas lived but a days journey from the eastermost villages of the Neutral Nation." This must have been near Lockport. A later Relation tells us that the Senecas had a village at Lewistown, on Niagara River, but this must have been after 1643, when the Senecas had completely vanquished the Neutral Nation. From that time, the Seneca villages extended westward beyond Buffalo, over the territory of the conquered Cat or Erie Nation; and, eastward, till they met the ancient ones on or near Genesee River. Justly then do the Relations say:

"The wisdom of God which draws good from evil made the persecution of the Huron Church become most useful to a great number of savage Nations. The scattered Hurons serving to transport all over Canada, (meaning Canada and Western New York,) the light of faith, westward, as we have seen, eastward, as we will see."

"The great aversion which the Iroquois had, to the preaching of the gospel, was removed by their Huron captives, of whom they have a great number. These poor captives knew how to find God in the midst of the barbarians. Not only did they make an open profession of our holy religion, but they also congregated as little flocks of Jesus Christ, assembling in their country cabins, to pray, and to perform all the devotions of religion which they could, without the assistance of a priest.

A French gentleman, who was captured by the Iroquois last summer, and who was sold by them, and afterwards released; bears illustrious witness of the religion and piety of these Indians; he says that they exhorted him, by signs, to unite his sufferings, with those which the Saviour endured on the cross, and that they waited on him rendering him all the assistance they possibly could, without any fear of exposing themselves to death. He was edified by the constant examples of their admirable charity, patience, piety, and attachment to the true religion.

The fruits of the zeal of these poor Hurons, has extended

still further than the country of the Iroquois. It is said
that even among the Cat Nation, five hundred leagues from
Quebec, a Huron preacher has caused Jesus Christ to be
known, and has established a church which is already flourishing. Many persons there, are favorable to the gospel.
This fervent christian is sixty years old, he collected every
Sunday all the faithful of his nation, he exhorts them to
virtue, instructs them in our mysteries, and causes them to
say their prayers, in the same manner, that he had formerly seen the Jesuits practice, at the time of his conversion.

The missions in the eastern part of this diocese opened
with still brighter prospects. The "Relations," speak in highest commendation of the country forming that eastern part.
After describing Onondaga, they say: "Twenty or thirty
leagues still further west, is the village of the Oiog-
uens (Cayugas,) composed of three hundred warriors; here
we had a mission which founded a little church, filled with
piety, in the midst of these barbarians, in the year 1657.

Towards the end of the large Lake which is called Ontario, dwell the Sonontagans, (Senecas,) the most numerous
of the five Nations of the Iroquois numbering about twelve
hundred men.

Their towns lie partly to the south and partly to the
West at a distance of one hundred, or a hundred and twenty leagues from the French settlements.

The land in general is very fertile, filled with beautiful
woods, which yield an abundance of chesnuts and walnuts;
it is intersected with lakes and rivers, which abound with
fish.

The climate is temperate; the seasons as regular as in
France, and the land in many places, capable of producing
all the fruits which are produced in Provence or Turin.

The snows are neither deep nor lasting; the three winters
we have passed among the Iroquois, have been mild, in

comparison to the winters in Quebec, where the snow is three or four feet deep, covering the ground for five months in the year.

It was towards these villages, that the footsteps of Fathers Chaumont and Menard were in 1656, directed. Fathers Menard and Chaumont left Onondaga towards the close of August, 1656, for the residence of the Cayugas, whither they arrived in two days, *going westward.* Menard remained there, and Chaumont proceeded westward, on the first visit of a Jesuit to the Senecas.

At the time of Chaumont's visit, the Senecas inhabited that beautiful and fertile region immediately east of the Genesee river, extending as far as Lake Ontario on the North, and the territories of the Cayugas on the East. They lived in four principal villages; one of the largest was situated on the commanding eminence south of Victor. The numerous graves and Indian remains found in this locality, attest the magnitude of the ancient village.

The other principal town was situated in *the great bend* of the Honeyoye outlet; the place is known by the name of Abraham's Plains. In the Seneca language, Honeyoye means "the bend." The third village lay on the west branch of the Chi-nos-hah-geth, or Mud Creek, at the crossing of the old Rochester Road, about five miles Northwest of Canandaigua. The fourth village was near a spring which forms the source of the little Conesus, about three miles southeast of Avon. They were all destroyed in the expedition of De Nonville against the Senecas in 1687.

"The levelling plough of the white man, and the wasting hand of time, have, in the lapse of less than two centuries, obliterated most of the traces of these, once flourishing towns, which sustained a population of more than seven thousand persons. In respect to the existence of the first three villages, the evidences were so fresh and abundant, at

the first advent of the settler, that no great difficulty has been experienced in identifying their position.

"The location of the fourth, was pointed out on a map of the Genesee country, by a Seneca chief, residing on the Tonawanda reservation. Although he had not visited the site for more than forty years, he was positive as to the correctness of the tradition, fixing the locality.

"In order to test his accuracy, the place he had indicated was recently visited, and his statements fully verified. The village had been built in a quiet and secluded valley, almost entirely shut in, by hills of moderate elevation. A copious spring, from which a small stream flowed, had supplied it with water. On one side of the stream, a broad and level plateau, had afforded a commodious site for the village. On the surface of this plateau, there have been ploughed up, from time to time, quantities of hatchets, beads, broken pottery, and other indubitable evidences of Indian occupancy.

"Higher up the side of the valley, in the edge of the forest, small hillocks and other signs were found, indicating the last resting place of the Indian. Impressed perhaps with the sanctity of the spot; or, it may be, with the appropriateness of the location, the first settler chose it also, for his burial place; and the remains of the early pioneers and their descendants, have been laid side by side, and their dust has commingled, with, that of the sachems and warriors of the proudest and fiercest tribe of the Iroquois confederacy."—O. H. MARSHALL.

When the Jesuit arrived at Gannagoro, on Boughton Hill, the chiefs assembled in council, to receive him, and hear his message.

He told them the object of his mission. The desire of the French to form a firm treaty of peace and alliance; and

the intention of the Jesuits, to establish a mission among
them. The usual presents were delivered.

"In addition to these presents," said the Jesuit, "I offer
"myself, as a guarantee of the truths which I utter. And
"if my life is deemed insufficient, I offer you, in addition,
"the lives of all the French I have left at Onondaga. Do
"you distrust these living presents? Will you be so simple,
"as to believe, that we have left our native country, the
"finest in the world, to come so far, and to suffer so many
"privations in order to bring you a lie?"

Thrilling was the effect of this address, CHAUMONT was
indeed borne up by Heavenly stength, for he had risen
from a sick-bed to deliver his address, and a few days after,
was surrounded by his companions, who, in dejection,
awaited his last moment. He was however spared. Full
of confidence in St. Peter, he invoked the aid of the Prince
of the Apostles, and soon rose from his couch, in health,
being destined in fact to out-live all those around him."

The Indians were moved by CHAUMONT's appeal; and
the council, after solemn deliberation, resolved to receive
the missionaries, and allow the Senecas to be instructed in
their mysteries. The Jesuit was followed from the council
by the chief, who begged to be instructed without delay, a
striking proof of the magic power which the missionary's
eloquence possessed, for an Indian must be deeply moved,
to show his feeling. Conversions followed; but the most
important was that of the great chief of the tribe, the
invalid ANNONTENRITAOUI. Visited, instructed, and baptized by CHAUMONT, his faith was rewarded by the sudden
cure of a cancer, that had baffled all art.

The Jesuit visited the other villages with similar success,
in one of which he found the principal sachem of the nation
(Ga-no-ga-i da-wi) bed-ridden with disease. He converted

him to the faith, and this distinguished chief, having subsequently recovered, became a powerful friend of the French and Jesuits. The name which he bore, and by which the French always mentioned him, is the title of a Sachemship, still preserved among the Senecas, and belongs to a chief now residing among the Tonawandas.

Before the Hurons were dispersed by the Iroquois, a little church had been formed by the Jesuits, in one of the Huron villages, upon which they had conferred the name of St. Michael. To save themselves from entire destruction, those composing this church, threw themselves upon the generosity of their conquerors, and were adopted, as a body, into the tribe of the Senecas.

On the banks of the Chi-nos-hah-geh (near the present Canandaigua) in the third village we have described, these exiles from their country, found a home among their captors. The name of their church, St. Michael, was transferred to this village by the Jesuits, and here, if we may credit their statements, among the surrounding practices of a pagan superstition, they preserved, in purity and faith, the doctrines of the church, unto which they had been baptized.

Here all thronged around the old companion of Broebeuf and Daniel. Not one pagan now held back from baptism, not one believing Christian from confession; now, through misfortune, not one was unconverted. To be thus able to minister to these poor exiles was, in itself, a reward for the toils of the missionary; but his joy was dashed by the loss of the faithful Le Moyne, who sank in death, on the beautiful shores of Lake Tiohero, rejoicing that it was given him to die on the land of the Iroquois, in the work of the gospel.

In these villages were found captives of the Neutral and Tobacco Nations, (many of whom became Christians,) living in harmony with the Hurons, under the protection of the Senecas.

While Father Chavmonot was visiting the Senecas, Mesnard, whom he had left at Cayuga, had not been idle. He so conciliated the favor of the people, that, in four days after his arrival among them, they commenced the construction of a chapel, which was completed in two days, and carpeted with mats, woven with rushes, from the Montezuma marshes. Here he displayed the symbols of christian faith, and the pictures of the Saviour, and the Virgin. A crowd of wondering savages. thronged around. him, and from morning until night, the devoted Jesuit explained to them the mysteries of his religion. But, after a while Mesnard, who had been welcomed by the chiefs was treated coldly by the tribe, and so little regarded, that he never appeared without being attacked by the children. To the day of his death, many years after, amid the forests of Upper Michigan, he bore the scars, with which these tormentors covered his face. Soon after, however, the simple guilessness of the Father won the hearts of these savages, and, when he had converted the chief, his chapel was filled with admiring and listening crowds. On its wall of mats, beside the altar, hung pictures of our Lord and his Blessed Mother, and explaining these, the missionary told the history of our redemption. Now too the children changed, and became his helpers in the missions, leading him to the cabins of the sick, and giving him the names of all, which before some had studiously concealed.

The Iroquois women, already moved by the virtues of the Huron female captives, were the first converts they brought their babes to receive baptism; they followed the instructions; and in, almost every cabin, could be found an Indian mother, teaching wayward children to lisp a prayer, to Jesus and Mary.

Mesnard meanwhile, was now rapidly acquiring the Cayuga dialect, under the instructions of an excellent family, in whose cabin he was a guest. His mission was advancing, his chapel was crowded with catechumens; however, he baptized few adults, and seldom but in case of danger. The first admitted to the sacrament was an old man on his death-bed; the second, once a prominent chief, now a cripple, eaten up by a cancer; whose conversion seemed due to the martyred BROEBEUF and LALEMAND. At their capture he had been struck by their appearance, and bought them with wampum; yet was he unable to save them, for his belts were returned, and the missionaries put to death. His conversion gave great influence to religion; for his authority always stood very high in the canton: and indeed all protection was needed by MESNARD, who was on several occasions threatened with death.

After a stay of two months, he was recalled to Onondaga; but his converts were inconsolable, and he was soon restored to their entreaties, and renewed his mission with greater success than ever. Everything promised complete success.

But in Cayuga and among the Senecas, as in Onondaga, political artifices, which aroused suspicion and armed the pagan Indians against the missionaries, were, for a time, successful. Many martyrs watered, with their blood, the shores of Cayuga and Seneqa Lakes. But, as at Onondaga, so, it is believed, at Cayuga, and in the Seneca country, converted chieftains and devoted Christians kept up "the prayer, until God again lulled the storm, and sent other missionaries to continue the blessed work. Nor was the martyr-land entirely abandoned by the Jesuit priest. Father LE MOYNE, at least, is found at his holy work, until another intrepid band of missionaries, recommenced their apostolic labors.

The "Relation" of 1660 says: "Not to speak of the upper Iroquois, among whom many missionaries might be employed, if the lower Iroquois were humbled and brought to duty—we have been invited for some years by the inhabitants of the village of St. Michael's (near Canandaigua,) who are good Hurons, formerly instructed by our fathers in their own land. It is a vineyard that formerly brought forth good fruit for Paradise, and which still brings forth good fruit, but 'in patience.'" Another relation tells us of the heroic and Christian death of an Indian of the "Loup Nation." Amidst the most horrid torments, borne without groan or murmur, he related that, in his youth, he had heard the Huron captives speak of their Christian religion, and believed in it. This was the germ of that precious grace, which, long years after, made him a baptised Christian, before he ascended the scaffold of torture.

A CATHOLIC Governor of New York, in the following letter, shows how he deceived, and was deceived, whilst he persecuted the Church of his Fathers, in order to secure British supremacy, which was so soon lost!

"GOVERNOR DONGAN'S REPORT ON THE STATE OF THE PROVINCE, INCLUDING HIS ANSWERS TO CERTAIN CHARGES AGAINST HIM.

* * * * * *

The five Indian Nations are the most warlike people in America, and are a bulwark between us and the French and all other Indians. They goe as far as the South Sea, the North West Passage, and Florida, to warr. New England, in her last war with the Indians, would have been ruined, had not Sir EDMUND ANDROS sent some of those Nations to their assistance. And indeed they are so considerable, that all the Indians in these parts of America are Tributareys to them. I suffer no Christians to converse with them, any where, but at Albany, and that not without my licence. * * * * *

If therefore his Majesty were pleased to have a line run from 41° 40' in Delaware River, to the Falls upon the Susquehanna. and to let Mr. PENN keep all below that, it would be sufficient for him, the bounds below it being conjectured to contain more than all England.

To preserve the Beaver and Peltry trade for this and Albany, and to be an encouragement to our beaver hunters, I desire I may have order to erect a Fort, upon Delaware, in 41° 40'; another upon the Susquehana, where his Majesty shall think fit, that Mr. PENN's bounds should terminate. And another at Oneigra, (Niagara), near the Great Lake, in the way where our people goe a Beaver hunting, or trading; or anywhere else where I shall think convenient; it being very necessary for the support of trade, maintaining a correspondence with the further Indians, and in securing our right to the country; the French making a pretence of owning as far as the Bay of Mexico, for which they have no other argument, than that they have had possession this twenty years, by their Fathers living so long among the Indians. They have Fathers still among the Five Nations aforementioned, viz: the Mohawks, the Sinicaes, Cayouges, Oneides, and Onondagues, and have converted many of them to the Christian Faith, and doe their utmost to draw them to Canada, where there are already six or seven hundred, and more are like to goe, to the great prejudice of this Government, if not prevented. I have done my endeavors, and have gone so far in it, that I have prevailed with the Indians to consent to come back from Canada, on condition that I procure for them a piece of land called Serachtague, lying upon Hudson's river, about forty miles above Albany, and there furnish them with Priests.

"Thereupon, and upon a petition of the people of Albany to mee, setting forth the reasonableness and conveniency of granting to the Indians their requests, I have procured the land for them, altho' it had been formerly patented to the people at Albany, and have promised the Indians that they shall have priests, and that I will build them a church; and have assured the people of Albany, that I would address to his Majesty and to your Lordships, that care may bee taken to send over at first, five or six priests, it being a matter of great consequence. These Indians have about ten or twelve castles, (as they term them,) and those at a great distance, one from another, so that there is an absolute necessity of having so many priests, that there bee three, always travelling from Castle to Castle, and the rest to live with those that are Christians.

"By that means the French priests will be obliged to retire to Canada, whereby the French will be divested of their pretence to the country, and then wee shall enjoy that trade without any fear of being diverted."

The Governor could get no Priests, he could only succeed in chasing those away, whom God had sent. The British sovereign, the parliament of England, many distinguished and zealous Protestants, all combined to aid the Indian Missions. Protestant churches were built in the Iroquois country. No priests were sent. The unhappy DONGAN could not have his promise accomplished. But Protestant ministers were sent; some from Albany, occasionally visited the Indians, who soon got tired of their missionaries, as their missionaries did, of them. The Rev. WM. ANDREWS, settled among the Indians; but after six years of labour, toil, and disappointment, he left them saying: "there is no hope of making them better. Heathens they are, and Heathens they still must be." Clark, Onondaga, Vol. I. p. 213.

The "Relations" tell us that the fugitive Christian Hurons went, some to St. Michaels, among the Senecas; some to the Islands north of Lake Huron; some to Lake Michillimakinac, whence, pursued still by the Iroquois, they entered "the bay of Puant," and advanced six days march south west of Lake Superior, and were received by a nation called Abiiniwee; they settled on the borders of a great river, as broad and as deep as the St. Lawrence. They afterwards removed to "Pointe St. Esprit," on a bay south of Lake Superior, where Father ALLOUEZ first, then Father MARQUETTE became their pastors: with Father MARQUETTE, they finally " returned to Michillmacinac, and founded the Mission of St. Ignatius which subsists to our time." Hurons from this post subsequently established themselves at Sandusky, Detroit, and Sandwich. The most unhappy of the Hurons, were those who sought refuge with the Cat or Erie Nation, on the Southern Shore of Lake Erie. The Erie or Cat Nation, says Father RAGUENEAU, speak the same language as the Hurons, and have fixed habitations." The refuge they gave to the Hurons provoked a war with the Iroquois. The Eries were defeated, and, together with the Hurons, almost all slaughtered. The most happy were those who went to the French colony near Quebec, after many migrations, they formed the "Old Loretto mission," which finally transfered to "the new or young Loretto," subsists in all Christian faith and practice to this day. See Relations Abreges, by Rev. P. F. J. BRESSANI, S. J., Ap. x.

CATHERINE GANNEAKTENCE, the hostess of BRUYAS, at Oneida, where she, *a girl of the Erie nation*, had been adopted, was instructed by Father RAFFAIX, and CATHERINE was requested by him, to begin at La Prairie, in Canada, a New Reduction. Joined by most of her family, she, on their conversion, came from Loretto, and founded the first Iroquois Reduction, about the close of 1669, under the name of F. Xavier des Pres.

The Relations of 1661, writing of the dark period between 1658 and 1661, says:

"About four hundred leagues from here, the Angels

beheld with admiration a poor fugitive church, which sough some asylum after the Huron disaster, in which it lost everything but its Faith. A brave old man, was the pastor of this wandering band; he led them far away, across the forests towards an infidel Nation, named Rignerounous; beyond the reach of the Iroquois. This Moses, the conductor of this little flock, performed here all the functions of a Curate, with care, fit to excite the admiration even of Angels, who beheld a savage, perform the functions of missionary, of bishop, and of universal pastor of his church. He assembled them every Sunday, taught them their prayers, instructed them in their catechism; some he reproached, others he encouraged with kind words, according to their wants; but with a zeal, to which God gave such authority, that these good people came to him with simplicity, and confessed to him, the faults that they had committed during the week, as they had been accustomed to confess to their Priests, before the Iroquois had beaten and killed the shepherds, and dispersed the flock. Thus the cruel enemy of the Faith, did not retard our progress. We found many other wonders in all these poor churches. The joy with which God softened the pains of those exiles, and the sweetness of devotion, with which he seasoned their miseries, caused them almost to triumph in sufferings.

But, although our enemies, on all sides, endeavored to hinder us from reaping fruits so sweet and so ripe, we have not let this year pass, without attending to our missions in the four parts of this new world, and going everywhere to seek our wandering sheep. To the South, Father SIMON LE MOYNE has gone towards these same Iroquois, to crimson with his blood, those lands, which have already been bathed with Jesuit labor and blood. To the West, Father RENI MENARD is more than three hundred leagues distant from here, either dead or alive; for it is two years since he set out on his mission, and we have no news from him; it is likely that he has been immolated.

The coming spring, that is in 1662, we hope to effect much good with the Iroquois chiefs; in at least two grand Missions; that of the Onontagues, in which Father Le Moyne had employed his winter, in advance; and that of the Sounoutouaerounous, Senecas, which will give us many settlements to cultivate; and, above all that of St. Michael, which is composed of Huron christians, who brought their faith with their colony to the conquerors, after the destruction of the old Huron mission. These two missions alone require more missionaries than we have here; were it possible that we could divide ourselves, be assured that we would be found, at the same time, in different places, this being impossible. We aid one-an-other in accomplishing this great work.

The Relation of 1662 has the following notice "Of the winter spent by Father Le Moyne, among the Upper Iroquois." (That is the Cayugas and Senecas.)

"Behold here a mission of blood and fire; of labors and of tears; of captives and of Barbarians. It is a country where the earth is still red with the blood of the French, where the stakes yet stand covered with their ashes; where those who have survived their cruelty, bear its fatal marks on their feet and hands; their toes cut off and their finger nails torn out; and where, in fine, Father Simon Le Moyne has been, for one year, to soothe the sighs of this afflicted church, and to take part like a good pastor in all the misfortunes of his dear flock.

He was occupied chiefly, during the winter, with three churches, one French, one Huron and one Iroquois; he preserved the piety among the French captives, and became himself the sole depositary of all their afflictions; he re-established the Huron Church, formerly so flourishing, in their own country; he laid the foundation of the Iroquois church, going from place to place, to baptise the children and the dying, and to instruct those who, in the midst of barbarianism, were not far from the Kingdom of God.

A little chapel, formed of branches and bark, was the sanctuary where God received, every day, the adoration of of those who composed these three churches. Here the French assembled, each morning, half an hour before daylight, to assist at the august sacrifice of the Mass; and every evening, to recite, in common, the rosary; and often too, during the day, to seek consolation from God in their misfortunes; joining their mangled hands, and lifting them to heaven, they prayed for those who had thus maltreated them.

The Iroquois of Cayuga, who are less cruel, and whom we have found more affectionate, were moved with compassion at our danger and, in order to save the Father, invited him to come and instruct them until this danger should pass. The Father was rejoiced at the offer, more for the salvation of the kind barbarians, than for his own safety, and went to serve them, for some weeks.

He was received with public acclamations, and found sufficient field for the exercise of his zeal. The lancet of a young French surgeon, who accompanied him, and whose skill God wonderfully blessed, during a dangerous and infectious disease, aided the good cause; for many, already dispaired of, were cured. This gained the favor of the people, and opened the doors of every cabin to the Father, who found the Indians in the best possible disposition.

One whole month scarcely sufficed to baptise all the children, and to console a great number of Huron Catholics, in whom a sad captivity of fifteen or twenty years had not destroyed the faith. They were living temples of God, in the cabins of their masters, mutually aiding each other, and sanctifying by praise and prayer the woods and fields around, in which Jesus Christ had not before received hommage. What joy for this little band, so well disposed, to receive again a pastor, in the good Father LE MOYNE! The mute language of the eyes, spoke more than the tongue could say, in this happy moment. Nor could the Father refrain from tears of joy and compassion, seeing these poor Christians weeping with devotion! Certainly, such tears from the eyes of savages, are sufficient to dry the tears, and sweeten all the labors of those, who go in search of the poor lost sheep. But the Father was obliged to leave this consoling mission, and return to Onnontage, where GARA-KONTIE, (under whose protection were the French captives,) having returned from Montreal, and having published the kind reception he had received, gave an entertainment to the good Father, making him presents, which consist of some pumpkins—which make a very delicious food, when bread is wanting, and when, as generally, the missionaries make but one meal a day of a little saggomet, composed of pure water whitened with a little Indian meal: for such was the ordinary diet of this good Father. GARAKONTIE did not cease to load Father LE MOYNE with presents; among others, he gave a necklace made by the hands of the Ursuline Nuns of Quebec, decorated with ornaments which please and delight these people, most especially when they are told that it is the work of nuns, who had crossed the ocean expressly to instruct their little daughters, and that they wait in Quebec for Indian girls to be sent there; and that all who went there would see other holy women, who would receive them, when sick, in a large Hospital, where the sick receive all care and attendance, such as the sick Indians had lately received in the Hospital of Montreal. This is what we have learned of the labors of the Father, from some savages, who, at the close of the winter, came to see us, and who promised to return here in the summer with all their French captives, as a pledge of the sincerity with which they desired to be united with us.

By such generous aspirations did the Christian missionaries requite the unjust suspicions and the barbarous cruelty, which now clouded their hopes. Jesuit priests, however, still, either free or as captives, watched over the afflicted Church. Father JEROME LALEMAND, from 1659 to 1662, tells us that Father LE MOYNE wintered in the country of the superior Iroquois (Senecas, Cayugas,) and relates the cruelties of the Iroquois towards the French, the torture of prisoners, and the persecutions of the Christians and the Church.

The Relations of 1667, say "Father JAMES FREMIN and Father PIERRON, are ready for the mission of the Agne tribe, of the Iroquois and Father JAMES BRUYAS for the Onnecout. And three other fathers, are all ready for the Onontagas, (Oioquens) Cayugas and Sonontagans (Senecas) the other Nations of the Iroquois, as soon as the deputies of these nations arrive here for them, as they have already promised.

The three fathers above mentioned having received the benediction of Bishop PETRIE; each burning with zeal for the salvation of the Iroquois set out, from Quebec, during the month of last July, with the ambassador of the Agne and Onnecout tribes. Having arrived at Fort St. Ann, they were surprised by a body of between fifty and sixty Indians, that we call, the Wolf nation, they were in ambush, in the lake, waiting to fall upon them.

This was a sad drawback, for those who wished for nothing more than to reach their cities, to plant the faith on the land already crimsoned by the blood of the first of our fathers, who had there been most cruelly tormented, or massacred.

They were obliged to remain in this fort for one month, until the enemy scattered.

As yet we have learned nothing more of them; but if God blesses this undertaking, we will go to rebuild the Huron and Iroquois Churches, which we had already raised long before, and we will have nothing now to do, but to reap the fruit of our former labors for the instruction of these poor barbarians.

These are some of the new missions, which open themselves on all sides, north, south, east and west. We pray God that He will assist us and send some noble souls, and make them worthy to live in such labors, and even to die amidst the flames, and tortures of the Iroquois.

This is the only attraction, that I present to apostolic men, who may come to this new world, to shed their tears, and their blood, for the salvation of so many poor souls, for which, Jesus Christ shed his blood and laid down his life.

During these last years we have received quite an increase of chosen men, whose state in France was considerable; but who, in Canada, lead a life, hidden amongst the woods, the rocks, and the snows; ever in hunger and fatigue; often suffering the loss of their strength; and yet feeling now, more consolation in one day, than they received before in a year.

Sweet is their joy in a happy privation of nearly all comforts, when thinking of these words of the Apostle: "You are dead to the world, and your life is hidden with Christ in God."

Another "Relation" says: Father STEPHEN DE CARHEIL and Father PETER MILLET, who, as we have seen were waiting to enter the Iroquois missions, set out to begin their labors and cares. The Cayugas are quick to acknowledge any act of kindness. We have had good proof of this; during the ten years we were with them; and the late father MESNARD, who was there pastor, was always praising their docility."

The Father built them a chapel in the middle of their little city which they continue to frequent with much affection, and this last summer the Indian, with whom we had lived, and some of his neighbors, set out on their journey to seek our Fathers, and to beg of them to re-establish the Faith, which we had already planted there. We satisfied their demands by sending Father DE CARHEIL, to erect this church composed of some Iroquois and a great many Hurons.

But their fear of the enemy obliged them to divide themselves, and a portion of them to go and live on the Northern shores of the Great Lake Ontario. This detachment of Oioquens, Cayugas, or rather, this new colony, had need of Pastors to confirm them in the Faith; this was worthily done by MR. DE FENELON and MR. TROUVE, two fervent Missionaries, who were sent thither by the Bishop. But as it was late in the summer, when these two Fathers went, they have not as yet been able to send us any account from these new churches.

It is more than a year since anything has been heard of Father ALLOUEZ, who is now almost two years with the Algonquin chiefs, and who travels with them in the large forests, that are more than five hundred leagues from Quebec. Perhaps, overcome by the extreme fatigues of his mission, he has followed Father RENE MESNARD, his predecessor, to heaven.

Father ESTIENNE DE CARHEIL arrived at Cayuga on the 6th of November, 1668, and there presented to Heaven, as the first fruits of his labors, a female slave of the Andastes. He had come in her company from Onondaga, and this journey, which they made together, enabled her to proceed, on her way joyfully, to Paradise; for having been instructed and baptized, during this journey, of two days, as soon as she had arrived at Cayuga, she was burned and eaten by these barbarians, on the 6th of November. Father Garnier accompanied Father Carheil on this mission. They were very assiduous in their labors. A chapel was soon erected; many were invited to the Faith, and a goodly number joyfully accepted the invitation. The mission was again dedicated to God under the invocation of Saint Joseph. [Without knowing this, two hundred years after, the first Bishop of Buffalo, obtained from His Holiness, Pope Pius IX., that St. Joseph should be the principal Patron Saint of the diocese.] The mission was ably conducted, and for a long time the church was truly prosperous. Besides the village of Cayuga which is the seat of his mission, there are two others; one, four leagues distant, and the other, nearly six. The two last are situated upon a river, which coming from the side of the Andastoque, descends, at four leagues distant, from Onondaga, on its way to empty into Lake Ontario. The great quantity of rushes bordering this river, (Seneca) has given the name of Thiohero, to the village nearest to Cayuga. The people of these great villages are composed in part of Cayugas, Hurons, and Andastes; the two latter being captives of the Iroquois. It is there that the Father exercises his zeal, and asks companions to assist him in his apostolic labors.

The great chief Garakontie exercised great influence at this new mission, as well as at Onondaga and Oneida. He encouraged the new converts by exhortations, and strengthened the hands of the missionaries by his zeal and perseverance in faith.

Father De Carhiel wrote, on the day of St. Catherine, that assuredly this great Saint interceded for him, and for his poor barbarians, who came in considerable numbers on that day to learn to pray, and to be instructed: "It was on that day," added he, "that I asked of this great Saint that she would obtain for me, to speak in the same manner, that she had formerly spoken, so as to overcome the teachings of the Idolaterous philosophers." From that time the chapel has increased, and has never been wanting in visitors who come to pray.

When the Father first arrived there were very few men who would come to his instructions, as they were occupied for the most part, either in fishing, or in the chase; but the report of the approach of an army of the Andastoques, soon caused them to return, and gave the Father an opportunity to preach the gospel to a great many. The report, which was spread, that the enemy to the number of three hundred men were coming to attack the Cayugas, proved false. But it did much for the misssionary Father, by proving to the Iroquois how much he loved them, and how little he thought of his own life, by remaining each night with those who kept watch. Those who thought that he had participated in the general fear were undeceived. Their warriors, their captains, and their ancients, in a public feast, gave evidence of the esteem which they had for the Father. And he well knew how to profit by this occasion, going from cabin to cabin. "Know my brethren," said he, "that persons like us, do not fear death. Why should we fear? We believe in God, we honor Him, we obey Him, and we are sure, after death of being eternally happy with Him in Heaven. It is you, my brethren, who ought to fear death, for up to the present time, you have neither known or loved God. You have not obeyed Him, and He will punish you, if you die without loving Him, and without keeping His commands, and being baptized." Being invited by a little child into a cabin, where there were assembled about twenty warriors, he addressed them thus: "I am rejoiced, my brethren, to find myself in the same danger that you are in. Be assured that I do not fear death, and that I would much rather die, than to see you die, without receiving baptism." He announced to them, that, on the next day, the day as they thought of the battle, they would see him go fearlessly among the wounded, to baptize those, who would be disposed, by a firm belief in our mysteries, and a true sorrow for their sins, to receive it.

These warriors showed by their actions that they were well pleased with these remarks, and although this turned out to be only a panic, it did not cease to have all its effects for the good of the faith. This church soon commenced to mutliply. It counted amongst its faithful, not only children, and women, but likewise warriors, who are, by far the most numerous. The same Relation speaks of the mission of St. Michael in the country of the Senecas: "This, of all the Iroquois nations in which we have been, is the most distant from us; being the least frequently seen by us, it is called the superior Iroquois. It is reckoned from us, about one hundred and eighty leagues. This country gives us the greatest hope of a successful mission, which has obliged Father JAQUES FREMIN, Superior of all the Iroquois missions, to go there to establish a new church. We have known this through the letters of other missionaries, he having set out from Mohawk, on the 10th of October, 1668. He visited other missions on his way, and on the 1st of November, arrived at the Seneca country, where he was received with all the honors rendered to Ambassadors Extraordinary. We have learned also that the chiefs have built a chapel, and that every one has shown an inclination towards Christianity. Upwards of sixty persons were baptized within four months. Thirty-three are supposed to be enjoying a blissful Heaven by a happy death. The "Jongleurs," in many instances, interposed, so that it was difficult to keep up an interest, in proportion to the merit of the work. Cayuga, we have named St. Joseph; Thiohero, St. Stephen; and Onontare, St. Rene.

Father FREMIN, also, set out, on the 10th October, 1669, for the Seneca country. In three weeks, he was in the Villages of the Western tribes. Received most honorably, he built a chapel, and began his labours by baptizing children, and hearing confessions.

At Cayuga, Father CARHEIL reduced the Cayuga language to roots or radical words, and composed his valuable works on the Huron and Cayuga languages. The Villages Goiogouen, Kiohero and Onnentare, were under his care. In all he found Hurons, some of them Christians and eager to profit by his Ministry. Gradually his Church began to increase in numbers, and sachems, warriors, women and children attended his catechism classes, and disputed for his little prizes. Baptisms of adults began to reward and console him. Just then he was attacked by serious illness, and obliged to return to Canada in 1671. Father PETER RAFFAIX replaced him at Cayuga.

The Reverend Father RAFFAIX, who was a missionary, describes the country, as it was in 1670, 1671, in the following terms:—"Cayuga is the finest country I have ever seen in America; it is situated in latitude 42½°, the needle dips there, scarcely more than ten degrees. It lies between two lakes, and is no more than four leagues wide, almost continuous plains, and the timber on their borders is very fine. * * * * * * More than a thousand deer, are annually killed in the neighborhood of Cayuga. Fishing, as well of the salmon as of the eel and other fish, is as abundant, as at Onondaga. Four leagues distance from here, on the brink of a river, I saw within a small compass, eight or ten very fine Salt Springs. It is there that numbers of nets are spread to catch pigeons; seven or eight hundred are often caught in one haul of a net. Lake Tiohero, which adjoins our village, is fourteen leagues long by one or two wide, it abounds with swans and geese. All winter and in spring, nothing is seen but continual clouds of all sorts of game. The river Choiquen, which rises in this lake, soon branches into several canals, surrounded by prairies, with occasionally very fine and pretty deep bays, where wild fowl flock. I find the inhabitants of Cayuga more docile and less fierce than the Onondagas and the Oneidas. * * * * * * They reckon over three hundred warriors, and a prodigious swarm of children. Relation 1671, 1672, p. 75. DE CARHEIL, after finding human skill unavailing, had recourse to God, and made a pilgrimage to the celebrated shrine of St. Ann, and obtained his cure. He immediately returned to Cayuga, and RAFFAIX proceeded to the Senecas. Soon after the celebrated Chief Saonchiowagan became a Christian, and was baptized. But in 1684, DE CARHEIL was plundered of everything by the Chief Horchouasse, and driven from the Mission.

One of the Seneca towns, Gandougara, or St. Michael's, was composed of Hurons, Neutrals and Onnontiogas. In 1669 Father GARNIER went to Gandachiragou; and Father FREMIN remained at Gandougara. In both places Mass was said daily. The Village Gandougara or St. Michaels was burnt, the Missionary lost his Chapel, and all it contained; but the zeal of the Christians repaired all: a new Chapel was built; prayers were now said publicly morning and evening in all the towns; the Christians firmly refused all participation in superstitious rites; and and many whom pride had kept from professing Christianity, began to yield. The Sachems of Gandachiragou publicly professed their wish to pray; but the rumor of a French invasion, and slanders against the faith, retarded the blessed movement.

Father RAFFAIX reached the Seneca Mission of the Conception in July, 1671. A third town, named St. James, contained several Christians, who anxiously begged a missionary. Father JOHN PIERRON, was sent to it, thus the

Seneca canton possessed three Missionaries. By their holy zeal, piety soon flourished in these towns, and the Seneca Mission, was scarcely inferior to the reductions founded on the banks of the St. Lawrence. Conversions of adults, however, went slowly on, being contested at every step by the Medicine Men. Father GARNIER was accused of sorcery, and as accusation and condemnation were nearly synonymous, they determined to tomahawk him. The executioner was named and paid, but God averted the blow.

The French occupation of Niagara by LA SALLE, in 1678, and his hostility to Father GARNIER, contributed to weaken the influence of the Missionaries, and excite the distrust of the French.

In 167*, the Senecas burnt the *quarters* (lodgements) which LA SALLE had built two leagues above the great falls of Niagara in 1668. The French marched against them, defeated them, and again took formal possession of the country in the name of the French King.

LA SALLE laid the keel of the first vessel on our western lakes, at the mouth of Cayuga Creek, 14 miles below Buffalo, and six miles above Niagara Falls. The place selected by LA SALLE for building this Pioneer, the "Griffon," continued long after to be used for building vessels or boats, and continues to be familiarly known by the name of the Old Ship Yard. The "Griffon" was launched in the Spring of 1679. Father HENNEPIN was there. She sailed on her voyage up the lake, on the 7th of August, 1679.

At the close of 1678, F. HENNEPIN started from Niagara, over the snows, and, after five day's march, reached Tegarondies, a large Village of the Fonnontouns, Senecas and Iroquois, 32 leagues eastward from Niagara. The day after, 1st January, 1679, "After the ordinary service, (the Holy Mass of course,) he preached in a little chapel made of the bark of trees. Father GARNIER and REFFAIX, Jesuits, were present."

Father HENNEPIN speaks of his "voyages," east and west of the "Falls" and says: "In all these comings and goings, I had always my portable Chapel on my shoulders, of course the Holy Mass was then said east and west of Buffalo. "The twenty-sixth, the keel of the vessel, and the other pieces being ready, M. LA SALLE sent Master MOSES, Carpenter, to beg me to drive the first bolt. My humble religious profession forced me to refuse the honor. He then promised ten *Louis d'or*, for this first bolt, to excite the Master Carpenter to hurry on the vessel During all the winter, *which is not half so severe here as in Canada*, I had a cabin to myself to celebrate the Divine Office on Sundays and Festivals. Many of our people understood the Gregorian notes, others could sing by ear." The Iroquois threatened to burn the vessel; some workmen wished to quit a hard service and go to New York; the evil was prevented by the prudence and zeal of HENNEPIN; "these unhappy men would have debauched our workmen were it not for the exhortations that I made every Sunday and Festival, showing that our enterprise was solely for the glory of God, and the success of Christian Colonies."

"Our vessel was soon ready to launch, and after having blessed it according to the Roman Rite, we launched it, though not quite finished, to save it from being burned, as had been menaced. The vessel was called the Griffon, alluding to the arms of Count Frontenac, two Griffons as support. The cannon saluted thrice, and we sung "Te Deum." Father HENNEPIN had much to discourage him; but he persevered, trusting in God. He ascended Niagara river, sounded the shoals, and found that he had been misinformed, when the savages assured him, that there was not water enough, to float his great vessel of sixty tons into the Lake.

Father HENNEPIN went to Fort Frontenac, he returned with Fathers GABRIEL and ZENODIUS, also Recollects, "they arrived at the mouth of the river of the Tsonnontouans which pours into Lake Ontario, they reached a little cabin in which to celebrate the Divine Office." Hence they could not reach Niagara before the 30th of July—and, in a frail *canot*, reach the Griffon than at anchor above Black Rock.

HENNEPIN started from Fort Frontenac, the 18th Nov., 1687, in a "Brigantine of ten tons burden." Sieur LA MOTTE commanded. On the feast of St. Nicholas, they entered the Niagara River, "In which never had such a vessel before entered." They sung the "Te Deum." The Iroquois, Tsonnontouans, Senecas, of all the little village at the entrance of the river, took more than three hundred fine fish and presented them to the strangers. They left their boat, and ascended to the mouth of Cayuga Creek, shovelled off the snow one foot deep, to make their fires; returned the next day towards the mouth of the river, meeting a great quantity of wild deer and turkeys. On the 11th Dec., 1687, they celebrated the first Mass that was ever said *there*. LA MOTTE returned to Canada; HENNEPIN steered the boat up to the Falls of Niagara.

On the 7th August, 1679, the Griffon, with three Franciscan Priests aboard, passed before what is now Buffalo; in passing they fired their seven cannons, and then sung the "Te Deum." Indians lined the shores; others who were on aboard joined with them, all cried—"Gannorin," "Admirable."

When the Relations close, Idolatry was generally discountenanced throughout the Cantons by the Indians, now fully instructed in the mysteries of the faith, but generally not courageous enough to embrace it. The life of the Missionaries for some time had been perilous, yet they had built and maintained their Chapels, and worked on patiently in hope; gradually gaining all, who were not corrupted by debauchery and intoxication; and baptizing all dying children whom they could reach. Now a new obstacle, the war between England and France, impeded all progress. In the ambitious strife for the Indian country, the Indian Missions were sacrificed. Still Father RAFFAIX labored among the Cayugas and Senecas till 1680, when he had to leave, and died in Quebec in 1703, broken down with years and toil. In the Spring of 1687, by the departure of Father JOHN DE LAMBERVILLE, the mission of the French was closed. The Governor of New York had long schemed and plotted for this. The treachery of the French Governor of Canada, hastened what the English had long been preparing.

In 1687, 14th July, the Marquis of Denonville routed the Senecas, cut down the corn around their four greatest villages, destroyed "about 400,000 bushels of Indian corn," killed "a vast quantity of hogs." The French estimated the number of Senecas at "fourteen or fifteen thousand souls." Formal possession was taken of the villages of "Totiakton, Gannagaro, Ganandota and Gannongarae; and a fort was established at a league's distance from the said village of Gannagaro."

On the last of July, 1687, the Marquis executed another act by which he took formal possession of Fort Niagara, "west of the Senecas, and twenty five leagues above them." In the act he recounts; "the taking possession of the said Fort Niagara, several establishments having been formerly made there, many years since, by the King's order, and especially by the Sieur LA SALLE having spent several years, two leagues above the great Falls of Niagara, where he had a bark built, of which the stocks are still to be seen. We have resolved to construct a fort there, in which we placed one hundred men of the King's troops to garrison the same, under the command of Sieur DE TROYES." Doc. His.

After the peace of Rysack, in 1697, missionaries again hastened to Cayuga and Seneca. In 1702, Fathers JAMES DE LAMBERVILLE, JULIUS GARNIER and M. LE VALLIANT renewed their labors among the Cayugas and Senecas. Fathers JAMES D'HEU, and PETER DE MARCEUIL joined the others and labored till 1703, when, "The English sent ABRAHAM SCHUYLER with four Dutchmen and some Englishmen, to sing the war song in the villages, and to present the hatchet to the Nations, on the part of the Queen of England."

SCHUYLER cunningly induced Fathers DE LAMBERVILLE and MARCEUIL, to quit the village of Onontague, and then engaged some drunken Indians to fire the Catholic chapel, "which he first caused to be pillaged." Doc. His. of N. Y. IX. 829.

Father D'HEU, who was then at Seneca, was also urged to fly. Later, "Sieur DE JONCAIRE assured me that forty Senecas were coming down, who were bringing with them Father D'HEU." Ib. 830. "The Iroquois not being able to resist the powerful solicitations of PETER SCHUYLER, had all finally declared in their favor."

On the 31st Oct., 1710, VANDRIEUL writes to Paris: "Sieur DE LA CHAUVIGNIERE, arrives from the Iroquois, where he had been well received by the Onontagues and Cayugas, despite all the new Governor of Manathe could say."

Versailles, 24th April, 1731. "His Majesty has approved of your having sent Sieur DE JOINCAIRE to the Senecas. . . His Majesty has also approved of your having, in concert with M. HOCQUART, sent Sieur RIGAUVILLE to Niagara, to command that post."

In 1731 a mutiny occurred at Niagara; some lay brothers of the Franciscan order, aided the mutineers to escape; the Superiors discountenanced their misplaced charity.

Letters in Doc. Hist. of N. Y., Vol. IX., show that friendly relations were kept up between the French and the Senecas and Cayugas, up to 7th November, 1744, during which time it is highly probable that zealous missionaries visited those nations. Under that date we read as follows: "As for the Iroquois of the Five Nations Sieur DE CELORON, the commandant of Niagara, writes me on the 20th of last month, that one of the brothers of Sieur DE JOINCAIRE, whom he had sent to the Senecas to examine what was going on there, returned within two days, and reports, that the result of the council, which the Five Nations, and the English, held at Orange, this summer, has been, a refusal to take up the hatchet which the English presented them to strike the French."

Reverend PIERRE DE MARCEUIL, is stated to have come to Canada in 1706. He remained in the upper Iroquois country, (Cayugas and Senecas) until the above date, when he was conducted to Albany by Lieutenant Colonel JOHN SCHUYLER, "the Governor's brother." On the 23rd June, the House of Assembly ordered "That the Commissioners for managing the expedition to Canada, &c., do take care a decent Provision be made for the French Jesuit and a servant that surrendered themselves to this Government from the Indians as the Governor and council shall direct." After experiencing every attention at Albany, he was finally exchanged towards the close of the year for Lieut. BARENT STAATS, a nephew of Colonel PETER SCHUYLER, who had been previously taken prisoner. He died in France, at the college of Louis le Grand, in the year 1742.

Extract of a Letter from M. de Beauharnois to Count de Mauressas.

"As for the Iroquois of the Five Nations, Sieur De Celoron, the Commandant at Niagara, writes me on the 20th of last month, that one of the brothers of Sieur De Joncaire, whom he had sent to the Senecas, to examine what was going on there, had returned within two days, and reports that the result of the Council, which the Five Nations, and the English held at Orange, this summer, has been a refusal to take up the hatchet which the English presented them, to strike the French, who might visit them, and particularly Sieurs Joncaire and La Chauvigniere; that the Iroquois invariably answered all their demands by saying, that they would not do anything; that they did not wish to take any part in the present war, against their Father Onontio.

Sieur De Joncaire the younger, has added according to Sieur De Celoron's letter to me, that, during his sojourn among the Senecas, two English messengers had arrived there with Belts, to demand a chief of each nation, to guard the house at Choneghen, but that the messengers received for answer that the English might guard it themselves, and on the messengers reproaching them, that plenty of them were at Niagara, the Senecas replied to them, that the chief was there, to settle any difficulties that liquor might occasion, among the Indians, in the work they had to do at the carrying place; but as for the rest, they did not wish to participate in their war with their Father.

The Senecas have likewise sent word to Sieur De Celoron, to assure me that, whatever proposals and advances the English may cause to be made to them, they will never declare in their favor; that they requested me to be at ease on that score, and, when they would recover from the affliction caused by the death of two of their chiefs, they should go to the Onontaques, to light up the council fire, and prevail on that Nation, to be as firm as they, in the resolution of neutrality, which they have adopted, provided always the Beaver traps at Choneghan and Niagara remain untouched: which are the words they used to me, this summer, at Montreal."

Extract from Memoir on the Indians of Canada as far as the River Mississippi, with Remarks on their Manners and Trade. 1718.

The Niagara portage is two leagues and a half to three leagues long, but the roads, over which carts roll two or three times a year, is very fine, with very beautiful and open woods through which a person is visible for a distance of six hundred paces. The trees are all oaks, and very large. The soil along the entire of that road is not very good. From the landing, which is three leagues up the river, four hills are to be ascended. Above the first hill there is a Seneca village of about ten cabins, where Indian corn, beans, peas, water melons and pumpkins are raised, all which are very fine. These Senecas are employed by the French, from whom they earn money, by carrying the goods of those, who are going to the upper country; some for mitasses, (ie the Algonquin word for stockings or leggings,) others for shirts, some for powder and ball, whilst some others pilfer; on the return of the French, they also carry their packs of furs, for some peltry. This Portage is made in order to avoid the Cataract of Niagara, the grandest sheet of water in the world, having a fall of from two to three hundred feet. This fall is the outlet of Lakes Erie, Huron, Michigan, Superior, and consequently of the numberless rivers discharging into these lakes, as well as of other lakes, towards the Sioux, with the names of which I am not acquainted. The Niagara portage having been passed, we ascend a river, six leagues in length, and more than a quarter of a league in width, in order to enter Lake Erie which is not very wide at its mouth. The route by the Southern, is much finer than that along the Northern shore. The reason that few persons take it, is, that it is thirty leagues longer than that along the North. There is no need of fasting, on either side of this lake, deer are to be found there in such great abundance; buffaloes are to be found on the South, but not on the North shore.

It is believed that missionaries visited, under great risks, the Seneca and other Iroquois countries, almost or quite up to the time when, under the administration of the Very Rev. JOHN CARROLL, priests of the Crucified God, again began to seek entrance into this State. An enemy attests it; for, in the year 1770, the Rev. CHARLES INGLES, who, after the Revolution, removed to Nova Scotia and became Bishop there, sent to Lord HILLSBOROUGH, a "Memorial Concerning the Iroquois," to which was attached a map by Col. GUY JOHNSON, from which it seems that all the present diocese of Buffalo was inhabited only by Indians. No mention, of course, is made of Buffalo. About where Rochester now stands, we find the Indian village "Chencessio;" then, eastward, Canadasegy; then, Cayuga; then, Onondaga, Oneida, Schenectady, Albany. All the other great names belonged, as yet, to the distant future.

Dr. INGLES admits that "Many of the Oneidas profess Christianity; being instructed partly by the Jesuits." But in the bounds of the present diocese of Buffalo, he says, of "the Cayugas, amounting to 1,040, the Senekas, to 4,000, the Tuscaroras, to 1,000, . . . Very few have any impressions of Christianity." He pleads strongly against the Catholic Priests; and strives to impress on the mind of the

Secretary of State that the converts of these Priests cannot be good subjects. He adds: "Under these circumstances, the affection of the Indians will be alienated from us more and more; to which the pomp and ceremonies of the Popish Religion, with which the savages are much captivated, will not a little contribute." Alas! his advice, too well followed, forced away the priest, left many a pagan Indian still savage, and forced the Christian Indian into exile.

CHAPTER XI.

EARLY INDIAN MISSIONS IN THE NOW DIOCESS OF BUFFALO CONTINUED.

God prepared for the persecuted Catholic priests, and Indians, Missions whither the Church might, "fly into the desert, to be nourished for a time, and times, and half a time." Along the St. Lawrence many such Missions called "reductions," arose. The Rev. FRANCIS PICQUET, a Sulpician, left a brilliant career, which opened before him in France, to devote himself to the Missions of North America, in which he labored thirty years. His austere life, and unsparing labors, gave to an enfeebled constitution, extraordinary vigor, and robust health, even to the end of a long and highly useful life.

God destined this zealous priest to found a "reduction," in which the Christian Indians of Western New York, might find a refuge. He came to the Indian Mission in 1733, and was the great Chaplin, during the war of 1742. When, in 1748, peace was restored, proposing to remedy evils which he had seen and deplored, he began a settlement or "Reduction," at "La Presentation," near Lake Ontario. The establishment, succeeded beyond his hopes, and has been the most useful of all those of Canada, (meaning also Western New York). The Fort of La Presentation, (now Ogdensburg,) is situated at 44° 50' north latitude, on the Presentation River, which the Indians named Soegasti, thirty leagues above Mount Real. Fort Frontenac had been built near there, in 1671, to arrest the increasing power of the English and the Iroquois; the bay served as a port, for the Mercantile and Military Marine, which had been formed there, where the tempests are as frequent and as dangerous as on the Ocean. But the Post of La Presentation appeared still more important, because the harbor is very good, the river rarely freezes, the barks can leave with northern, eastern and southern winds, the lands are excellent, and that quarter can be fortified most advantageously.

Besides, the Mission was adapted, by its situation to reconcile to us the Iroquois savages of the Five Nations, who inhabit between Virginia and Lake Ontario. The Iroquois to the South, and the Micissaquis to the North, were within its reach. Thus it eventually succeeded in collecting the Indians together, from over a distance of one hundred leagues. The officers, interpreters and traders, however, regarded the establishment as chimerical. Envy and opposition would have effected its failure, had it not been for the firmness of Abbe PICQUET. On the 20th October, 1749, he had built a Fort of pallisades, a house, a barn, a stable, a redoubt, and *an oven*. He had lands cleared for the savages. His improvements were estimated to cost thirty to forty thousand livers, but in all, he introduced as much judgment as economy. He so animated the workmen that they labored from three o'clock in the morning, until nine at night. As for himself, his disinterestedness was extreme. He received at that time neither allowance nor presents, supporting himself by his industry and credit. From the King he had but one ration of two pounds of bread and one half pound of pork, which he, and his fellow priests, could scarcely cut, this made the savages say, when they brought him a Buck and some Partridges, "We doubt not, Father, but that there have been *disagreeable expostulations in your stomach*, because you have nothing but Pork to eat. Here is something to put your affairs in order." After this, the hunting became good; the hunters furnished him wherewithal to support the men. The savages brought him trout, weighing as much as eighty pound.

At first, in 1749, he had only six heads of families; eighty-seven families the year following; three hundred and ninty-seven, in 1751. All these, were most ancient and influential; they numbered three thousand. Mr. Picquet took advantage of the peace to increase that settlement. He brought it, in less than four years, to great perfection, despite the contradictions and obstacle which he had to surmount, and the gibes and unbecoming jokes which he was obliged to bear; but his happiness and glory suffered nothing therefrom. People saw with astonishment several villages start up almost at once; a convenient, habitable and pleasantly situated fort; vast clearings covered with the finest maize. More than five hundred families, still infidels, who congregated there, soon rendered this settlement the most abundant of the colony. Depending on it, were La Presentation, La Galette, Suegatzi, L'Isle au Galope and L'Isle Picquet, in the River Saint Lawrence.

The most distinguished of the Iroquois families were distributed at La Presentation, in three villages; that which adjoined the French fort contained, in 1754, forty more bark cabins, some of which were from sixty to eighty feet long, and accommodated three or four families. The location pleased them on account of the abundance of fishing and hunting. * * * * * * The Bishop of Quebec, wishing to witness, and assure himself personally of the wonders, related to him of the establishment at La Presentation; went thither in 1749, accompanied by some officers, royal interpreters, Priests, from other Missions, and several other clergymen, and spent ten days examining, and causing the Catechumens to be examined. He himself baptized one hundred and thirty-two, and, during his stay, ceased not to bless Heaven for the Progress of Religion among these Infidels. Scarcely were they baptized, when M. Picquet determined to give them a form of government. He established a council of twelve ancients; chose the most influential among the Five Nations; brought them to Mount Real, where, at the hands of the Marquis De Quesne, they took the oath of Allegiance, to the great astonishment of the colony, where no person dared to hope for such an event.

In the month of June, 1751, M. Picquet made a voyage around Lake Ontario, with a king's canoe and one bark, in which he had five trusty savages, with the design of attracting some Indian families, to the new settlement of La Presentation. There is a memoir among his papers on the subject, from which it is purposed to give an extract. At the Bay of Quinte, he visited the site of the ancient mission which M. Dollier De Klees and Abbe D'Urse, priests of the St. Sulpice Seminary, had established there. The quarter is beautiful, but the land is not good. He passed thence to Niagara. He examined the situation of that fort. It is well located for defence, not being commanded from any point. The view extends to a great distance. They have the advantage of the landing of all the canoes and barks, which land and are in safety there. But the rain was washing the soil away by degrees, notwithstanding the vast expense, which the King incurred to sustain it. M. Picquet was of opinion that the space between the land and the wharf, might be filled in; so as to support it, and make a glacis there. This place was important as a trading-post, and as securing possession of the carrying-place, Niagara, and Lake Ontario.

From Niagara, M. PICQUET went to the carrying-place, which is six leagues from that post. He visited on the same day the famous Falls of Niagara, by which the four great Canada Lakes discharge themselves into Lake Ontario. This cascade is as prodigious by its height, and the quantity of water which falls there, as by the variety of its falls, which are to the number of six principal ones, divided by a small Island, leaving three to North, and three to the South. They produce of themselves a singular symmetry, and wonderful effect. He measured the height of one of those falls from the South side, and found it about one hundred and forty feet, (these are French feet, longer than English ones.) M. PICQUET negotiated with the Senecas who promised to repair to his mission, and gave him twelve children as hostages, saying to him, that their parents had nothing dearer to them; they followed him immediately, as well as the chief of the Little Rapid, with all his family. He set out with all those savages, to return to Fort Niagara. M. CHABERT DE JONCAIRE would not abandon him. At each place where they encountered camps, cabins and depots they were saluted with musquetry by the Indians, who never ceased testifying their consideration for the missionary. M. PICQUET took the lead with the savages of the Hills. Messrs. JONCAIRE and RIGUILLE, following with the recruits. He embarked, with thirty-nine savages, in his large canoe, and was received on arriving at fort Niagara, with the greatest ceremony; even with the discharge of cannon which greatly pleased the Indians. On the morrow he assembled the Seneca's, for the first time, *in the chapel of the Fort*, for religious services. M. PICQUET returned along the South coast of Lake Ontario. Along side of Choiquen, a young Seneca met her uncle who was coming from his village with his wife and children. This young girl spoke so well to her uncle, though she had but little knowledge of Religion, that he promised to repair to La Presentation, early the following spring, and that he hoped to gain over also, seven other cabins of Seneca's of which he was chief.

Twenty five leagues from Niagara, Father PICQUET, visited the River Gasconchagou (Genesee) where he saw a number of Rattlesnakes. The young Indians jumped into the midst of them, and killed forty-two, without having been bitten by any.

He next visited the Falls of this River. The first which appear in sight in ascending, resemble the great cascade at Saint Cloud, except that they have not been ornamented, and do not seem so high, but they possess natural beauties, which render them very curious. The second, a quarter of a mile higher, has beauties truly admirable, by its curtains, and falls, which form also, as at Niagara, a charming proportion and variety. They may be one hundred and some feet high. In the intervals between the falls, there are a hundred little cascades which present likewise a curious spectacle; and if the attitudes of each fall were joined together, and they made but one as at Niagara, the height would, perhaps, be four hundred feet; but there is four times less water than at Niagara Falls, which will cause the latter to pass, for ever, as a wonder, perhaps *unique*, in the world.

The English, to throw disorder into the new band, sent them a good deal of brandy. Some savages did, in fact, get drunk, whom M. PICQUET could not bring along. He therefore desired much that Choiquen—Oswego—might be destroyed; and proposed erecting a fort near there, at the bay of the Cayugas,—Sodus Bay,—which would make a very good harbour and furnish very fine anchorage. M. PICQUET next returned to Frontenac. Never was a reception more imposing. The Nipissings and Algonquins, who were going to war in company with M. DE BELLESTRE, drew up in a line of their own accord above Frontenac, where three standards were hoisted. They fired several volleys of musketry and cheered incessantly. They were answered in the same style, from all the little craft of boats. M. DE VERCHERE and M. DE LA VALTRIE, caused the guns of the Fort to be discharged at the same time, and the Indians transported with joy, at the honors paid them, also kept up a continual fire with shouts and acclamations, which made every one rejoice. The Commandants and Officers received our missionary at the landing. No sooner had he debarked, than all the Algonquins and Nipissings of the Lake, came to embrace him, saying that they had been told that the English had arrested him, and, had the news been confirmed, they would soon have themselves released him. Finally when he returned to La Presentation, he was received with that affection, that tenderness, which children would experience in recovering a father whom they had lost.

War was no sooner declared, in 1754, than the New children of God, of the King, and of M. PICQUET, thought only of giving fresh proofs of their fidelity and valor, as those of the Lake of the Two Mountains had done the war preceding. They distinguished themselves, especially at Fort George, on Lake Ontario, where the warriors of La Presentation alone, with their bark canoes destroyed the English fleet commanded by Capt. Beccan, who was made prisoner, with a number of others, by M. DE VILLIERS, who was at Isle Galope. The war parties which separated and returned continually filled the mission with so many prisoners that their numbers frequently surpassed that of the warriors, rendering it necessary to empty the villages, and send them to head quarters.

The "Relation" then shows the success of the bands from La Presentation, particularly in the expeditions of Sarasto (Saratoga), Lake Champlain, Pointe à la Chevelure (Crown Point), the Cascades, Carillon (Ticonderoga), Choiquen (Oswego), River Corlac (Mohawk), Isle au Galope, etc.

In the month of May, 1756, M. DE VAUDREUIL got M. PICQUET, to depute the Chiefs of his Missions, to the Five Nations of Senecas, Cayugas, Onontaguis, Tuscaroras, and Oneidas to attach them more and more to the French. But at length the battle of 13th Sept., 1749, in which the Marquis of MONTCALM was killed, brought ruin on Quebec; that of all Canada followed. When all was thus lost, M. PICQUET terminated his long and laborious career by his retreat on the 8th May, 1760, with the advice and consent of the General, the Bishop, and Intendant, in order not to fall into the hands of the English. He had determined never to swear allegiance to another power. He passed to Michilimachina, between Lake Huron and Lake Michigan; pro-ceeded thus by way of Upper Canada to the Illinois country and Louisiana, and sojourned twenty-two months at New Orleans.

On his return to France, he passed several years in Paris. A hernia, which afflicted him a long time, having become aggravated, finally caused his death at Verjon, on the 15th July, 1781, aged 73. In his life time he was complimented with the title of "Apostle of the Iroquois."

At Ogdensburg, as will be seen by the following letter, a lingering relic yet remains of his works:

Letter from L. Hasbrouck, Esq., to Dr. O'Callagan, Ogdensburg, St. Lawrence Co.

APRIL, 1849.

DEAR SIR,—Observing by the papers that you have been

collecting information relative to the early occupation of this country by the French, I take the liberty of sending you a copy of the inscription on the corner stone of the barracks at this place, (called I believe *Fort Presentation*,) and which was found at the base of the stone buildings.

My father was one of the early settlers here, about 1800, and it was given to him as being the "oldest inhabitant." The stone is now in my possession and corroborates your history.

    In nomine + Dei omnipotentis
    Huic habitationi initia dedit
     Francis Picquet, 1749.

   In the name + of Almighty God,
  To this edifice a beginning was given, by
     Francis Picquet, 1749.

On the departure of M. PICQUET, the Mission was entrusted to the pastoral care of REV. PETER PAUL DE LA GARDE, a Sulpician. After many trials, those who did not remove to Canada, were by the English Government located, first at Johnstown, than at Lisbon Point, on American ground; here they had a little village, which was finally dispersed in 1806 and 1807. The faithful Indians retiring to the Mission of St. Regis in Canada.

A letter written in 1770, by a Protestant Divine, Dr. INGLIS, alluded to in the last Chapter, shows that then, there were still practical Catholics among the Iroquois. Dr. INGLIS pleads against permitting Catholic priests to be with them, "Because the Savages are much captivated with the pomp and ceremonies of the Popish religion."

Alas! In many lands has the same enmity to Catholicity, blasted the fairest promise for "Glory to God, and peace on earth." An excellent work, just published, in Canada, says: "CECIL CALVERT, Lord Baltimore, a convert from Protestantism to the religion of his forefathers, sent two hundred Catholics, in "The Ark, and the Dove," under the Spiritual guidance of the Jesuits, Father ANDREW WHITE and JOHN ALTMAN. They arrived in Chesepeak Bay, the 22d Nov. 1633; bought, from the Indians, land on which they began to build the city of St. Mary, with its humble Chapel. Many Indians were converted. Whilst Catholics held power, toleration for all, and blessed peace existed. But the Puritans got footing, in that Catholic land of universal toleration; and, whilst still a minority, through English influence, they persecuted the Catholics, and seized the Missionaries, whom they sent in chains to England. When persecution and death, had taken away the zealous pastors, the Savage tribes relapsed into barbarism. On the borders of the Potomac, as on those of the St. Lawrence, Catholic teaching produced the same blessed fruits. Unhappily for the honor of the Christian name, Protestantism, brought persecution into Maryland and prevented Catholic Missionaries from continuing their work of civil and religious regeneration."—Earlan, Canadas, 1 Vol. 288.

From the Relation of Abbe PICQUET, already noted, and from the inventory of Fort Niagara, when it was left, as given in Doc. Hist. of N. Y. Vol. 1 pg. 69, it is certain there was a Chapel and religious exercise in Fort Niagara from early times. The words of the PICQUET "Relation," as will be remembered, are: "He set out with all these savages to return to Fort Niagara, and was received on arriving at the Fort with the greatest ceremony. * * * On the morrow he assembled the Senecas, for the first time, in the *Chapel of the Fort*, for religious service."—Doc. His. Vol. I., pg. 284.

When on the 25th July, 1759, Fort Niagara, defended by 486 men, was taken by Gen. WM. JOHNSON, Article IV. of the capitulation stipulates: "The French ladies, with their children, and other women, as *well as the Chaplain,* shall be sent to Montreal, &c.

The old French Fort at Niagara, begun in December, 1678, by the celebrated explorer La Salle, as one of his line of posts, had been more or less regularly attended by chaplains from that date. It was visited in 1679 by the romantic Father Hennepin, of the Order of Recollects or Reformed Franciscans, and by the still more distinguished Fathers Gabriel De La Ribourde and Zenobe Membre, of the same Order, both martyrs to their zeal in endeavoring to plant the faith amid the wilderness. Here, on his departure for the West, La Salle left as chaplain another Recollect, Father Melethon Watteau, with a small party. Hither La Salle returned on foot, baffled, but not discouraged, in April, 1680; and he set out from it again, in 1682, on his memorable expedition which had the glory of first descending the Mississippi to its mouth. On the disastrous end of La Salle, his post at Niagara was abandoned, and the Jesuit missionaries in the Seneca country, of whom we have already spoken, were the only priests of Catholicity in Western New York. The Marquis De Denonville, in spite of the protests of Gov. Dongan, took possession of the spot, in July, 1787, and began to rebuild the Fort. Denonville had just returned from his Seneca expedition, and restored Niagara, as a check upon the enemies of France. The Jesuit Fathers John de Lamberville, was the first Chaplain of the new Fort, having reached it in September 1687. But the garrison closely blockaded by the Indians, was attacked by the scurvey, and the missionary, sick himself, was dragged on the ice to Fort Frontenac which he reached, almost in a dying condition. He was succeeded by Father Peter Milet, who remained until the evacuation of the Fort in September 1688. The official account of the commandant at that time, states that he demolished the ramparts, leaving the houses and cabins, to prove possession; and, in the midst of the Fort, a cross eighteen feet high, which the officers had planted, on Good Friday, after it had been solemnly blessed by Father MILET. This cross bore the inscription "Christus vincit, Christus regnat, Christus imperat:" and it remained to foretell the future truimphs of religion, where almost beneath its shadow, now raises the noble Cathedral of Buffalo. The Chaplain's cabin is thus described "Father MILLER's cabin furnished with its chimney, windows and sashes, shelves, a bedstead and four boards, arranged inside, with a door furnished with its fastenings and hinges, the whole cabin being made of twenty four boards."

In 1721, The French resumed possession of Niagara, which they held till the fatal battle, in which the gallant AUDRY was defeated, in his attempt to relcive it. The Fort then surrendered in 1759. During this interval of thirty eight years, the Fort had undoubtedly a Recollect chaplain, because the King assigned one, to every post holding over forty men, and the Garrison at Niagara always exceeded that number; we do not however find any, mentioned by name, except the celebrated Father EMMANUEL GRESPEL, and the register of the Fort is lost, having probably been carried to Albany after the surrender. Father EMMANUEL GRESPEL, of the Order of St. Francis, came to Canada in 1723, was chaplain at crown point, and then at Niagara. He also visited Detroit, and attended an expedition against the Fox Indians, in Wisconsin, in 1728. He set sail for Europe in 1742 but was wrecked at the mouth of the St. Lawrence. Those who reached the shore, almost all perished of cold or hunger. Father GRESPEL survived, and on his return to Europe, published an account of his travels which is remarkably interesting.

What BANCROFT, in his History of the United States,

says of early missionaries, was true, in some part, or in many parts, of what is now the Diocese of Buffalo, down at least to 1759. BANCROFT, Vol. III, p. 14, says:

"A chapel was built at Onondaga, another on Cayuga Lake, etc.; and then in the heart of New York, the solemn service of the Roman Church, was chanted as securely as in any part of Christendom."

The Jesuit Relations speak of their masses, their solemn services, their sacred hymns and fervent singing, in various points of their wide missions. The voice of their sacred chant mingled with the roar of Niagara's cataract.

The French had a fort at Schlosser; a stockade at the present ferry between Lewiston and Queenstown: and another stockade just above the Falls, half a mile above the residence of the late Judge PORTER; the place is still known by the name of the "French Landing." In all those ports, regular, or occasional Catholic service was held. It is also known that after the events of 1759, the English abandoned the old French military works, and constructed others, where the present cluster of buildings stand, at the end of the road leading to Lewiston. The large chimney around which a small building is erected, belonged to the English messhouse, as it was called; it was a large, inconvenient structure, very high between joints: the frame of this building was prepared at Fort Niagara, while in possession of the French, for a Catholic church at that place, the English hauled it over to Schlosser, and put it up there. This was the residence of Judge PORTER for several years, after he removed to the Niagara frontier, it was burned down by the British, when they invaded the country, in December, 1813.

In tracing the solicitude of the Prelates of the Church, evidences are afforded, that, in the succeeding dark interval of forty or fifty years, missionaries often traversed this country, and, like their Divine Master, it is to be hoped that they were "doing good," even if only as in "passing" through the land. This will be seen, in tracing the source of jurisdiction for our America.

In 1615, the Franciscan Fathers received their jurisdiction, in America, from the Pope, through the Nuncio in Paris.

In 1648, F. VINCENT arrived at Quebec, with the title of Vicar General of the Archbishop of Rouen: "*this has not been approved.*" In February 5, 1654, Pope Innocent X., addressed a Brief, erecting the Confraternity of the Rosary in the Church of Quebec, thus: "Ecclesiæ oppidi Quebec, nullius diœcesis." In June 11, 1658, ALEXANDER VII., issued a Brief, giving to Mgr. DE LAVAL, the powers of Vicar Apostolic of New France.

March 31, 1659, ANN of Austria, Queen Regent of France, wrote to command that the Bishops of Petree, whom the Pope had named Vicar Apostolic of New France, should have full jurisdiction through the whole Province. Subsequently jurisdiction passed through the Bishop of Quebec.

In 1787 Mgr. DESEYLY, Bishop of Quebec, wrote to his grand Vicar, in London, stating that by the treaty of 1783, the south of the St. Lawrence, from the 45° of latitude belonged to the "Anglo Americans," and consequently, that since the said treaty, he, the Bishop of Quebec, had sent no *permanent* missionary thither or to the country of the Illinois. It seems that then the "Prefect Apostolic" of New England, sent thither M. DE LA VALENIERE, and M. DE ST. PIERRE. The Bishop of Quebec adds: "I do not know the extent of their powers, nor have I a wish to question them." In October, 1788, Mgr. HUBERT, Bishop of Quebec, wrote to Very Rev. JOHN CARROLL, Prefect Apostolic, regarding the same subject, and adds to the names of the two priests, above noted; a third, Rev. M. GIBEAU, requesting Mr. CARROLL to continue his care over that district.

On 13th January, 1791, Pope Pius VI. issued a Brief, confiding the jurisdiction over all the country, in the limits of the United States, to the Bishop of Baltimore.

On the 14th January, 1796, Mgr. HUBERT, Bishop of Quebec, wrote to the Right Rev. JOHN CARROLL, Bishop of Baltimore, saying that Rev. M. FRECHETTE, pastor of Detroit, but member of the clergy of Quebec, desired to be recalled to Quebec, and requesting Bishop CARROLL to provide a pastor in his place. Bishop HUBERT also states that the Rev. Mr. BURKE, at "Riviere aux Raisins," was willing to continue pastor of the place, even after its approaching surrender to the Americans, and that the Bishop of Quebec left him at the disposal of the Bishop of Baltimore. Bishop CARROLL answers, in date of May 2, 1796. Expressing how much he would have been consoled, if both pastors could have been left, and declaring that he will do all in his power to find a pastor for Detroit, &c. In this hasty, and often interrupted collection, it can only be hoped that provision may be made for future more extended history of this early interesting epoch.

Before the removal of the Indian missions, Catholic priests from Europe, Baltimore and Philadelphia, had begun to penetrate New York, in despite of cruel penal laws. At this period of our history, it becomes a duty to show from authentic documents what remains of good from the heroic apostolic zeal of early Catholic Missionaries, And the reader will be consoled to learn from truthful and zealous Rt. Rev. and Rev. Catholic Missionaries that the number of Catholic Indians, perhaps *never diminished*, certainly *is now far greater than ever.*

A respected missionary in the Diocese of Quebec writes:
"There are at Montagnais, in the Diocese of Quebec, on
the north shore of the River and Gulf of St. Lawrence,
two hundred and eighty families, containing about eleven
hundred individuals. Mostly all of the adults are able to
read and write. They were taught reading and writing,
more than a century ago, by some of the Jesuits; books
have been since printed in their language. Each family
carefully preserved the knowledge they received from preceding generations, without the aid of schoolmasters.
Except the Hurons of Lorette, all the Indians belong to
the Algonquin family. I do not think that there is in the
Diocese of Quebec a single Protestant Indian."

In the Diocese of Quebec 2386
" " " Milwaukee, Menomees . . 2000
" " " Sault Ste. Marie, over . . 3000
" " " Michigans, Hurons, Ottawas,
　　　　　　　Pattowatamies, Menomees . 4000
" " " Hamilton and Owen Sound . 80
" " " " " Monitoulin . 1000
" " " " " Garden River . 80
" " " " " Fort William . 80
" " " " Montreal, St Regis . . 1256
" " " " Sault St. Louis . 1400
" " " " Deux Montagnes . 800

"An old Indian missionary of Montreal, writes
　thus: "It may be said that the Catholic
　Indians of the diocese of Montreal are, for
　the most part descendants of the Senecas; the
　others less numerous are Cayugas, Ouantagas and Oneidas."

Catholic Indians in State of Maine 1000
In Kansas, the number of Catholic Indians,
　Pend'oreiles Kalissas, is　　　　　　　　4000

West of Rocky Mountains, Catholic Indians   6000
Other Catholic Indians, east of Rocky Mountains, and in Minnessota, California, etc., but not reported, supposed   5000

32082

Besides very many descendants of Indians, who intermarried with Europeans in Missouri, Illinois, Indiana, Louisiana, etc., and whose children's children are faithful Catholics, as their Indian parents were, two-hundred years ago.

It is consoling to read the annotations of several Right Rev. and Revd. correspondents, who attest to the number and piety of their Indian christians. Thus the Right Rev. Bishop Baraga, of Sault St. Marie, says: "Their number amounts to more than two thousand faithful Catholics, and all of them, except small children, are communicants." And again: "The number of our Chippewa Catholics is over one thousand, and all of them are practical Christians and communicants, except the children."

A most respectable missionary, thus states the condition of other Indian settlements: "The contact with the whites, whiskey, and Protestantism, have been at work among others of the ancient Indian tribes, and have made sad havoc among them." The following applies specially to the Manitoulin Islands, but is partially true for some other places. Extract of a letter will show *'how the thing is done.'*

"How the Indians became Methodists and Protestants, is a fact which deserves a brief mention here. The writer of these notices heard it from the mouth of the old chief of the tribe. When the English Government gave us to understand that we should have to become Christians, and join a Church, otherwise that we should lose all claim to the land,

and to the support of the Government. In consequence of which, a petition was sent, in the name of the tribe to the Governor, praying that the same *Black Gowns*, who had converted our Fathers, should be sent again to their children. The Governor, or rather the Government agents, in answer sent them a Protestant minister, who being dressed in a *black coat*, was pawned on them as a great " black gown." The simple Indians, who had never seen before a Catholic priest, fell into the snare, and were thus made Protestants. "But," did I reply to him, "why don't you correct your mistake now that you know better?" "Oh!" answered he, " If we would change now, we would be deprived of our annuities and of the protection of the Government, and perhaps our reserves." Such was his answer verbatim, about ten years ago. I suppose their situation is about the same now, perhaps worse. The same trick and the same means were employed in some other settlements, and with the same results, namely to prevent the Indians from joining the Catholic Church.

The Iroquois tribe of Sault St. Louis (Caughnauaga) was composed by emigrations, coming from the five Iroquois cantons of the United States, namely: the Agnez, the Onneyots, Onantaguas, the Geoquens and the Tsonnontuans, who spoke different dialects. The villages increased and especially that of Sault St Louis, which became very prosperous particularly since it sent to heaven the Iroquois Virgin, CATHERINE TEAGHOKUITA.

Now-a-days the Iroquois are much degenerated from their ancient fervor; nevertheless they keep ardently to the religion of their fathers, so that it has not yet been heard of, that any one ceded to the reiterated attempts, which some heretics made to deprive them of their faith. The village of Sault St. Louis numbers about three hundred families, nearly 1400 souls, of which there are about 800 communicants.

The Savages of St. Regis amount to 1324 of the Catholic population in the two, *Royalist* and *American* parties, as they call them, where they live in the same village. Of the number 1324, eighty-eight are Protestants, who apostatized some years ago, the others are Catholics.

The Savages of St. Regis are descendants of the famous Iroquois nation, have emigrated from Sault St. Louis in 1759, under the direction of the Jesuit Father Gordon, and have founded the village known under the name of mission of St. Regis. Afterwards when the village of the Presentation (now Ogdensburgh) founded by Father Piquet, under French domination was abandoned by the savage Iroquois inhabitants, a part of them emigrated to St Regis.

There are no Hurons at St Regis, only some Abenaskis families of the village of St. Francis, in the District of the the Three Rivers.

The Indians, so far as reported, practising the Catholic Religion within the limits of the United States, number 20,000. It is supposed that at least 5000 might be added for California, Minnesota, &c., &c., where no circulars have been sent. In Canada, from near the site of the first Huron mission, down to the diocess of Quebec inclusive, 7082 faithful and fervent Catholic Indians are reported, many of them descendants of the Seneca and Cayuga tribes. From the diocese of Ottawa, in which there are many Catholic Indians, no return has been obtained. Most of the others, are descendants of the Algonquia and Huron Iroquois tribes; among whose fathers the first Franciscan and Jesuit missionaries laboured.

Thus it is evident that *then* and *now*, there are more faithful Catholic Indians, than in the palmiest days of the Martyr Apostolic Fathers, in the early Missions of this country. So that the taunt; "Look over the world and read the history of the Jesuit Mission: after one or two generations they have always come to naught. * * * Must there not have been something wrong in the whole system—some grevious error mingled with their teaching, which thus denied them a measure of success proportioned to their efforts:" Kipp, (now Bp. of California,) is unjust.

The strong hand of power and persecution, thwarted many a promising hope, compelled Missionaries to shift from place to place, until they found a safe spot for their altars. * * * But their work continued. Under the most adverse circumstances, the number of their faithful Indians has increased not decreased. Whilst, in the same land, Protestant Ministers aided by the Sovereign, by Parliament, by laws, by all that could protest, encourage, and excite, "after one or two generations have come to naught."

Sixteen hundred years ago Tertullian said of the Sects of his day: "They can pervert, but not convert; that is, of Catholics, they make non-Catholics; of Children of One Church, they make Sectarians and Schismatics; of Christians, non-Christians; of believers, infidels; but to convert one nation of heathens to Christianity, *is beyond their power.* Such is the testimony of history in favor of the Catholic Church." Such also its testimony now, in America. Only when non-Catholic Ministers preach mere Deism, or quasi paganism, can they hope to convert Indians back, *to nearly their old paganism.*

From 1759, on the American or Canadian side of the St. Lawrence, in the Jesuit "Reductions," the Catholic Indians practiced faithfully their religion. Their priests, probably, also, visited the poor faithful Indians, that could not get away. Amidst persecutions and cruel penal laws, priests also visited their proscribed flocks in the city of New York. The law passed under Bellamont, Governor of New York, against Popish Priests and Jesuits, adjudged them to suffer *perpetual imprisonment;* and death, should they, after escape, be again captured. All who harbored priests were to pay a fine of two hundred pounds, and stand three days in the pillory. Queen Anne, in 1703, granted liberty of conscience, in the State of New York, to all, *except Papists.* The persecuting *spirit was general.* Thus, in Maryland, among other barbarous laws having the avowed intention of preventing the growth of Popery, a duty of twenty shillings was imposed upon every imported popish servant.

The last Chapter completed all that seems useful, in the spirit and view of this history, to give a general idea of early Indian Missions, and to connect the present with the distant past. Lest it might however be thought that the facts heretofore stated are presented in ultra Catholic light: It may be well to append the statement of an Englishman and a Protestant. He is called the "Indian's Friend,"—has lectured in Buffalo, and in many other places—and, though neither Priest, nor Catholic, for his age and holy zeal in a good cause, goes by the name of "Father BEESON." In his paper, *The Calumet,* he says:

"It is admitted by all who have travelled extensively among the Indians, that the Catholic missionaries are by far the most successful among them. Under their control, the inhabitants of New Mexico are chiefly Indians. While in New England, where they were once so numerous, they are now extinct. In California they were living in thrifty communities, owning vineyards and cultivated fields, and vast herds of cattle and horses, and were blessed with peace and plenty; but now they are peeled and scattered like sheep without a shepherd. In Arizonia they were living in villages, raising grain and cattle, and corn and cotton, weaving excellent blankets, and sustained the most pure democratic form of government on the continent; but now they are driven from their fertile valleys to perish upon the sterile mountains, and their usurpers report that ' we must kill or feed the *Savages.*'

"In Northern Oregon, some of the largest tribes believe that the frauds and outrages which have been perpetrated upon them was a sequence of missionary establishments, and therefore will have none but Catholics, in whom they have confidence—and, as if to spite the poor Indians for their preference, during the war against them they were driven from the Catholic mission; the Priests' robes were used to decorate the horses of the invaders, the premises were burnt at a loss of $30,000, and several poor sick creatures who could not make their escape were put to death and their bodies used as targets to shoot at; and the life of good Father Pandozy was sought after, because like a good shepherd he kept with his flock in its distress, while in Southern Oregon, the Bible was quoted to justify the extermination of the Indians. Need we wonder that they regard the Bible as their death-warrant, and your religion as a curse? Gentlemen, I appeal to you as men, not as ministers, for with the creeds which many of you hold, you are, as such, as effectually shorn of your strength as was Sampson, after Delilah had sat upon his lap with her scissors at his beard. The Philistines, in the quickened common-sense of the world, are upon you, and unless you obey the voice of God in nature, you will die as he died, an inglorious death."

CHAPTER XII.

INDIAN MISSIONS IN THE DIOCESE OF BUFFALO CONCLUDED.

A new era commences. In 1776, our country became independent of England. The penal laws of England against Catholics, more or less fully established in every State, quailed before true liberty. But with Independence, those laws were not at once abrogated; the spirit of the people, so far more kind, so far better, than the laws, made them generally become a dead letter before they were repealed. That law which condemned Catholic Priests to perpetual imprisonment or *death*, was repealed by the New York Legislature only in 1784, when there was not a single Catholic congregation in this State. It is curious that the law, under which alone Catholics can now incorporate, was enacted in 1784, and, of course, was not intended for them: yet whilst almost all Protestant churches or sects refused to use that act of 1784, because, as the preamble to their petition states, *it was contrary to Church discipline;* yet Catholics are still required by a penal law, enacted in 1855, to incorporate under that very law, not intended for them, and which Protestants generally refused to use, having obtained other laws which suit their discipline. In our "Revised Statutes," it is said, at each revision; "Law passed in 1813—in 1821, etc., etc.;" but this is a fiction: no such law passed at those epochs. The only excuse for the assertion is, that the Revision was completed and presented to the Legislature in those years.

In spite of the cruel law, missions had been kept up; for priests would risk their life to visit the sick, or to aid a soul that yearned for truth and for God. But missions could not spread when Catholic or Protestant laymen, were liable to a fine of $1000, and three days in the pillory, for giving shelter to a priest.

As soon as the Catholic priest could appear, without danger of death, or ruin to his friendly host, the work of God advanced most rapidly. In 1784, there was not a single Catholic church or Catholic congregation in the State of New York. In 1862, they form about one-third of the total population of the State.

For many years before a Priest came to Rochester or Buffalo, the Catholics in this West part of our State, were accustomed to go, at least once a year, about Easter, to Albany—a journey of three hundred miles—to accomplish their duties of the Christian Passover, and to get their children baptised. When, with other Commissaries, De Witt Clinton explored, in 1810, the location of the present Erie Canal, Rochester had no existence. In 1812, two houses were built. Nathaniel Rochester, William Fitzhugh, and Chas. H. Carroll surveyed the one hundred acre tract which they bought in 1802, at seventeen and a half dollars per acre, and laid it out as a site for a village.

Mr. Scranton built the first house, occupying the site of the present Eagle Hotel, on the corner of State and Buffalo Streets. The increase of inhabitants was at first slow, as may be seen from the fact that the future city, in 1816, numbered only three hundred and sixty-one inhabitants.

But emigrants from the Eastern States and from Europe, found their way thither, and swelled the number of its inhabitants, in a few years, to a degree equalled by no city in Europe, and by very few in this country.

In 1820, it possessed 1,500 inhabitants; in 1825, 4,274; in 1830, they increased to 10,863; in 1836, to 17,160; in

1838, to 20,000; in 1840, to 30,000; and now its census shows the respectable figure of above 50,000 inhabitants.

The City of Rochester, may boast of having been the first spot, in the present diocese of Buffalo, blessed with regular visits of a Catholic priest. The Rev. PATRICK MC-CORMACK visited it in 1818. The following year the Rev. FRANCIS KELLY made a second visit.

In 1798, when the surveys of the Holland Purchase first commenced, all the travel between the Phelps and Gorham tract, and Buffalo, was along the old Indian trail; but the legislature passed an act, appointing CHARLES WILLIAMSON a commissioner to lay out, and open, a state road from Connewagus, on Genesee river, to Buffalo Creek, on Lake Erie; and to Lewiston, on the Niagara River.

Buffalo, in October, 1798, consisted of the log house owned by MIDDAUGH and LANE, a double log house—about two squares from Main Street, a little North of the present line of Exchange Street; Captain JOHNSTON's half log and half framed house, a little east of the main building of the present Mansion House, near Washington street; a two story hewed log house, owned by Captain JOHNSTON, about Exchange street, from six to eight rods west of Main street, where a tavern was kept by JOHN PALMER; this was the first Tavern in Buffalo. ASA RANSOM'S log house west of the Western Hotel; WINNE's log house on the bank of little Buffalo, south of the Mansion; MAYBEE's little Indian store in a log building on west side of Main street, about twenty rods north of Exchange street, and a log house occupied by ROBBINS. The flats were open ground; a portion of them had been cultivated. Such was Buffalo—and all of Buffalo—in 1798.

DAVID MATHER, says "I settled in Buffalo in April 1806, there was then sixteen dwelling houses, principally framed ones; eight of them were scattered along Main Street, three of them were on the Terrace, three of them on Seneca, and two on Cayuga Streets. There were two stores, one, the 'Contractor's,' on corner of Main and Seneca streets, (east side of Main,) Vincent Grant kept it. The other was the store of SAMUEL PRATT, adjoining Crow's tavern. Mr. LE COUTEULX kept a drug store in a part of his house on Crow street. DAVID REESE's Indian blacksmith shop, was on Seneca Street; and WILLIAM ROBBINS had a blacksmith shop on Main Street. JOHN CROW kept a tavern where the Mansion House now stands, and Judge BARKER kept one on the site of the market.

"I remember very well the arrival of the first public mail that ever reached Buffalo. It was brought on horse back by EZRA METCALF, he came to my Blacksmith shop and got his horse shod. He told me that he could carry the contents of his bag in his two hands,"

From 1809 to the commencement of the war, many settlers came into Buffalo and many buildings were put up. Mr. LECOUTEUX came to reside in Buffalo in the year 1804, and soon after employed some Canadians to construct him a frame house opposite Mr. CROWS, on the site of the building now known as the "Le Couteux block," and in which he lived until the burning of Buffalo, with his second wife, whom he married a short time after his release from captivity.

He was soon after employed by the Holland Company as an agent for the sale of their lands in Buffalo and its vicinity, and was appointed first Clerk of Niagara County, the 28th of March, 1808, which office he continued to hold until the war of 1812. In December, 1813. Buffalo contained one hundred houses. All, except two, were burnt down by the British.

Some of the early settlers were Catholics. LOUIS STEPHEN

Le Couteux De Chaumont, of a noble family in Normandy, France, was a distinguished benefactor to charitable and religious institutions.

The first recorded visit of a priest occurred eight years after Buffalo had been burned down by the British. The Right Rev. Henry Conwell, Bishop of Philadelphia, then passed thro' on his way westward, and baptized a child of Patrick O'Rourke, whose pious wife still remembers and relates the facts. The few Catholics of this place, were next visited, in 1821, by the Reverend Mr. Kelly, of Rochester, who said mass in St. Pauls, the Episcopal Church; only five Catholic families being in attendance. From this time occasional visits were made by clergymen stationed at Rochester.

The Catholics of Auburn, then numbering some four or five families, and having several children to baptize, sent to New York for a Catholic priest. The Revered Mr. Gorman came. This was the first visit, that Auburn had ever received, from a Catholic clergyman. He remained but a few days, having celebrated the Holy sacrifice of the Mass, and preached a sermon, in the court house; he could stay no longer, since he had to visit other scattered children of the church; nor did the little Catholic family of Auburn see a Catholic priest again, for the space of five years, when they were visited from Rochester by the Reverend Francis Kelly.

The Rev Michael McNamara labored to erect a church in the city of Rochester. He collected for it, in New York, Philadelphia and Baltimore, Washington, and divers other places. The Rev. Dr. Farnham of Utica, then also visited Auburn. Seeing the want of a church he encouraged the Catholics to build one, Mr John H. Beach, a respectable Protestant, gave a lot for the purpose, between Chapel and Van Anden streets. The pious Catholics immediately commenced the work. The walls of the foundation were built, but Rev. Dr. Farnham came no more, the poor Catholics were discouraged, and gave it up.

The Reverend Michael McNamara settled in Rochester, and became the first resident pastor. His mission must have been excessively onerous, comprising, as it did, Auburn, Ithaca, Owego, Canandaigua, Geneva, Palmyra, the counties of Monroe, Ontario, Wayne, Tompkins and Steuben. He had to visit them, periodically baptizing and administering the sacred rites of the church to his scattered flock; and, at the same time, directing the building of his church in Rochester.

The Rev. Mr. Badin, the first priest ordained in the United States, visited Buffalo, in 1828, remaining six weeks, officiating sometimes in the Court house, and at other times at the residence of Louis Le Couteulx, Esq.

Mr. Le Couteulx had acquired a considerable extent of property while it was yet cheap in Buffalo, and at the solicitation of Father Badin, on the 5th of January 1829 he executed a deed of a piece of land, in trust for the Catholics of Buffalo, to Rt. Rev. John Dubois, Bp. of New York, and his successors, for a Catholic church and cemetry, and sent it to the Bishop as a New Year's Gift.

Bishop Dubois made his first visit to Buffalo in the year 1829; an account of it, may be found in his letter to the Society for the Propagation of the Faith, (annals vol. IV. p. 454) where he states that he found seven or eight hundred Catholics, instead of the seventy or eighty he had been led to expect. By means of an interpreter, he heard the confessions of some two hundred Swiss; preached in the Courthouse; administered the sacraments of Baptism and Matrimony, proceeded to the above mentioned ground, and dedicated it to the object for which it was given; this ceremony was the first of the kind, ever performed in

Western New York; after the consecration, the Catholics called upon the Bishop and urged him to send them a priest which he promised to do; accordingly in the fall of that year the Revd Mr. Mertz arrived in Buffalo.

Father NICHOLAS MERTZ who had collected upwards of three thousand Dollars in Europe with the intention of building a church elsewhere, erected in 1831, with part of this money, on the consecrated lot, a small wooden church called, "the Lamb of God," the name being suggested by the figure on a bronze tabernacle, which he brought with him from Europe and placed in the new church.

When first Father MERTZ arrived in Buffalo, he resided in a small log hut, on the west side of Pearl street, between Court and Eagle streets, and held Divine service in an old Frame house near by, which the Catholics rented and used until their church was finished.

Father MERTZ visited Lancaster, and Java, from time to time, consoling the poor Catholics, by administering to them the rites of their holy religion.

In 1832, the Rev. J. McGARRY, was appointed Pastor of Rochester. In his case, as the records show, there was furnished a proof that the present Archbishop of New York was wise in suppressing the obnoxious Trustee system. The Board would not receive Mr. McGARRY. The venerated Bishop DUBOIS, was obliged to interpose his authority; and being disobeyed, finally interdicted the Church.

The good and holy Bishop wrote letters and issued a pastoral; the answer of the trustees was not respectful. A church incorporation law, which almost all Protestants rejected, because it was contrary to Church discipline, misled even good men. But whilst defending the sacred discipline of the Church, the good Bishop had evidently at heart the interests of St. Patrick's Church. Under date of August 14, 1832, he writes thus to Father McGARRY: "As for the salary, remember that I will not consent to more than five hundred dollars being allowed yearly, until the Church is completed, vestments provided, and debts paid. I also wish a house to be built, for the accommodation of the priest, adjoining the Church." The awful scourge of the cholera began; sudden deaths, *that seemed like judgments of God*, restored obedience and peace.

Some time afterwards the venerable Bishop arrived in Rochester; the pastor met with no more trouble. The interdict was removed; and the priest labored with zeal in the performance of his ministerial duties.

The following list will show the different pastors that governed the Church from the beginning, and also the time of their visit or residence.

Rev. PATRICK McCORMACK, from 1818 to 1819.
" FRANCIS KELLY, " 1819 1823.
    No pastor during   1823 1825.
" MICHAEL McNAMARA " 1825 1832.
" J. J. McGARRY " 1832 1833.
" BERNARD O'RIELLY " 1833 1834.
" J. J. McGARRY " 1834 1835.
" BERNARD O'RIELLY " 1835 1849.
" WILLIAM O'RIELLY " 1849 1854.
" MICHAEL O'BRIEN " 1854 1859.
" MARTIN KAVANAGH " 1859 1860.
" MICHAEL O'BRIEN " 1860 to the present.

In 1831, Bishop DuBois, accompanied by Rev. Mr. RAFFEINER, visited Buffalo. Some German leaders complained of the venerable Mr. MERTZ. A deputation was sent to the Bishop to complain that the pastor would not allow them to manage the money affairs of the church, giving the usual reason, that it was their own moneys, and that they had a right to see to its disbursments. Rev. F. RAFFEINER simply inquired of each deputy, how much he had contributed towards the erection of the church. "Nothing;" was the answer. The complaint was dismissed, and peace restored.

Mr. RAFFEINER several times after visited the Germans, and was always joyfully received.

Buffalo was incorporated as a city in 1832, with a population of about eight thousand, nearly one tenth of whom were Catholics; consisting of nearly equal numbers of Irish and German emigrants, with a few French; all assembling to hear Mass on Sundays in the same little church of "The Lamb of God."

The demon of discord having, even at this time scattered the seeds of disunion, a small number aspired to be leaders and rulers. They commenced with a pretended desire to promote the interests of the church. At first they did nothing, without consulting the wish of the pastor, but at length, they acted on their own responsibility, often grieving him by their wordly and unjust pretensions; even claiming the church as *German*; but the pastor, though himself a German, promptly rebuked their selfishness, declaring that it was not the church of a nation or of a party but simply a Catholic church, for all the Catholics of Buffalo.

In Rochester, in 1833, whilst St. Patrick's Church was under interdict, the old church of St. Mary, situated on North St. Paul street, was purchased from the Protestants and opened as a place of worship for the English speaking Catholics; and after the interdict had been removed, it was still retained by the Catholics who lived on the eastern side of the city, and was attended by the Rev. F. FOLEY. The Rev. FRANCIS DONOUGHUE stationed at Salena, occasionally attended Elmira, Ithaca, Auburn and Greece, and through his encouragement and zeal, a very comfortable frame

M

church was, in 1834, purchased in Auburn, from the Methodists. Father Donoughue soon became the first resident pastor of Auburn.

The number of Catholics in Buffalo, increased to such a degree, as to make it necessary to find more church room, to accommodate them. The Irish people, pained also by petty annoyances, to which they were exposed at St. Louis' Church, resolved to withdraw from it, and procure, if possible, a pastor of their own, from whom they might receive more frequent instruction in English. They accordingly rented a hall, on the Terrace, for Divine service and, in 1837, the Rev. CHARLES SMITH was sent from Albany as their Pastor. At first, he said mass in Buffalo, only one Sunday in the month; as the congregation was small; and devoted the rest of the time to Java, and other adjacent places.

As these Catholics no longer received any benefit from the first donation of a church lot for all, Mr. LeCouteulx, deeded to them a spacious lot of ground for a church. This site was not then convenient, or suited to the wants of the scattered people. Bishop Hughes, on his next visit to Buffalo, recommended the purchase of a lot, on the corner of Ellicott and Batavia Streets, which was effected October 15th, 1839. Yet most of the purchase-money was paid by Bishop Timon, who completed the payment in 1852. St. Patrick's Church was soon built. Rev. C. Smith, soon after returned to Brooklyn.

The Catholics of St. Mary's Rochester, not being able to collect the purchase money in 1835, lost possession of the Church, and returned to St. Patricks, thus increasing the already crowded congregation of that Church. Up to this time the German Catholics also attended St. Patrick's Church, and formed with the English speaking portion, one peaceable congregation. The first German priest, who visited his countrymen, was the late Vicar General of Brooklyn, the Very Rev. John Raffeiner. Finding so many German Catholics, he at once exhorted them to build a Church for themselves, especially as St. Patrick's was too small even for the English portion. But most of them being poor, they felt discouraged at such an undertaking.

Soon after the Rev. Mr. Prost, of the congregation of the Most Holy Redeemer, passing through Rochester on his way to Ohio, addressed his countrymen in their native tongue, and exhorted them to the above mentioned undertaking. He found, on his return in the fall of the same year, to his great satisfaction, a brick church already purchased. With the consent of Bishop Dubois and of his Superior, Father Prost remained in Rochester, as first Pastor of this Church, which he placed under the protection of St. Joseph. He also opened a school and appointed a male teacher for that purpose.

Father Prost, with a lay brother, began in Rochester, the first regular house of the celebrated and pious Society of the Most Holy Redeemer. The first record found on the book of baptism of that Church, is dated 24th July, 1836. Another entry attests the solemn dedication of St. Mary's Church, in Ely street, in 1837.

In 1838, Father Czackert, from Ohio, came to assist Mr. Prost. But the efforts of a few so discouraged the pious missionary, that he left the city of Rochester, and started for Pittsburg; leaving the Church under the care of Father Czackert, who remained but a few months, and left the trustees to rule, with full glory, in an empty Church.

For one year after this; no German priest celebrated Divine service in Rochester.

The Revd. Simon Sandrel, a missionary among the Indians, in upper Michigan, came (with a tribe of Indians on their way to Lower Canada, where they settled,) to Rochester, and, having been frequently invited by the pious

Germans of Rochester, with the consent of his Superiors, who gave up the Indian Missions, he became pastor of St. Joseph's Church. He, also, came in conflict with the trustees, because, as he said, they could not give a satisfactory account of the Church income and expense; and he declared, from the pulpit, that he would no longer acknowledge trustees.

The Right Rev. Bishop HUGHES, of New York, visited Rochester to consecrate St. Patrick's Cemetery. He called a meeting of the Irish Catholics of the city, in St. Patrick's Church, to take into consideration the erection of a second Church for the congregation then worshipping there. The project was not favorably received by many; but the Prelate encouraged its friends to proceed in their praiseworthy efforts; and the old Church of St. Mary's was repurchased in the Fall of 1841. The Right Revd. Prelate at this time, also gave permission to Father SANDREL to build a new Church, as St. Joseph's congregation had, during the last two or three years greatly increased; and the little church, besides being in a dilapidated condition, was far too small. Father SANDREL called a meeting of the congregation and stated, that, if they would hand over to him the Church treasury, and assist him with their contributions, he would build them a fine large Church. Some difficulty was made, and he determined to quit the Church. The Irish Catholics who had just purchased old St. Marys, having no resident-pastor, Father SANDREL accepted charge of it, and shut up his St. Joseph's Church. But at a meeting of the St. Joseph's congregation the people voted in favor of Mr. SANDREL's proposition; the trustees resigned, and handed over to him the treasury of the Church consisting of $630 in cash, and a balance of pew rents amounting to $500. With this money he purchased a lot and commenced the erection of the New St. Joseph's Church, whose title was vested in the congregation of the Most Holy Redeemer. But those members residing in Western Rochester were dissatisfied with the selection of the lot, because it was not central for them; and they also opposed the vesting of the title in the congregation of the Most Holy Redeemer!

From the year 1834, to the year 1840, the Rev. BERNARD O'RIELLY was pastor of St. Patrick's, Rochester, thence he visited occasionally, Java, Canandaigua, and Lockport, until Father MANIGAN became resident pastor there, and began its first church. Mr. O'RIELLY also attended occasionally Mount Morris, and Palmyra.

In Buffalo, the very small number, who, perhaps unconsciously, tried to sow discord in St. Louis Church, had been frustrated in their first attempt. Yet they only awaited a more favorable time; and in the year 1838, some of them, having gone through the legal forms, incorporated under the above-named general law of 1784, which Protestants rejected. The Bishop was grieved; for, in sending the Rev. Mr. PAX, he said: "The usurpations of trustees are not there to be feared; for the ground belongs to me." The residuary heir of the donor, P. A. LECOUTEULX, Esq., a man of great honor and probity, also declares that his father never wished *such* an incorporation. This was an event productive of evil to the pious members of the congregation, of annoyance and grief to ecclesiastical superiors; and, until lately, of almost incessant discord and embarrassment to the Church. The Rev. J. N. MERTZ, their Pastor, left that Church, and removed to Eden. The Rev. ALEXANDER PAX, by the wish of the Right Rev. Bishop DUBOIS, undertook the pastoral charge. This worthy clergyman, finding the Church too small, and being assured by the Bishop that, as the ground belonged to him, no annoyance was to be dreaded from trustees, began to build the present spacious edifice, with the hearty co-operation of the people.

About this time, the Female Orphan Asylum of Rochester was founded, and, for the first two years, conducted by a Matron and Assistants, under the supervision of Rev. B. O'RIELLY, pastor of St. Patrick's Church.

Father C. D. M'MULLEN, pastor at Lockport, finished the Church of Lockport, erected a pastoral residence, and purchased a Catholic cemetery.

In 1828, the first Catholic came to Java. In 1829 the Rev. Mr. MERTZ, of Buffalo, visited Java. In 1836 the Rev. BERNARD O'RIELLY visited it. In 1837 Rev. CHARLES MANGAN attended it and continued till 1840, when Rev. Mr. ——— took charge till 1842. Rev. CHARLES SMITH succeeded, formed a Congregation and built the Church of Java in 1843. From 1843 to 1846, Rev. P. RATICAN was pastor. From 1846 to 1852, Rev. THOMAS McEVOY took charge as pastor, attending the surrounding missions at the same time. He also attended Portageville.

At Mount Morris, three hundred Irish Catholics working on the Canal, were visited by Rev. MARK MURPHY, and, to suit their convenience, Divine Service was held near Brushville. Judge CARROLL donated a piece of ground, upon which was built a poor chapel, or rather a shanty, where the pious Catholics met to adore their God, and to practice their holy religion.

The Church of Auburn was successively placed under the care of Revs. Fathers DONOHUE and CONNOLLY, who were succeeded by Rev. WILLIAM GRACE; after whose death, the Rev. Father BRADLEY became pastor, and from Auburn attended Geneva, Ithaca, Elmira and Jefferson.

The Revd THEODORE NOETHEN succeeded the Redemptorist Fathers at Lancaster and became the first resident pastor there.

Scarcely had the New Church of St Louis been built by the Rev. Alex. Pax, when the trustees of the congregation broke out in opposition to Church discipline, by refusing to comply with the statutes of the Diocese, and the faction so harrassed their clergyman, that his health became impaired, and he was obliged to return to his native country, to endeavor to recover it.

His letters of this period, to Bishop Hugues, breathe nothing but grief and despondency. In that of Dec. 26, 1842, he says: "This time I write to you, with a broken heart. . . I read your pastoral letter, that part which treats of the administrations of ecclesiastical property, occupied me two Sundays, because I was obliged to correct the most malicious interpretations, spread among the people. W. B. Le Couteulx is the head of the opposition party. Misrepresentations of the worst kind, and lies of every description, were resorted to. Their continued agitation produced a frightful excitement," &c.

He subsequently narrates how, some persons unknown, thus maddened, attempted his life, by throwing large stones through the window, at which he generally sat. And that placards were afterwards posted up, with the words: "We tried you once with stones; if you return we will try you with balls." The trustees wrote a letter of exculpation, and rented a house, down in the city, in which the Rev. Pastor could remain without danger, because it was surrounded with other habitations.

It is well known that, on weak minds, whilst reading history a deep impression will be made, that almost all in life is evil; so much being said of war; whilst what regards peace and prosperity, is discussed in a few brief lines. But the attentive reader knows, that many years of peace, with all its blessings, may be sufficiently said in the two words of the cheering cry, "All's well;" whilst, to render history what it should be, a lesson of experience and wisdom, pages must be employed, to point out the causes, the actions and the consequences of a month's war; so also must be this history; whilst briefly narrating the onward struggle of God's Church militant, in this diocese. But we will now say, once for all, that, generally, the pastors and the flocks, amidst dangers and difficulties, of which extreme poverty was not the least, displayed deep piety, disinterested zeal, a generous spirit of self sacrifice, the Christian virtues which always accompany it, and, even in poverty, charity like that of the poor widow, whom the Saviour praised for casting her last mite, into the treasury of God's house. Even the strife, which history to be useful must record, was, in every instance, caused by some twenty or thirty, (often fewer) leading men. These men, too, were generally good men; but men deceived in their estimate, both of the importance of Church discipline, of the extent of their powers, and of the propriety of pushing to their utmost meaning, the words of a church incorporation law, which almost all Protestants refused to use. A very few of the leaders, Catholics but in name, were men, who never approached the sacraments; men to whom the words of Bishop Hughes, might well apply: "In such cases, only let one enlightened, talented, intriguing, and irreligious mind get among them, and then, whatever *he* concocts in his infidel mind, he induces them, under specious pretexts to adopt; and then *he* gives it out, as the act of the board; and *this* again, as the act of the congregation."—Letter of Bishop Hughes, in the "Commercial" of N. York, April 4, 1845.

After many useless efforts to induce the trustees to submit to the discipline of the Church, the Right Rev. Bishop Hughes, was obliged to interpose his authority, to save the Church laws, by interdicting the Church of St. Louis.

Men who never approached the sacraments, exclaimed

against the cruelty of depriving the congregation of holy
sacramental helps. W. B. LeCouteulx, Esq., who seems
to have been the master-spirit in opposition to Bishop
Hughes, wrote several letters to his Bishop assuredly in no
Catholic spirit. In one, dated 4th August, 1841, he says
to the Bishop: "In case that, contrary to our expectations,
you should have given your consent to the above propositions, I feel bound to inform you that it would be a dero-
gation to the clauses specified in his [his father's] act of
donation, and would therefore put me under the obligation
to claim the property back again." It is a sacred duty to
say the truth, in giving this history to the public, but to
say it in such a manner as to give the least possible pain to
the living, or to the friends of the dead. The subject of
St. Louis Church would have been passed over, truthfully,
yet only in general, hasty views; but this mode of treating
it can now no longer be just to the worthy dead, to the
living, or to posterity. The worldly-wise and very cunning
sometimes overact their part; thus the enemies of the
Catholic Church have already forced into history false and
injurious statements on this subject. In the New York
Gazetteer for 1860, published by J. H. French, page 287,
we read: "There are fourteen Roman Catholic Churches
in the City of Buffalo. . . . The Roman Catholic
Church of St. Louis, in this city, has been prominently
before the public, from the refusal of its Trustees to *convey*
their church-property to the Bishop, and the extraordinary
but ineffectual efforts made by the Roman Pontiff to induce
obedience *to this order*. In 1853, Cardinal Bedini visited
America, having this as a prominent object of his mission;
but the Trustees were inflexible, and still continue the own-
ers of the property." No Priest or Bishop ever asked the
Trustees to *convey* the lot to them, nor has there ever been
a dispute about *the deed*; the dispute, from first to last,
was solely about church discipline.

On the 5th of January, 1829, nearly ten years before any Trustee's church existed, the deed of that property was made to the Bishop, *and he holds it still.* On the 3rd of August, 1850, when Bishop Timon forgave the first series of resistance to church discipline, under his administration, the Trustees pledging themselves to abide for the future, by the discipline of the church, say: "On our part we acknowledge that, according to the laws of the State, the titles of the temporalities of the church are vested in the Bishop and his successors in office, in trust for the sole use and only purpose of the congregation." With Bishop Hughes and Bishop Timon, the sole contest has been about the discipline of the Church. Bishop Hughes, no doubt, has said in substance to the Trustees, what Bishop Timon often did—that no pay they could give would induce him to accept the administration of their revenues. On seeking reconciliation, the trustees granted all that Bishops Hughes or Timon ever asked. Bishop Timon wished to have the revenues administered, and church affairs conducted, according to law and discipline; the people heartily agreed to this. As matters of history, it is now a duty simply to state facts, and justify the vast majority, who always were deeply and sincerely Catholic, while the chief agent in discord was a member of a secret society, who never approached the sacraments. His example drew some after him, and they were his best helpers. Immediately after the publication of the Interdict, some of the most respectable Germans sent a petition, through George A. Deuther, Esq.; Bishop Hughes answered it as follows:

New York, April 5, 1843.
Mr. George A. Deuther.
Dear Sir:—
I have received your petition and letter yesterday, and lose no time in forwarding my reply. Of course I always knew, that there were a great many true and

faithful Catholics, in the congregation of St. Louis in Buffalo. Indeed, on my visitation of the Diocese, that congregation was, by its piety, my joy and my consolation. It was my pride and my boast, on my return to New York.

But when a congregation, through its officers, allows its pastors to be thwarted in doing good, to be harrassed, and be made miserable, then I cannot expect that any priest will stay with them. The Trustees of a congregation are only its servants, and when these servants undertake to reject ecclesiastical laws of the Diocese, and to make laws themselves, as if they were Bishops, in God's Church; then it is time for those, who are Bishops and priests, to withdraw in peace, and leave them also in peace, to govern those who are satisfied to be governed by them. They say the congregation supported them in their proceedings—if this be so, which I cannot believe, unless they deceived the congregation by false statements,—then *so be it.*

Much as I feel for the good pious people, I cannot allow any priest to officiate in the Church of St. Louis, until I am assured that the Congregation, in its Trustees as well as in its members, are *Catholics,—true Catholics, in their soul,* as well as by their outward profession. If they choose to have it otherwise, I shall not quarrel with them. But, in the meantime, I have no priest to send them; and if I had, I should not expose him in such a situation. Our priests are for Catholic congregations, and no other. Now there are many other good German Congregations without a pastor, and until I have German priests enough for them all, it will be my duty to provide for those congregations, who make it their pride to be governed by their pastors, instead of attempting to govern them.

When I had written thus far, one of our city papers was brought me containing an article from the "Buffalo Gazette" which is false in almost every particular, and which I have answered here. I hope the editor of the "Buffalo Gazette" will publish my answer, in order that the good and pious people of the Congregation, may see how much they have been imposed upon, by means of falsehood.

The People must *oblige their Trustees to do right*, or else they must be prepared to suffer for what their *Trustees do*, in their name, wrongfully. I shall have no dispute with any Congregation, but whenever a Congregation allows its Trustees to behave so badly that the Pastor must leave, I will allow them no other.

With the same kind feeling towards all, as your true friend and father in Christ, I remain sincerely,

✝ JOHN, Bp., N. Y.

The trustee party made other false statements, through the public prints. Bishop Hughes answered in the following letter to the New York Commercial Advertiser, of April 4, 1843, which was copied from it into the Buffalo Gazette:

[From the N. Y. Commercial Advertiser.]

Messrs. Editors—In your "Commercial" of Monday you published from the "Buffalo Gazette" an article purporting to be a statement of the difference between the congregation of St. Louis Church and myself. It stated that I claimed to have "the property of the church vested in my hands, and that the claim was resisted by the congregation." This is entirely untrue. I never advanced such a claim, and of course it could not be refused. It is stated that in consequence of this refusal I "called away the Rev. Alexander Pax, and left the congregation destitute." This is equally untrue. On the contrary nothing but my persuasion was able to prevail on him to stay for the last eighteen months or two years, under the ill treatment of a few worthless men who call themselves the congregation. It is stated that the congregation of St. Patrick's, in Buffalo, have "complied with my requisition." This again is untrue. The trustees and congregation of St. Patrick's will bear me witness that I never made any such requisition. I advised them as a means of putting an end to quarrels among themselves, to dispense with trustees, and to avoid the rock on which St. Louis is now splitting. These are the principal statements; and the honorable confidence of the editor of the Buffalo Gazette, has been sadly abused by those, who have employed his authority for statements, which they knew to be unfounded in truth. He should demand proof of them, and if they cannot furnish it, to which I challenge them, he should publish their names, and vindicate his own. He has been deceived. I attach no blame to him. If his deceivers can furnish no proof that I ever made such a demand, I can furnish proof, in their own writing, that I never did.

It is surmised, says the statement, "that the Bishop has gone so far as to forbid any priest from performing divine service in St. Louis Church until its congregation shall fully comply with his demands." I forbade only one clergymen, whose inexperience might have been taken advantage of, by the same artifice which trifled so foully with the good faith of the editor of the Gazette. And secondly, what are called my "demands," in the statement, never had any existence in reality."

Surely the editors of the Buffalo Gazette will feel a glow of virtuous indignation, when they discover how much they have been imposed on.

The only difference between the congregation of St. Louis and myself, is, that its trustees have thought proper, not to be governed by the ecclesiastical discipline of the diocess, and expect me to supply them with priests who shall be governed by a different discipline, of which they shall be the authors. The congregation of that church are pious and exemlary Catholics, to whom their holy faith is dearer than life. Even, this may be said of a large number of the trustees.

But it sometimes happens that our trustees may be honest and upright in their intentions, and yet men of simple understanding, and without education. In such cases, only let an enlightened, talented, intriguing and irreligious mind get among them, and then, whatever he concocts in his infidel mind, he induces them, under specious pretences to adopt; and then he gives out the depraved purposes of his own heart, as the act of the board, and this again, as the act of the congregation! From the moment this arrives, woe to the flock, and woe to the pastor, who are at once divided from each other, and yet kept together by such a link of iniquity.

The pious and amiable Mr. Pax was not called away by me, but I left him at liberty to leave whenever he felt that he could stand it no longer. It appears to me that the time has arrived. I have no German pastor to send in his place. But if I had, it would be with instructions to rent a barn, get up an altar in it, and administer the sacraments of religion with that freedom from restraint and guidance of unauthorized laymen, with which God made the ministers of his church free—but which is not to be enjoyed it appears, in the church of St. Louis.

The neighboring clergymen could not officiate in it without neglecting their own congregations, which have the first claim on their ministry. Besides, I deem it my duty now to forbid all clergymen of this diocess to officiate in that church, until it shall be determined whether it is to be governed by the ecclesiastical regulations of the diocess, or by "the *resolves*" of its trustees. I trust, Messrs. Editors, that you will publish the above in your valuable paper, as an act of reparation which I may claim on the score of justice. I ask an insertion in "the Buffalo Gazette," which I am sure

the editor will not refuse. I appeal to the honor of such other editors, as may have copied the false and injurious statement first published in the Buffalo Gazette, for a similar favor. +JOHN HUGHES,
Bishop of New York.
New York, April 4, 1843.

The pious portion of the German Catholics, now met for worship in the basement of St. Patrick's church, having a Redemptorist, Father ALLICK, for their Pastor. Bishop Hughes gave the Order a deed for a lot on Batavia street, where they at once erected a temporary church, residence, and school-house.

The Interdict on St. Louis Church in Buffalo continued from 4th April, 1843, to 10th August, 1844. During that epoch, many of the peace-loving, pious Catholics of Saint Louis Church had attached themselves to the rising congregation of St. Mary's. The trustees became alarmed, asked forgiveness of the Bishop, and published, in English, in the *Commercial Advertiser* of August 10th, 1844, the following:

"A CARD.

"We, the undersigned, Trustees of the Church of Saint Louis, Buffalo, having had the honor of an interview with the Rt. Rev. Dr. HUGHES, Bishop of New York, in relation to the difficulties which have existed between the congregation and the Bishop for some time past, and having received from him a true explanation of certain parts of his Pastoral Letter, and finding thereby that we have been laboring hitherto under a misunderstanding of the same, hereby express our willingness that the Church and congregation of St. Louis be regulated according to the provisions of the said Pastoral Letter, and the true explanation received from the Rt. Rev. Author; and we promise, in our own name, and (so far as we can) in the name of our successors, that the administration of temporal affairs of our Church and congregation shall be conducted conformably to the same.

"We further take occasion to say, that if our course in this matter has given any scandal or offence to our Catholic brethren, we regret it; adding merely that our action proceeded from mistaken impressions, and that we should be the last to oppose the authority of our religion, either intentionally or deliberately.

     T. DINGENS, Presd't Board Trustees.
     JOSEPH HABERSTRO,
     BARTHOLOMY RINK,
     JOSEPH STEFAN,
     NICHOLAS HAAS,
     MARTIN FISCHER,
     CHARLES ESSLINGER, Secretary."

The Bishop next day, Sunday, went to their Church, preached, gave absolution and his blessing.

As few of the Germans then read English newspapers, some who still adhered to uncatholic usurpations, spread a report that the Bishop had been forced to give up, and acknowledge himself in the wrong. Several who had been deceived by such reports, mentioned it to GEORGE A. DEUTNER, Esq., who most prudently said nothing until he could produce documents. In a few days he found it. He had the English translated into German, and published in the German newspaper, cut out the *Card* and posted it up conspicuously at the door of St. Mary's Church. This had the good effect of silencing the lovers of discord.

In Rochester during the spring of 1842, twelve men of St. Joseph's Congregation, held a nocturnal meeting to consult about building another church to be governed according to their own principles. They sent one of their number to Bishop Hughes, to ask permission to build a second German Church, in Rochester. The Bishop thought it strange, that they should require a second church so soon, but, thinking it might be needed before long, gave permission in writing, but on condition that the Redemptorists would not oppose it.

They purchased a lot on the corner of King and Maple streets, the title was vested in two of their members. The organization of the congregation took place in the Public School No. 2, where sixty three members bound themselves for the erection of their church, making their property responsible for the payment thereof. They sent an invitation to the Redemptorist priest to lay the corner stone, which he refused. They then applied to the Rev. B. O'Rielly, who also declined; therefore, for want of Bishop or priest, they performed the ceremony themselves. A document was put in the cavity of the corner stone, reading as follows:

"Whereas, we have been much deceived by the Redemptorist Fathers, we are going to build in spite of them, a Catholic Church, not to be sold, alienated, or transferred or given away to any person, whomsoever as long as the church members, one to three, oppose it."

When the Church was finished, they sent a letter to Bishop Hughes informing him that the church was finished and petitioning for a priest. He replied, that he had no German priest to give; and, if he had, that he would not send him, because they had erected their edifice in the spirit of strife and discord; however, he added, that he would appear personally in Rochester, in a few weeks, and see what was to be done. He kept his word and arrived there before the end of December. After having heard testimonies on both sides, the Bishop addressed both parties, and left the room.

With the unanimous consent of the congregation, one only excepted, Messrs. ZEUG and FOGELE, on the 26th of January, 1843, transferred to Bishop HUGHES, and his successors in office, a deed in trust of the New Church. The Bishop was satisfied, and sent as pastor of St. Peter's Church, Rochester, the Rev. FRANCIS JOHN LEVITZ, of the order of St. Francis, formerly Missionary in Syria, who arrived on the 23d of April, 1843. The Church was dedicated, on the 29th of June, 1843, by Father LEVITZ.

The Rev. WILLIAM WHALON, pastor of the English speaking Catholics of Buffalo, held a meeting, May 16, 1841, at St. Patrick's Church, to urge on the finishing of the Church then building for the Irish Congregation.

Rev. Father ALIG, C. S. S. R., was pastor of St. Mary's Church, Batavia street, which was formed, during the interdict of St. Louis Church, from its faithful members.

The Reverend PATRICK BRADLEY was stationed at Auburn from which place he attended Geneva.

The Reverend CHARLES D. MCMULLEN, pastor of Lockport, attended Albion, Lewistown, Niagara Falls and Medina.

The Reverend THEODORE NŒTHEN, pastor of Williamsville, attended Lancaster, Batavia, Northbush, Transit and Tonawanda.

Rev. BERNARD O'RIELLY, pastor of St. Patrick's, Rochester, also attended Canandaigua and Greece.

Rev. LAURENCE CARROL, pastor of St. Mary's Rochester, attended Scottsville.

The Reverend RUDOLPH FOLLENIUS, pastor of Eden, attended White's Corner.

The Reverend THOMAS MCEVOY, pastor of Java, attended China, Aurora, Scio, Greenwood and Portage.

Rev. BENEDICT BAYAR attended St. Joseph's, Rochester, Rev. GEORGE BERANCK succeeding him, when he was obliged to visit Europe, on business, in 1844.

On the 10th of August, 1844 the Reverend NICHOLAS MERTZ, departed this life at the advanced age of eighty-one years. He was a native of Germany, and as a Seminarian, his fervor in devotion, his punctuality in the observance of rules, the ardor with which he applied himself to his studies, his humility and sauvity of manners, endeared him to all.

In the year 1791, the twenty-eighth year of his age, he was ordained priest. With unfeigned devotion and zeal he labored for the first twenty years of his ministry, in Europe. In the year 1811, this zeal led him to cross the Atlantic. He labored in the city of Baltimore for fifteen years, making himself all to all, that he might win all to Christ. In the year 1826 we find him pastor of Conewago, Adams county, Pennsylvania. He remained pastor of that mission for three years, when he became pastor of Buffalo, and Eden. His zeal led him across the Atlantic for the purpose of collecting means to build a church for the latter place. Having succeeded in collecting some $3,000, on his return he built, with a portion of it, the first Church that was ever built for the Catholics in Buffalo, and remained its pastor for eight years. The consolations he had from a pious and faithful people, were greatly diminished by annoyances from a few, who wished to rule the priest, and the Church. He retired to Eden and became its pastor, and built its old church and schoolhouses. His life was that of a true priest of the living God, so much so, that the leading Protestants said of him "if ever a man was clothed in Justice, it was Father MERTZ." Shortly before his death, he heard that the Bishop was making a visitation of his diocese; he prayed most earnestly that Almighty God would, in his mercy, spare his life, until the Bishop would arrive in Buffalo. On the forenoon of Saturday, the Bishop arrived, and in the evening of the same day, having been consoled by the rites of our holy religion, he calmly breathed his soul into the hands of his Creator!

On Monday his remains were piously conveyed to the tomb, after having been exposed in the church, during the solemn Requiem Mass, at which the Bishop, and a number of the clergy attended.

Rev. Father LEVITZ had to suffer much in Saint Peter's, Rochester, from the rulers of the congregation; upon which account, he secretly left them, during the night, and presented himself before his Bishop in New York. The Bishop sent his Vicar General, Mr. RAFFEINER, to make inquiry into the state of affairs. He, calling a public meeting, discovered that the majority were in favor of their beloved Pastor, and that only a few leading members were his opponents. Whereupon the Bishop sent Father LEVITZ back again; but he did not succeed. An old man, harrassed and worn out, he left Rochester forever in May, 1848, after having served this Church for three years. He died in his native country, Hungary.

After his departure, the Redemptorist Fathers served that Church, for about three months. In August, 1846, Count ANTONY BERENYI, of Hungary, took charge of this congregation. Under him, the Church was in a flourishing condition; the number of member increased from 842 to 1676; many debts were paid; some fine vestments purchased, as also an organ for the sum of $5.0. The congregation were united, peaceable, submissive, and bought for him, as a token of their love and gratitude, a riding horse, which he, who lived like a hermit, refused to accept. Still, a midnight party, consisting of grocery-men and tavern-keepers, was organized to destroy the harmony which prevailed. They went to Father BERENYI, and persuaded him to announce an election of seven men, for the purpose of inquiring into the account-books of his Church Committee, alleging that they had reason to believe that the Committee had not acted honestly. In reality, their object was to procure a charter for an incorporation of trustees. Father BERENYI was ensnared, and had already twice announced the election, when one of the party, in a state of drunkenness, discovered the secret. Father BERENYI then strictly forbade the election; so the evil was for a time postponed.

Rev. Father WHALON, Pastor of St. Patrick's, Buffalo, discharged his duties with zeal, until, worn out by care and sickness, and fortified by the devout reception of the last rites of the Church, he departed this life on the 27th of April, 1847, to receive the reward of his labors.

This being the year and about the time that the new Diocese was formed, a bird's-eye view may here be taken of the state of the Church in the Diocese of Buffalo, when the Rt. Rev. JOHN TIMON began his administration:

In the new Diocese there were then sixteen priests and sixteen churches; though most of those churches might rather be called huts or shanties. Many of them have since been replaced by brick or stone churches, in plain but good architectural style.

There were but four Catholic schools, taught by seculars, generally in a poor state; no Religious Ladies of any Order or community, for instruction or charity, except one house of the Sisters of Charity, in St. Patrick's Orphan Asylum, Rochester. The Redemptorists had a house in Rochester, and another, poor indeed and miserable, in Buffalo; with a church, that surely did not deserve the name of a church, but which was ever densely crowded, and in which the zealous Fathers did great good.. No other religious bodies of men or women were in the Diocese.

The Bishop had no house to live in. The pastor with whom he lived, and to whom he paid board, a few weeks after his arrival, told him that the trustees wished the Bishop to seek other lodgings, as they did not like to have the Bishop there. But when the Bishop was about leaving, to board with the Pastor of St. Patrick's Church, in his rented house, the same trustees sent to offer the Bishop $400 per annum, as his salary, if he would remain. In St. Patrick's Church, the only one for Irish and English-speaking Catholics, the communicants were then only three hundred. A Bishop, perhaps, never began under circumstances more discouraging.

CHAPTER XIII.
BUFFALO AN EPISCOPAL SEE.

The divinely constituted Hierarchy of the Church, completed, in each district, by the consecration of a Bishop with the appointment and approbation of the successor of St. Peter, always brings special blessings of progress in the spiritual, often too in the temporal order. This has been exemplified in Buffalo and in the wide district, of which Buffalo then became the centre. The diocess was established on the 23d April, 1847, by our venerable and saintly Pope Pius IX., with the following limits: all that part of the State of New York which lies west of the eastern limits of Cayuga, Tompkins and Tioga counties. The Very Rev. John Timon, then Visitor of the congregation of the Mission, in this country, was named the first Bishop. It was known that his nomination was before the Holy See for other bishoprics; but neither had he nor the public ever guessed that he would be appointed to Buffalo. He was consecrated in the Cathedral of New York, by Bishop Hughes,

assisted by Dr. WALSH, Bishop of Halifax, and Dr. Mc-
Closky, Bishop of Albany; Dr. F. P. Kenrick, Bishop of
Baltimore, preached the Consecration Sermon.

It will be seen in these annals how the blessing of
"Increase and multiply," followed this creative act of the
"Great Bishop of souls," through His Vicar on earth. As
every drop, too, aids to swell a river; so, for all, but for
Buffalo especially, many necessary visits to its Bishop,
many, settling down more willingly and more frequently,
when religious comforts became abundant, more money
spent for many establishments, etc.—all aided to increase
the prosperity of the city and turn attention towards it.

The climate of Buffalo is more agreeable than that of
any other American city in the same latitude. The winter
and spring months are boisterous; but, in winter, the ther-
mometer never sinks as low as it does in other cities much
to the south of Buffalo. The summers are cool and
pleasant. Owing to this, and to admirable system of
sewerage, Buffalo is a very healthy city. There are many
fine buildings in this city. Of St. Joseph's Cathedral, the
"New American Cyclopœdia" says: "This Church contains
a stained glass window, lately made at Munich, (at the
Works of the celebrated MAYER,) which is the finest specimen, in this department of art, in the country."

The population of Buffalo was,

In 1810,	1,508
In 1820,	2,095
In 1830,	8,653
In 1840,	18,213
In 1845,	34,656
In 1850,	40,764
In 1855,	74,214
In 1858, estimated	90,000

On the 17th October, Sunday, Feast of the Maternity of
the Blessed Virgin Mary, Bishop TIMON was consecrated·

He immediately named the Rev. BERNARD O'RIELLY, his Vicar General; wrote to Buffalo to the Rev. F. GUTH, that the Bishop would be there on the evening of the 22d, and accompanied by Bishops HUGHES, WALSH and McCLOSKEY, and by the Very Rev. B. O'RIELLY, started on the 20th for Buffalo. Boats or trains did not run then as now. They reached Rochester at 2 A. M. On the 22nd Bishop TIMON said his first Mass in the Diocese, in St. Patrick's Church Rochester, at 8 that morning, preached and gave his blessing to a large assemblage of the faithful, who, at such short notice, had already met to welcome their BISHOP.

His Right Rev. Friends, fatigued by the night journey, wished to remain till morning, particularly as the weather was unpleasant. Bishop TIMON thought the wish reasonable, invited them to remain, and rejoin him next day, but desired that, having sent word that he would be in Buffalo, by the train that left Rochester at 3 P. M., of the 22nd, he felt himself strictly bound to keep his appointment. The other Rt. Rev. and Rev. gentlemen then generously resolved to accompany him. The trains moved slowly: an accident further retarded them; so that they reached Buffalo after sunset but an immense crowd awaited them. A procession was formed of, it is supposed, about ten thousand persons: hundreds of torches illuminated the route. The drizzling rain seemed not to check the enthusiasm. It was 10 P. M., when the procession entered St. Louis Church. The Bishops, clergy and people, in silence adored the Blessed Sacrament, then Bp. TIMON delivered an appropriate discourse gave his blessing, and the crowd joyfully dispersed at 11 P. M.

The Bishop had no church to which he could safely assert a right, nor had he a house to lodge in. He agreed to board, at a certain fixed price, with the pastor of St. Louis Church, and betook himself to understand the condition of the new diocess: he named Rev. Francis Guth, Vicar General for the Germans.

In a few days, the Trustees of St. Louis Church, called on him, and requested him to consecrate their Church: he answered that it was a fine Church, and well worthy of being consecrated; but that he was bound by Church dicipline, as decreed in the Council of Baltimore, not to consecrate any Church unless the title was in the Bishop. The trustees assured him, that the Church had been deeded to the Bishop, and belonged to him, in trust for the Congregation; and, to remove all his scruples, they brought him, in a few days, an authenticated copy of the deed of Louis LeCouteulx de Chaumont, Esq., to the Bishop. This was sufficient.

After several days of labor and preparation, the Bishop having to do almost all himself, for a ceremony so new to those that assisted at it, on the 21st Dec. 1847, consecrated the Church of St. Louis, preached at the consecration, and after Vespers preached again, and confirmed 227 persons. Shortly after the Consecration, the Revd. Pastor of St. Louis Church, informed the Bishop that "the trustees wished him to find other lodings, as they did not like to see the Bishop there." The Bishop felt sad; after twenty years of arduous ministerial labor, he found himself poor, advanced in age, and without a shelter on earth. He told the good priest to say to the trustees, that he never intended to remain permanently at St. Louis Church; for he wished to go and labor, where his beloved flock were in greatest want. That at St. Louis Church, the faithful had nearly sufficient help; but that the Irish Congregation was greatly in need of help, and that he had already determined to make St. Patrick's Church his home.

On the 10th November, the Bishop began a pastoral retreat for the Clergy of the diocese, conducting it himself.

On the 11th, he gave benediction with the Blessed Sacrament, for the first time in St. Patrick's Church. Immediately after the retreat he held his first Synod. Both Retreat and Synod were in the Church of St. Patrick.

On the 23rd the Bishop moved to the rented house of Rev. P. BRADLEY, pastor of St. Patrick's, and made St. Patrick's his temporary Cathedral.

On the 28th of November, the Bishop began a retreat at Rochester, in St. Mary's Church, which produced blessed fruit. There were nine hundred communicants. On the 6th of December, he confirmed in St. Peter's Church. On December 12th, the Bishop gave another retreat in Java.

On the 20th, he began one in St. Patrick's, Buffalo. In all his retreats preaching thrice each day, making two meditations for the people, and passing the rest of the time, except a few hours for food and sleep, in the Confessional. The results of the retreat in St. Patrick's of Buffalo, induced him to prolong the sacred exercises for nearly three weeks, at the end of which time, that congregation, which had counted but 300 Communicants, saw upwards of 1,500 approach the holy table.

On the Sacred feast of the Immaculate Conception of the Blessed Virgin Mary, the Bishop preached his first sermon in German, in the Church of the Redemptorists, during the Pontifical High Mass, which he celebrated there. It was, indeed, a strange but a touching sight. The building was a very long, narrow, brick cottage, very low, crowded to suffocation. How different from the present noble Church of the pious and zealous Redemptorists! But, now we would find difficulty to understand how then, so many who went to Communion, could penetrate the crowd and reach the altar. In that long, narrow gut of a Church, the Bishop confirmed 173 persons.

The trustees of St. Louis Church, asked his permission to

enlarge their Church so as to prevent streets being run through their lot. He refused, thinking that it would spoil the Church, which was already the largest in the United States, and shewing them how they could build, tower, priest's house, &c., to suit them better.

The first year was thus passed in giving retreats, and in visiting the whole diocese, preaching, saying mass, &c., in the few Churches that existed; or, in Schoolhouses, or in Protestant Churches, when their use was permitted him; and in a shanty, or in the open air, when no shelter was attainable. This first year he Confirmed 4,617 persons, of which about half were adults. Williamville, Lancaster, &c., were visited.

In Lockport the Bishop gave a retreat of fourteen days, beginning on the 9th of January. During it, he opened one also for the French, wishing to get a French congregation there as he had done in Buffalo and Rochester.

He Confirmed 170 persons, of whom 150 were adults. Finding the Church far too small, he advised an addition, which the pastor, Rev. C. D. McMullen, with energy and zeal soon effected.

At Buffalo and in Lockport, by his efforts and advice, the Conference of St. Vincent of Paul was established, for the relief of the poor.

At his visit to Auburn, the Bishop gave a short retreat of three or four days. Here, as in most parts of his missions, the extreme poverty of the people had prevented their providing Ostensorium or Cope, for Benedictions, even Ciboriums were very rare, and the sacred vestments few and poor. Efforts were immediately made to remedy this.

For many years, purposely, scarcely any notices have been sent to the Catholic papers though the Bishop still continues his visits, often preaching three, four, or five times a day. But the following, published February, 1847, may serve as a specimen of labors and progress :

Diocese of Buffalo.

On the 24th, the Bishop arrived, at 11 A.M., at Seneca Falls—found the Catholics assembled in the Church, gave them an instruction, Fathers O'Flaherty and Sheridan began to hear confessions; the Bishop aided them in the same holy function in the evening and preached at 7 P.M., the little chapel being crowded to excess. The exercises continued till the 28th at mid-day, 53 persons were confirmed, and 200 received the holy communion. The want of church-room for our poor Catholics may be gathered from the following numbers. The Church of St. Patrick at Buffalo will not contain more than 1000 persons, and then it must be greatly crowded. During the retreat, in it, of that congregation alone we had 1500 communicants. The church of Lancaster will not contain more than 200, in it during the retreat prior to the confirmation there were far more communicants; the church of Lockport will contain about 900, in it we had 1300 communicants; the church of Auburn will contain 900, in it we had 300 communicants; the church at Seneca Falls will contain 200, in it we had 200 communicants.

On the 26th, the Bishop arrived by private conveyance at Geneva, at 3 P.M. He and Rev. Fathers O'Flaherty and Sheridan began to hear confessions; at 7 P.M., the Bishop preached to a large congregation, and in this retreat 200 persons received the holy communion, and fifty-three were confirmed.

On the 29th the Bishop arrived at Jefferson, at southern end of Seneca Lake. A church once used by the Presbyterians had been purchased; it was not yet fitted up. The Bishop and Father Sheridan worked till near night in fixing the altar, etc. And the church, beautifully seated on an eminence over the lake, was called "St. Mary's of the Lake." At 7 P. M. the Bishop preached.

On the 30th, the Bishop confirmed twelve persons; many approached the holy table. A convert, a very respectable lady, remarked that, having been exceedingly terrified at Methodist preaching about hell, so that she was afraid to sleep; she felt her terrors removed by a dream, or vision in a dream. She saw a bright arm extended as if to help and a voice pronounced distinctly the words, "Do penance, and you shall be saved." Never having heard those words, she knew not where to find them or what they meant. In vain did she read over her Protestant Bible; after long search, she found in a Catholic Bible; then examined the Catholic faith, and became an edifying member of the Church.

On the 1st February, the Bishop confirmed three persons at Gen. KERNANS', thence proceeding to Hammondsport, preached for a long time to a very crowded audience, and confirmed eighteen persons; starting thence at 4 P. M., he arrived at Jefferson at 9 P.M. After blessing and distributing candles at St. Mary's of the Lake, and confirming one adult, the Bishop started with Father SHERIDAN for Ithaca. They arrived at 7 P.M., and drove straight to the town hall, where they found a large and respectable congregation assembled. The Bishop preached. At 9 the service was over. Father SHERIDAN then went to hear confessions and administer the sacraments of matrimony. At 11 the day's labor was over.

On the 3rd, the Bishop and Mr. SHERIDAN heard confessions in a private house; as we have no church in this place, many went to communion there at the Bishop's mass. At 11, Father SHERIDAN said mass at the town hall, the

Bishop preached on the Holy Mass, and after it on Confirmation; twenty-four persons, mostly adults, were confirmed. At 2 P.M., the service was over. At 4, the Bishop and Mr. Sheridan started for Owego, which place they reached at 10½ P.M.

On the 4th, began a retreat at Owego, saying mass and preaching in a small chapel at a private house; each night, also, the Bishop preached in the court-house to a large and respec'able audience. On Sunday the early mass and communion were in the private chapel; at 11 mass was said by Father Sheridan in the court-house, the most respectful and religious attention was observed; the Bishop preached at the Gospel on the Holy Sacrifice, and, after mass, on Confirmation, eighteen persons were then confirmed A very large audience again assembled in the court-house at 7 P.M., the Bishop preached on the Sacrament of Penance; many seemed very much struck with the proofs he adduced.

On the 7th, after mass, the Bishop and Rev. Mr Sheridan started in a sleigh for Elmira. The sleighing was good for a few miles, then gradually failed. Whilst seeking the road-side, where some snow remained, the sleigh upset, the Bishop was thrown on the hard frozen ground, much stunned and cut, but after a few moments he strove to continue his route, the sleigh broke, a wagon was hired, the horse than gave out, and after great fatigue the missionaries were forced to stop at Factoryville. The Bishop taught catechism and heard confession that night. Whilst friends were seeking a wagon and team, next morning the Bishop said mass in a private house, gave instructions to the Catholics there, preached to a large audience, mostly of Protestants, in the school-house, then started for Elmira; heard confessions there the same night, next morning said mass in a private house and preached for the assembled Catholics. The Rev. Mr. Sheridan said mass in the court-house, the

Bishop preached at the Gospel on the Holy Sacrifice, and after mass, on the Sacrament of Penance. The confirmation was deferred to the next visit, as those who wished to receive it were not prepared. After the service, the Bishop started for Corning. No place could be found for preaching or Divine service, except the Methodist Church; the people had already begun to assemble in it. The Bishop then repaired thither as soon as he arrived, and preached to a very large audience on general views of the Catholic Church and its holy sacraments. When he had finished, a poor Irishman approached and said, " God bless you! but, och, how good it would have been, if you had said more about confession; *they do mock us so much about it.*" The Bishop immediately cried out, at the top of his voice, " To-morrow morning, at 10 o'clock, I will say mass here and preach on Confession and the pardon of Sin." Wrapped up in his cloak, the morning being very cold, the Bishop was being shaved in the barber's shop, when two gentlemen entered, and said laughingly to the barber, " Well, Tom, ain't you coming up to hear that Bishop, and to get your sins pardoned; better bring plenty of money with you." The conversation went on for a while in this way, no one suspecting that the Bishop was present. As the Bishop began his sermon, he saw the two gentlemen come in, just as he was mentioning this fact, without giving names, which indeed he did not know. The audience seemed quite satisfied, at least that Catholics had been greatly wronged on this point. And, in the Bishop's appeal for help to build a Catholic church, many Protestants came forward to subscribe; three hundred dollars were at once subscribed. A most respectable Protestant company gave the lot, and very soon a Catholic Church was erected.

There being then no railroad in that quarter, the Bishop was about entering a carriage for Bath, when he was called to a dying man, in a small shanty, some distance off. He started on foot. An ex-Presbyterian Minister, who had assisted at the whole service, asked permission to accompany him, it was easily granted. In a miserable shanty, on a rough straw bed, laid on the ground, the sufferer awaited his final deliverance; the family retired as far as they could, some went out, the minister stood watching, but distant as the others. The dying man's confession was heard, the holy Viaticum administered, the Extreme Unction given, and a few words of prayer and consolation, all in the simplest manner of such Catholic ministrations, but the Presbyterian seemed deeply moved, and as the Bishop left the shanty, he, took his hand saying; "God bless you, that was very touching." It is to be hoped, that God continued to give him light and grace, thus perfecting the good work, then begun in him.

At 7½ that night, Feb. 10, the Bishop preached to a large audience, mostly Protestants, in the Court House of Bath; he heard confessions, said mass and gave communion in a private house; and at 11 A.M., again preached in the Court House; then started in intensely cold weather for Greenwood. A good man had given a large lot, a log church had been erected, but not finished. The congregation appeared truly fervent. The Bishop heard confessions, said mass, preached, gave communion to many and confirmed 55 persons. On the 14th, he started for Scio, 20 miles distant; found people assembled, catechised the children, made an instruction, &c. The Rev Thos. M'Evoy accompanied the Bishop, his labour must have been herculian, having to attend so vast an extent of country. He has gone to his reward, and we hope and pray, that the mercy of God will there crown him; for his apostolic merciful zeal was great. Many a poor stray sheep he brought back to the fold, whilst his recreation, and his exercise was at every spare moment to go far and wide, through the tangled forest, through thorns and briars to find the bad negligent Catholic and bring him to feast with his God; or to preach, in his winning persuasive way to prodigal non-Catholics, who often as suits the generous American character, nobly acknowledged that they had been wrong, and sometimes embraced the faith which innocently they have despised.

At Scio, the Bishop confirmed 42. In the evening drive to the next post, they got lost, and stopped at a tavern, and whilst taking dinner, the good aged host and hostess, told them frankly all the bad that they believed of Catholics. The Bishop kindly corrected their statements; Mr. McEvoy took their part, and pressed the Protestant arguments strongly on the Bishop, who thus had an opportunity, which he did not expect, of removing many prejudices from the minds of these good people. When the time came for starting, the Bishop asked them to say frankly, what and who they thought their guests to be. They answered that they thought Mr. McEvoy to be a lawyer, and the other, a Catholic Priest.

It was 9 o'clock at night when they reached their post, near Hornby House. The wagon in which they rode, was almost miraculously saved from sliding down the icy precipitous road, which then led from the top of the precipice over the tunnel, to Smith's Mills, near Portageville.

Hornby House was used for a Chapel. The Bishop and Mr. McEvoy heard Confessions from early morning, till 2 in the evening, when the Mass began; the Bishop, as usual, preached before the Mass, to explain to the many Protestants, not without use even to many Catholics, the sacred act, and its venerable ceremonies; again at the gospel, on the

Eternal truths, then after Mass, on Confirmation, or Baptism. A great number, some who had not approached for many years, went to Communion; 41 were Confirmed. They were almost all adults. About 5 P. M, breakfast was prepared for them.

On the 19th February, the Bishop returned to Buffalo, from his visit of more than a month, through part of the diocese. On the way to his lodings he met W. B. LE COUTEULX, Esq., in the street, who immediately accosted him thus: "I am glad to see you. I rejoice to be able to tell you that we have begun our addition to St. Louis Church, the work is already far advanced. I am now about another important business, for the good of the Church. Here is a petition I am going to present to the Common Council, to request them to deed to St. Louis Church, the grave yard that was given for it. I have searched all the records, and I find that the deed was never made out, so that it might be taken from us. I went to your house, to show you the petition before it would be presented, but you were not home." The Bishop smiled, as he knew that his absence on the visit was well known in the city. He read the petition, and then told Mr. LE COUTEULX that the petition contained things most untrue, and most offensive to the Congregations of St. Mary's and of St. Patrick's. That, to his intimate knowledge, the faithful of both Churches had been orderly and quiet at their burials; that the grave yard was given for all the Catholics in the city, and, further, that he, the Bishop, held the deed, duly executed, and duly recorded. The Bishop invited the gentleman to come to his house, and see the instrument, which he did, noted the page of records, and dropped the matter.

The Bishop than went to the Trustees, expostulated with them for having, after his express prohibition, begun the walls, which were already two or three feet out of ground; he required them to demolish the work, and, if they wished to build, to build according to any plan they might prefer, but for the objects he had sanctioned, not for the enlargement of a Church, already very large. He then spoke to the Very Rev. Mr. Guth, to whom the trustees had referred him, as having sanctioned the work. Mr. Guth expressed himself much grieved and very sad, acknowledged that he had sanctioned the work; and declared that, if now demolished, he could never hold up his head again, but would have to withdraw to hide his shame. The trustees came, they begged pardon, but as so much was done, they entreated that they might be permitted to finish the part begun. The Bishop, deeply touched at the grief of Mr. Guth, whom he greatly respected, hesitated. At length he said that he could not approve, but he would overlook, and not notice the act, provided no more was attempted, than the part already begun. The promise was given, but not kept.

About this time, the Bishop rented a larger house, much nearer to St. Patrick's Church, and immediately began, in it, a Theological Seminary, being himself for some time the Professor. But he soon found a learned priest to perform that duty, whilst he continued to be Professor of Ceremonies.

In March, the Bishop went to Baltimore, and obtained a promise of two Communities, three in each, of Sisters of Charity, one for a hospital, the other for an Orphan Asylum in Buffalo. Rev. Mr. Winslow had deeded his house, next the Church, to the Sisters of Mercy, for a Charitable establishment; but the Sisters of Mercy could not think of going to Buffalo; a deed of the property was then made to Bishop Timon, but he found it of no use; actual possession of another party kept him long out; afterwards the nephew of

Mr. Whelon instituted a suit against his uncle's estate, for attending him on his death bed. The claim was for $600, and was considered unjust, the Bishop consequently defended the Sisters' claim; but the suit went in favour of the Plaintiff. The house was sold under execution, and the Bishop had it bought in for the Sisters.

The Bishop looked around for a house in which to begin the Charity Hospital. He, with his other few priests, had often to visit the sick in the Poor House, than on Prospect Hill, where the Oblate Fathers now are; and he well knew how little Spiritual Comfort the dying could receive under the system then too common.

In the meantime he gave a retreat for the pious Catholics of St. Patrick's Church, Rochester; and was much edified by the fervor of the people. He also, in the same Church of St. Patrick, gave a retreat for the French and Canadians. He had done the same before, in Buffalo, and though he preached each day in French for them, the result was not satisfactory. Seeing then the necessity of getting a French Church, in which they could be taught Catechism, and every Sunday hear the word of God, in their mother tongue; he laboured thenceforward for this, and at length rejoiced to see a French Church in Buffalo, and one in Rochester.

The Church of Sheldon being nearly finished, the Bishop went out on the 14th April, travelling through a storm of snow, sung the Pontifical High Mass, preached in French and German, and succeeded in settling difficulties that had arisen there.

On the 24th in Buffalo, the Bishop laid the foundation stone of St. Mary's Church, on Batavia street, for the Redemptorists, preaching on the occasion.

On the 28th the Bishop purchased land, which was soon used for St. Joseph's Cemetery. Then continued his visitation of the Diocese through Dansville, Scottsville, Greece, etc., preaching, confessing and confirming in each place.

On the 6th of May, 1848, the Bishop reached Canandaigua, fixed an altar; on the 7th, sung Pontifical High Mass, and dedicated the Church, which had been begun by the lamented Bishop O'RIELLY, then pastor of St. Patrick's, Rochester, and nearly completed by his brother the Rev. WM. O'RIELLY.

The Bishop reached Rochester on the 11th May, much fatigued; but a messenger came for a sick call at Portageville, a journey of 14 hours. As Rev. WM. O'RIELLY was hearing Confessions of the Children, the Bishop started at 8 A. M., 12th May—reached the sick person at 10 P. M., after continuous and fatiguing travel, found that there was no real need, and returned in time to sing the High Mass in St. Joseph's, Rochester, and to confirm 190, preaching in German, before and after Confirmation. In the evening he sung Pontifical Vespers in St. Mary's Church, preached and confirmed 167. At night he lectured in St. Patrick's Church.

After various visits to different Churches, on the 28th the Bishop went to Eden, said mass, preached in German, Confirmed 109, visited the tomb of the Rev. Mr. MERTZ, whom the Bishop had known in early youth in Baltimore. Being, according to his will, the heir of that holy priest, the Bishop gave Mr. MERTZ's vestments and sacred vessels to the Church of Eden, and his books to the actual pastor, Rev. R. FOLLENIUS. On returning the Bishop visited the Congregation of White's Corners, called Hamburg, and settled some little troubles of that pious Congregation. On his return to Buffalo he bought the lot on which the Church of St. Michael now stands, as a site for a Cathedral.

In June, 1847, the Right Rev. Bishop Smith, of Glasgow, in Scotland, came to collect for his Church; Bishop Timon gave him permission, but when the charitable Prelate saw the poor yet crowded Church, and the rented house of Bishop Timon, so poor, so small, and yet so crowded, and the evident poverty of the Catholics who assisted at Mass, he generously declined making an appeal to them.

On the 3rd of June, six Sisters of Charity—three for an Orphan Asylum, and three for a Hospital—reached Buffalo. By great efforts the house where St. Vincent's Orphan Asylum now stand was prepared for them. But there was no house for the Hospital.

On the 21st June, the Bishop bought from the managers of the Buffalo Orphan Asylum, the house and lot which they then occupied, as they wanted to build on a large lot, which Louis LeCouteulx, a good Catholic, had given for a General Orphan Asylum to this Corporation; having subsequently put two Orphans under their care, and having been refused permission, to send a Priest to instruct them, when well, or aid them on their death bed, he w 1.- drew the children. The Bishop was informed that most of the children in that Asylum were Catholics, but that no Priest could have access to them. After getting the deed, and making the first payment, he found it difficult to get possession when it was known that he had bought it, for the Sisters of Charity and for a hospital. After fixing various days for giving possession, and failing, on the 5th July, the Bishop went to the Director, from whom he had bought it, and said: "This delay is a great inconvenience, as the Sisters for this house have now no place.

You say that you cannot find a suitable house: I will, then, take all your orphans, put the girls with the Sisters of Charity, and keep the boys in my own house; and, when you find a suitable place, you can take them back: only, I will request you to leave the Catholics with me, and to take back the Protestant orphans only." The next day, they began to move; and, on the 8th July, the Sisters entered into the Hospital, in which, under God's blessing, they have saved many lives, and done an immense amount of good.

This Charity Hospital had scarcely been opened over one year when Buffalo was attacked with epidemic cholera. As no Cholera Hospital then existed, the Sisters of Charity promptly tendered to the City Council the use of that Institution for cholera patients. All who came or were sent, were very kindly received; and, though the City soon took measures to establish a Cholera Hospital, yet, as the Buffalo *Medical Journal* says, "The number of patients received in this, the City Institution, was 243, of which 115 recovered. The Sisters' Hospital, however, received 134 patients, of which 82 recovered. Considering the character of hospital cases," continues the *Medical Journal*, "the results of the Charity Hospital, as declared by the rate of mortality, certainly affords grounds for much satisfaction. . . . We are free to say that, whatever credit is due to the Institution for the large proportion of recoveries, belongs to those, under whose immediate charge the Institution is placed. . . . Each patient admitted to the Hospital was, at once, placed under the charge of one of the Sisters, and received her unceasing and assiduous care, as long as it was requisite. Scrupulous exactness in the execution of all medical directions, and fidelity in the administration of remedies, could be confidently depended upon, together with all other attentions and appliances, which the circumstances of the case might suggest. The degree of patience and endurance exhibited by the Sisters of Charity, in their unwearied labors of mercy, during the period of the epidemic, was a matter of astonishment, not less than of admiration. Night after night, as well as on successive days, they were at their post, never manifesting weariness or diminished zeal; and during the whole period, not one was debarred, by illness, from the exercise of her voluntarily assumed duties."— Buffalo *Medical Journal*, Vol. V., No 6, pp. 319 and 332.

The good Sisters of the Hospital were not the only ones, whose zeal was put to the test by this epidemic. The three Sisters, in charge of the Female Orphan Asylum, might be seen receiving with tenderness and compassion, the poor orphans, whom, under the direction of the Bishop, the Very Rev. BERNARD O'RIELLY sought after and collected, with the zeal and eagerness of a Vincent.

During this year St. Joseph's College, Buffalo, was established under the clergy of the Bishop's residence. It was commenced in two brick houses on Niagara street, near Main. The houses were rented with privilege to connect them, by opening doors in the separating wall. In the basement of this building, owing to the scanty means of the young diocese, St. Joseph's Male Orphan Asylum was begun. The poor boys had been left destitute orphans, by the cholera.

Whilst Buffalo was rapidly advancing in Catholic spirit and practice, the Bishop continued his visits through the diocese, that all might equally progress, for the glory of God, and salvation of souls. On the 17th June, 1848, the Bishop visited Youngstown, preached, said mass, heard confessions, and confirmed twenty-four persons. Thence he went to

Lewiston. The Universalist church had been promised to him, but on his arrival, he found it occupied by Methodists, who would not yield. He then preached, heard confessions, said Mass, and confirmed, in the unfinished house of Mr. KELLY. He got at once a subscription of $250 for a church. At Niagara Falls, he could get no place, but an old, and rather small Methodist church, in which he exercised all the functions of the holy ministry, confirmed seventeen persons, and began a subscription to build a church. With great difficulty, principally through the aid of P. PORTER, Esq., he got a lot from Judge PORTER, for a Catholic Church.

At Pendleton and Transit, the Bishop officiated as in other places, and urged on the building of the present churches, in which the truly pious Germans of those districts now worship.

From Ellicottville where the Bishop made the first confirmation in a poor school-house, he went to the Cattaraugus Indians. The intelligent and respectable Indian, Mr. PARKER accompanying him. He found the majority attached to what they call the "National Religion." The Bishop briefly explained the Catholic religion to the chiefs, who seemed pleased; he gave a crucifix to each one. They said that they thanked the Great Spirit for sending him, and would consult.

In Randolph, the Bishop officiated in a Baptist church, and confirmed twelve persons; passed then to a wild mountainous country, and said mass, officiated, and confirmed ten persons, in the house of Mr. P. DORAN. The Bishop, in both places, made efforts to get a church lot. At Jamestown, he sought in vain for a place in which to officiate, and therefore started for Maysville, and preached in its courthouse. In Dunkirk and Silver Creek, no place could be had for Divine service; the Bishop then went to Fredonia, where he preached, said mass, and baptized some converts. The Bishop and Rev. Mr. McEvoy started in the carriage of Mr. Devereux for Ellicottville: the carriage broke down. The Bishop took out one of the horses, and rode about some miles, back and forward, through a wild mountainous country, until he found a house, and hired a wagon, the carriage was fixed to it. Mr. McEvoy, being much fatigued, was placed in it, the Bishop continuing to ride horseback, until the party, after dark, reached a village, engaged workmen to repair the carriage during night, and then retired, excessively fatigued, to rest. Resting next morning at Ellicottville, they proceeded on to Cuba, and addressed the Catholics assembled there. They were hospitably entertained that night in the noble mansion of Judge Church, and early in the morning went over to Angelica, fixed up an altar in the court-house, said mass, preached, heard confessions, confirmed seventeen, etc. Here, as in other places, the Bishop was struck, with what must have been most pleasing to God, to Angels, and to men of faith. The Protestants soon filled the Court House; their faces turned to the temporary altar; on each side of it sat a confessor, the Bishop or Rev. T. McEvoy; the Catholics, before the wondering crowd, would come up, kneel down, make their humble confession, then, after receiving absolution, turn, and with countenances bearing the impress of recent deep and holy emotion, seek to regain their place, and kneel to bless God for his mercy. Ah, who can tell how many and how glorious, were then the triumphs of faith and duty, over timidity, and the modest instinct of wishing to hide the soul's deepest feeling, from curious eyes!

Through Java, where the Bishop again officiated and preached, they proceeded to Akron, and visited the Indians of the Tonawanda Reservation. The principal chief,

"Blacksmith," told the Bishop that only 15 out of 600 had joined the Baptists; who then had charge of the mission and its emoluments. He himself strongly adhered to his "National Religion." As he described it, it spoke of one Great Spirit, other spirits or subordinate Gods, good and evil, their idea seeming to make them much like our good and bad angels, a Providence of God, the power of prayer, and sacrifice, their greatest one being that of the white dog, during the full moon of February. The dog is immolated, the sins of the whole nation being put upon him, the body is burned, the ashes scattered to the winds, and the nation is purified! The Bishop told the old chief his religion, and requested leave to send a teacher. "Your talk is good," said the old Chief; "but now I will make mine. The Great Spirit make his white and his red child. He put the white child on the other side of the great waters; He gave this side to the red child: it was not right for the white child to come on this side, and seize the property of his red brother. The Great Spirit gave a religion to his white child, we will admit that it is very good for him. He also gave a religion to his red child, it *is* good for him, *and he will not change it.*" The Bishop answered: "Brother, you have said much that is true. It is very true, that the Great Spirit made his red and his white child, we are brothers! It is true; that he gave each of them a religion, but that religion, was only a bud, a germ; and it was the same for both. But the white child held it fondly in his open hand, and let the light of heaven, and the summer's sun shine on it, whilst the dews from above moistened it. It grew and produced leaves and flowers and fruit, and the white child fed on that fruit, and grew strong; but the red child held the germ tight in his closed fist, the light could not shine on it, the sun could not warm it, the dew could not moisten it, it remained always only a germ, a bud, it never had fruit, the red child had nothing to eat; and this is the reason why the red man becomes weak before his white brother." The old Chief said that he liked the *talk*, and would think of it.

About this time, great changes began in the diocese; zealous and pious priests were straining every nerve to multiply Churches, to furnish them with sacred vessels and neat priestly vestments. It will become a duty, as it is a pleasure to note in detail the generous efforts and holy sacrifices of worthy priests, and devoted flocks. To do this properly and fitly, a pause will here be made. A Second Volume will contain interesting details of the holy works above indicated.

www.ingramcontent.com/pod-product-compliance
Lightning Source LLC
Chambersburg PA
CBHW021351230426
43666CB00006B/485